SO-AKY-697

Applying Personal Leadership Principles to Health Care:

The DEPO Principle

by Michael S. Woods, MD

An ACPE Publication

the Woods Development Institute

American College of Physician Executives
4890 West Kennedy Boulevard
Suite 200
Tampa, Florida 33609
813/287-2000

Copyright 2001 by Michael S. Woods, MD. All rights reserved. Reproduction of this work in whole or in part without the expressed permission of the author is prohibited. Requests to reprint material from the book should be directed to the Permissions Editor, American College of Physician Executives, Suite 200, 4890 West Kennedy Boulevard, Tampa, Florida 33609.

ISBN: 0-924674-87-3

Library of Congress Card Number: 2001095704

Printed in the United States of American by Evatone, Clearwater, Florida

Dedication

This book is dedicated to Denny and Lila (deceased) Hardman, RG "Shep" and Edie Jean Sheppard, Hugh and Jo Woods, and the Smith Center Medical Group (1952–1987), whose members successfully practiced, played, and lived together in rural Kansas in harmony for more than 35 years.

To my parents, who taught me everything that's important, and to Marcia, who reminded me how important those things really are.

Acknowledgments

This book began from a simple collection of thoughts, but ultimately resulted from the thinking of many people. The impact of the work of Stephen Covey, Dee Hock, Alfie Kohn, and Robert Quinn on my thinking and the book itself is apparent. Reading their material provided me a mechanism by which to organize—in fact understand—what I was trying to say in many cases. I indebted to them, as is all of society, because they each have messages that can transform our world, if we only listen and act.

Kim Jackson of Assessment Plus has been a continuing source of information, strength, and support for this work during the trying times of starting a business, as has Kathryn Jashinski of A.S.K. Marketing Communications. I might well have given up without them. Marshall Thurber of MetaQuality probably gave me the single most important editorial comment, when he suggested I "tone it down." His reviews of important books in business and leadership, edEdge.com, proved invaluable as well. A simple "thank you" to the Smith County Medical Group of Smith Center, Kansas, whose demonstration of personal leadership in everyday life was out for everyone to see, seems an insignificant gesture compared to the incredible richness they provided to this book.

Finally, thanks to my wife, Marcia, who had the faith to let me quit my "real job" and undertake writing the book and developing a business that few seemed to understand when I walked out the door of corporate America. She really is a model of personal leadership, and I'm privileged to be able to be with her and learn from her every day.

What Reviewers Are Saying...

"Michael Woods has developed a practical thesis for the development of physician leadership, based on a synergistic combination of personal experience and proven leadership/organizational change principles. Importantly, he has emphasized in this book that the true interest of the physician leader should be positive and sustained organizational change...the type of change that benefits all the stakeholders (patient, payer, and provider) in the symbiosis of this country's largest service industry, health care. In particular, he has carefully outlined the frequent, common mistakes made by those physicians attempting the leadership journey and has, most carefully, outlined a rationale and a plan for correcting such mistakes. This work is unique precisely because the author has carefully described why the personality and training of physicians is often both counterintuitive and, therefore, counterproductive to the development of competent organizational leaders. If for no other reason, this book should be read by any physician seriously interested in the transformational development of leadership and organizational change."

> —**Richard Schwartz, MD,** Professor of Surgery, Commonwealth Professor of Physician Leadership, and Assistant Dean, Process Improvement, University of Kentucky, and Associate Chief of Staff, Lexington (Kentucky) Veterans' Administration Hospital

"*Applying Personal Leadership Skills to Health Care* is right on. Leadership has not been taught or emphasized in medical school, and it is an important area of study for anyone interested in personal growth and success. Medicine is now a team effort and every physician and health care worker needs to understand the DEPO principle."

> —**George D. Ferry, MD,** Professor of Pediatrics, Baylor College of Medicine, and Chief, Ambulatory GI/Nutrition Clinic, Texas Children's Hospital.

"Applying Personal Leadership Principles to Health Care is a book that meets a great need for the health care leader of the future. It should be in every health care professionals office!"

> —**Marshall Goldsmith,** co-editor of the best-selling *Leader of the Future* and *Coaching for Leadership* and co-founder of the *Financial Times Knowledge Dialogue*

"I found the book very interesting and almost a "retreat," forcing me to be objective and introspective of my own 'leadership' style(s). I would recommend the book to all professionals, irrespective of their profession, as it allows one a template for self-analysis.

> —**M. Brian Fennerty, MD,** Professor of Medicine, Oregon Health Sciences University, Portland, OR

"Qualities of personal leadership that seemed almost instinctive to an earlier generation of doctors must be consciously and deliberately learned by today's physicians. In his challenging new book, Dr. Michael Woods dares, prods, and finally guides his generation in the direction it needs to go. Fail to travel on the journey with him at your own risk."

> —**Wayne J. Guglielmo,** Senior Editor, Medical Economics Magazine

The Desiderata

"Go placidly amid the noise and haste and remember what peace there may be in silence. As far as possible without surrender be on good terms with all persons. Speak your truth quietly and clearly; and listen to others, even the dull and ignorant; they too have their story.

"Avoid loud and aggressive persons; they are vexations to the spirit. If you compare yourself to others, you may become vain and bitter; for always there will be greater and lesser persons than yourself. Enjoy your achievements as well as your plans.

"Keep interested in your own career, however humble; it is a real possession in the changing fortunes of time. Exercise caution in your business affairs; for the world is full of trickery. But let this not blind you to what virtue there is; many persons strive for high ideals; and everywhere life is full of heroism.

"Be yourself. Especially, do not feign affection. Neither be cynical about love; for in the face of all aridity and disenchantment it is perennial as the grass.

"Take kindly the counsel of the years, gracefully surrendering the things of youth. Nurture strength of spirit to shield you in sudden misfortune. But do not distress yourself with imaginings. Many fears are born of fatigue and loneliness. Beyond a wholesome discipline, be gentle with yourself.

"You are a child of the universe, no less than the trees and the stars; you have a right to be here. And whether or not it is clear to you, no doubt the universe is unfolding as it should.

"Therefore be at peace with God, whatever you conceive him to be, and whatever your labors and aspirations, in the noisy confusion of life keep peace with your soul.

"With all its sham, drudgery, and broken dreams, it is still a beautiful world. Be careful. Strive to be happy."

—*Found in Old Saint Paul's Church, Baltimore, Maryland; dated 1692.*

About the Author

Michael S. Woods, MD, was born and raised in Smith Center, Kansas, where his father and two partners practiced for 35 years, serving as role models for Dr. Woods in life and medicine. Dr. Woods earned his doctor of medicine and completed a general surgery residency at the University of Kansas. This was followed by a fellowship in hepatobiliary-pancreatic surgery at Virginia Mason Clinic in Seattle, Washington. Dr. Woods is board-certified in surgery and is a fellow of the American College of Surgeons.

After practicing surgery for three years at the Wichita Clinic in Wichita, Kansas, Dr. Woods joined Johnson & Johnson, where, within 3 years, he became the Global Medical Leader responsible for clinical research performed in support of one the largest pharmaceutical programs in the history of Johnson & Johnson. It was during this period that Dr. Woods became interested in personal leadership, and a large portion of his private time was devoted to reading and studying the literature on leadership and personal leadership development.

Dr. Woods began to formulate his concepts of leadership in medicine and the importance of increasing personal leadership skills of physicians in 1999, leading to the writing of this book. He left the pharmaceutical industry in January 2001 to complete his book, start The Woods Development Institute, Inc., and devote himself to working with individuals and health care organizations interested in achieving greater levels of success by developing the personal leadership and interpersonal skills of physicians.

Dr. Woods believes the "on-the-ground" physician—the physician seeing patients day in and day out—can have the greatest impact on health care and that enhancing the personal leadership skills of these individuals will result in greater patient and provider satisfaction; reduce employee turnover; lower personal and organizational malpractice liability; and provide greater satisfaction for, and intrinsic motivation of, the physician. Dr. Woods consults on a wide spectrum of issues (personal and organizational effectiveness, patient and health care employee satisfaction and retention, and malpractice liability and risk assessment) to individuals, health care organizations of all sizes, and the malpractice insurance industry. He has clients in the United States and Europe. He can be reached by email (mwoods@wdi-inc.com) or by telephone (610-294-8151, extension 201).

Introduction

Marshall Thurber, a friend and colleague, read one of the early manuscripts of this book and commented: "Mike, perhaps you should think about how to deliver your messages with the same degree of compassion that you are trying to instill in your audience." Sage advice, Marshall, sage advice. I can honestly say I have attempted to follow his advice in writing this book.

Some messages, however, are hard to hear, regardless of the degree of compassion with which they are delivered. Difficult messages are always harder to hear when delivered poorly, but telling a patient he or she has terminal cancer, for instance, is a tough, unpleasant job regardless of how well it is done and who is doing it, even if it oozes compassion.

I decided conveying the message of this book is a bit like informing the terminally ill patient of his or her fate. Some of the messages and concepts I am trying to convey, and the therapy that is required, are difficult messages for those in health care, regardless my success or failure in attempting compassionate delivery. It is my sincere hope that those who read this book focus on my good intentions, and forgive me for those parts where I appear to have either forgotten or failed to be as compassionate to the reader as I hope the reader is, or will be, to patients, staff, and family.

I never wanted to do anything other than to become a doctor, except for a six-week period in Junior High School when I wanted to become an architect. This took care of itself, of course, when I found I couldn't really draw anything in a reproducible, recognizable, or representative fashion.

I went into medicine because of my father's influence. Not influence in that he pushed me—he never did, but the way *he was,* day in and day out. The embodiment of compassion mixed with competence and an unquenchable thirst for learning, he set the level that I hoped to one day attain. My father and mother (brilliant in her own right) mixed those qualities with great senses of humor. I had fabulous role models at home while growing up.

If I went into medicine because of my father, I went into surgery because of my father's partner, who, in my eyes, demonstrated an amazing combination of interpersonal skills and uncompromising technical competence. He was, and still is, the finest technical surgeon I have ever had the pleasure to see work.

My vision of what "medicine was all about" was formed as I grew up. I saw three men and their families, in rural Kansas, practice together for more than 35 years without fighting about money, who was "more valuable" to the group, or who should control "this or that." They socialized together and their families grew up together. They balanced their professional and personal lives as well as could be achieved in their situation. They took care of the people in six to eight counties in two states, never neglecting their responsibility, despite occasionally being tired and disheartened, and never being compensated the way physicians were in more populated areas. Certainly they were not compensated the way physicians expect to be compensated today. (I remember my father marveling at the fact that the VA Hospital he practiced in at the end of his career paid him two-times more than he ever earned in private practice.)

I found the practice of medicine nothing like what I expected and had dreamed of. Of course I was naïve. Were my expectations unrealistic? Was medicine really that different, or had I simply made decisions about my career and the way I was that resulted in my dissatisfaction?

There are many successful physicians in medicine. In fact, most physicians are successful by conventional measures. But successful people are sometimes successful in spite of themselves. Few in the profession would disagree that other things—negative things—are found in the medical world of today: self-serving behaviors related to "turf" and money; in-fighting between and even within groups; political maneuvers by individuals to leverage peer review systems in attempts to eliminate competition; physicians with significant personal behavioral problems or disorders who are abusive of peers, staff, and students. The experience I had in practice seemed foreign to me—politics and financial greed had overwhelmed civility, mutual respect, and intellectual honesty, especially when compared to how I had seen my father and his partners practice together. What I saw and experienced was antithetical to my naïve beliefs. I was on the way to complete disillusionment and disgust with myself, physicians, and medicine.

I left medicine for what can only be called a "refuge"—a full-time research position in the pharmaceutical industry. One of the benefits of this move was more free time, which I utilized to read about leadership, especially personal leadership. I thought it would be important for me to know as much as I could about current leadership thought so I could "climb the corporate ladder." After all, I was in business now, not medicine. It was a different game. But as you will see, I began to ask myself, "Is it really that different?"

In this self-development process, I began to think about my past experiences in medicine. It became clear to me that one of the biggest issues in medicine was an under-appreciation of the importance of personal leadership and interpersonal skills. This is what my father and his group understood so well—perhaps intuitively—and what seems increasingly needed in today's medical climate.

It is my belief that this phenomenon—successful people who could benefit from enhanced personal leadership—has occurred because of the way we select and train physicians. We have developed a world view, as individuals and as a profession, that is not suited to the development of effective interpersonal relationships or business practices, both crucial for success in today's complex medical environment.

We have lost control of the profession. It seems we do not control our own destiny. Yet we are responsible for the decisions we have made, so we are responsible for our situation. For physicians to regain some of the control they have lost over their destiny, a cultural change related to personal leadership development and interpersonal skills must occur across all levels of medicine—practicing physicians, physician administrators, and down into medical school and even premedical training. This will require nothing short of a social movement within the medical profession, beginning with the acknowledgement that there is a problem. In some ways, it will require "occupational rehabilitation."

But recognition of this problem isn't enough. Individuals, and the profession as a whole, must take the next step of committing to change—to improving individual leadership skills, consciously and deliberately. There are no quick fixes. A "shot of penicillin" won't cure the problems we see today. Denial or resistance by some—perhaps many—within the profession is certain. The change will be slow and painful, but everyone can improve their personal leadership skills, no matter how good they or others think they already are.

The reader should not misconstrue my ideas as coming from a personal belief or position that I have mastered personal leadership. In fact, the contrary is true. My ideas have crystallized precisely because of reflection on my own career in medicine, my own failures, my own integrity gaps, and my own failures in personal leadership. I forgot what I learned from my father (and mother) and his partners. This book might be titled: "Everything I ever needed to know about medical practice I learned from the Smith County Medical Group." And I learned it before I ever went to college or medical school. Further, I don't believe that improving personal leadership and interpersonal skills will solve all problems that we face in medicine today. But it is the crucial first step that must be taken to solve the other issues in medicine.

If there is anything unique about what I have done, it is that I began to systematically dissect my behaviors and the results of my behaviors, providing me with a greater understanding of why personal leadership in medicine "is the way it is." Subsequently, I began to observe other physicians and their behaviors, and reflect upon past interactions and experiences, and I began to notice common behavioral traits of physicians. It hit me: it wasn't just *my* behavior. I casually spoke with hundreds of physicians—all successful in their own rights—relating my ideas and concepts, and they immediately understood what I was saying. Almost all physicians I have talked to understand the need for enhancing personal leadership in medicine and how it can help make successful people even better. The Seven Common Leadership Missteps℠ of Physicians is the codification of my thinking, ultimately distilled from 20 original "missteps" I identified as being common across the profession.

Some who read this book may be tempted to say it is only a "catharsis" of my own failures and an attempt to gain some peace with myself—if there is any truth to this assertion, it is only a partial explanation. The "cathartic" part of this book is an attempt to institute real, positive, measurable, and sustainable change in personal leadership and interpersonal skills for physicians and the profession, for the benefit of their staffs, their patients, and ultimately society. My hope is that individuals will read this with an open mind and understand and embrace these goals.

I have relied heavily on the work of others in the field of leadership and medicine, extensively including their words where it seemed appropriate. I draw primarily from Stephen Covey, Dee Hock, Robert Quinn, Kevin Cashman, and Alfie Kohn. I also have drawn substantially from David Hilfiker's book "Healing the Wounds." I saw no reason to not pull the best information from the best sources I knew, including lifting their words directly to illustrate my concepts and ideas. It is far better to use them as a direct source than for me to attempt to paraphrase things they have already communicated in a manner superior to what I could. I think this has simply added to the power of the material, and I hope you find it has been woven into the book in an interesting and compelling fashion.

The book has five sections. The first section focuses on the business leadership literature, the impact of good personal leadership on business results, and how the same type of results can be obtained in medicine by enhancing the personal leadership and interpersonal skills of physicians. The second section focuses on The Seven Common Leadership Missteps℠ of Physicians. In-depth exploration of why physicians develop these missteps and how they trip us up in our daily lives is provided. Section three presents data from the business and medical literature, as well as some data collected by The Woods Development Institute, concerning patient, health care employee, and physician satisfaction. The fourth section outlines an action plan for successful physicians and organizations to achieve positive, measurable, and sustainable change in personal leadership skills and interpersonal behavior. The final section is an amalgam of information, including women and their leadership in medicine, and a plan for instituting leadership development in medical schools as a step to begin to shift the entire leadership culture in medicine.

The leadership culture in medicine can be changed—for the benefit of our office staffs, our practices, our universities and medical schools, and ultimately the profession, with direct benefits to our patients. In pure economic terms, if you enhance your personal leadership skills, more likely than not it will reduce the cost of turnover in your organization and office, reduce your malpractice liability, and increase your personal and organizational bottom line. More important, enhancing your personal leadership skills will improve your personal satisfaction and happiness with your profession and life in general. It will reconnect you to the intrinsic motivations that first led you to the profession.

I have hopes that this book will be read by a broader segment of the population than just physicians. I've tried to occasionally inject humor into material that may seem lethally boring to some. It is intentionally written in a manner that will appeal to any person working in health care and to the health care consumer (formerly known as "patients"). I believe if there were a greater understanding of some of the issues I raise by the population at-large, it would enhance the relationship between doctors, their staffs, and patients.

When John F. Kennedy, in the early 1960s, said that within "a decade" the United States would put a man on the moon, the technology to accomplish such as task did not exist. Yet, by the end of the decade, Neil Armstrong had left the footprint of a human in lunar dust. It was accomplished. I have a pretty good idea of how to change the entire leadership culture in medicine, and those ideas are contained in this book. While the ramifications of this work may not result in the same dramatic world-changes as the first moon shot, the premise is the same: without a goal, nothing happens, and nobody is mobilized.

Some of you will have noticed that the "Desiderata," which hung on the wall in my father's office for decades, is the first page after the table of contents and the Hippocratic oath is the last page before the references. Why? Because I'm thinking we in medicine need to pay more attention to the former. If we do, the latter will take care of itself.

Contents

SECTION ONE
Leadership and its Impact on Business

Section One

Leadership and Its Impact on Business

CHAPTER 1 ⬭⬭⬭⬭⬭

About Leadership

Leadership is leaders inducing followers to act for certain goals that represent the values and the motivations—the wants and needs, the aspirations and expectations—of both leaders and followers. And the genius of leadership lies in the manner in which leaders see and act on their own and their followers' values and motivations.
  —James MacGregor Burns in Leadership.[1]

The Literature on Leadership in Medicine

There is little published—at least that I have been able to clearly identify—on the conscious development of personal leadership and interpersonal skills in medicine. There are few attempts to describe, understand, or improve the ability of physicians to develop good personal leadership and interpersonal skills. Most of the available literature is about leading medical organizations—in other words, management.

Gill, in a review of literature regarding physician leadership, found: "To date, the physician leadership literature is based on normative traits of basic responsibilities, rather than on a definitive set of role competencies associated with strict professional entrance requirements. This trait-based description of role responsibilities in the physician leadership literature trails organizational leadership research and trends by almost 20 years, which calls for much more rigorous research about physicians in leadership roles.[2]

The literature vacuum is probably worse than Gill stated. Much of the best leadership literature seems to emanate from the past 20 years. Covey's seminal work was done in the '80s, with *The 7 Habits of Highly Effective People* being published in 1989.[3] Works that set a firm base for the leadership writers of the past two decades, from Peter Drucker and others, antedated Covey's work. One problem in medicine is that personal leadership and interpersonal skills haven't' even been on the radar screen of physicians or organized medicine as an issue, at least until very recently. Where they are on the "radar screen" the focus is on "physician managers/administrators," with no emphasis on, or even an understanding of, the importance of personal leadership at the individual physician level—the "on-the-ground" leaders in medicine.

Motivated by curiosity, and having been raised in an evidence-based medical system in which one must, if at all possible, make decisions on the basis of what is documented in the literature, I did a PubMed literature search on "Leadership + Medicine." There were 1,951 "hits" from 1975 up to April of 2001.* Of the articles found in the search, published in peer-reviewed journals, few were available online as abstracts. Many of the articles were published in nursing journals. Brief, random perusals of the titles in this search indicated that rarely were they really about leadership *as an individual.* They were about management, roles in managed care or practice development, health care reform, and even "innovation."

After a bit more searching, some published articles about personal leadership or leadership in medicine were found, written by physicians or other medical personnel. One of the best papers is the text of an address given by William E. Berger, MD, MBA, a professor in the Department of Pediatrics at the University of California, Irvine.[4] In his lecture, he unequivocally draws on the non-medical business leadership literature to make an argument that we, in medicine, would be better off following established leadership principles from the business world. He speaks of the "substance of leadership" as being made up of "three basic elements: character, competence, and commitment." This seems to be drawn from Covey's work. He also draws on Jack Welch, the CEO of General Electric Company, and lists Welch's "six rules for successful leadership":

1. Control your destiny, or someone else will.

2. Face reality as it is, not as it was or as you wish it were.

3. Be candid with everyone.

4. Don't manage, lead.

5. Change before you have to.

6. If you don't have a competitive edge, don't compete.

---

*An earlier search in August 2000 was perused in greater detail. Of the articles found in peer-reviewed journals, only nine were available on line as abstracts. Only two were in journals meant for U.S. physicians; two were in non-U.S. publications, and the remaining five were in nursing journals. Of the nine articles with abstracts, none of the titles indicated that the articles were about leadership as an individual.

The most relevant bits in this lecture are some of Berger's thoughts concerning enhancing personal leadership in medicine:

"We must constantly remind ourselves that resistance, fear, diversion, weariness, and ignorance only serve to move the focus away from the [leadership] change that is required."

"Change is not a logical, linear, or intellectual process. It operates on various emotional and interpersonal dimensions that are essential to mastering change. It challenges long-held assumptions and encourages nontraditional thinking."

"Good enough never is. Superb execution and performance naturally come, not so much as an end goal, but as the residual result of a never-ending cycle of self-stimulated improvement. It must be viewed as a long-term investment for the future. In reality, there is no ultimate finish line for success. According to William Faulkner, 'Don't bother just to be better than your contemporaries or predecessors. Try to be better than yourself.'"

All of these statements are focused on personal leadership and the difficulties in getting physicians to recognize the importance of good personal leadership, let alone actively enhancing their personal leadership skills. Berger clearly sees the need for change in leadership in medicine, as evidenced by these passages. Further he appreciates the various problems associated with such change: fear, resistance, and diversion. And he appreciates something that is difficult for many physicians to grasp: *change is not logical, linear, or intellectual.* Failure to understand these concepts converts them into barriers to seeing the need for and embracing change.

Wiley W. Souba, MD, ScD, MBA, has published at least three articles on leadership, especially leadership in the surgical specialties.[5-7] Some very good information is contained in Dr. Souba's work. Most important, however, he is attempting to put leadership in medicine "on the radar screen." He understands the need for personal leadership in medicine, and the shortcomings of the current training system, despite the profession's outwardly visible success. The following quotes from his article demonstrate some crucial principles:

"…my interest [in leadership] has grown because my observations have led me to believe that leadership is what academic medicine needs more than anything else. And unfortunately, it is in short supply."

"Lacking a clear sense of what leadership is all about, competent leaders [in medicine] fail to develop."

"…the nurturing and development of leadership talent in academic surgical departments have not been a high enough priority."

However, Souba's work seems to have only part of the picture (albeit a very important one) in focus. The most obvious problem is that the comments are confined to academic institutions and to surgery. *All* of medicine should take note of what Souba is saying. In fact, it may be that more rapid, sustainable change in leadership may be driven by community-based physicians, not academia, because there may be direct financial repercussions to suboptimal personal leadership and interpersonal skills that private practitioners will understand and see first. (The basis for this comment is laparoscopic general surgery, which was adopted much more rapidly in the non-academic medical world.) Academia's role, as Dr. Souba points out, is, ultimately, to ensure that leadership training is incorporated in the curricula.

The best quote from Souba's article, however, is a cogent summary of what really is needed: "The successful department of surgery of the future will have to integrate leadership development with its historical missions of patient care, research, teaching, and community service. Leadership will be the synthesizing force that unifies these traditional missions, generating equilibrium among them, balancing cross-subsidization, and providing direction. Time, energy, and resources will have to be invested in the leadership development process: role models will be vital, broad-based empowerment will be essential, and the notion that failure is unacceptable will have to be eliminated."

Leadership training and effective leadership will be the strategic focus and competitive edge in medicine for the foreseeable future.

The Literature on Leadership in Business

The supreme quality for a leader is unquestionably integrity.
—Dwight D. Eisenhower.

Like a physician approaching a clinical problem, one should first describe what one sees, and attempt to understand and interpret the problem. Most articles and books found in extensive literature searches of leadership and leadership in medicine address issues that are not about the kind of leadership on which this book is focused. They talk about management, administration, innovation, or "doing something first," often putting the words "leader" or "leadership" into the title. Their authors fail to understand the difference between leadership and these other terms, and none of them are about personal leadership.

Many examples from the business world confirm that being the most innovative, being first—or even being the best—does not translate into market leadership. Apple Computer, the innovator in personal computers and widely accepted to have developed the best computer operating system, lost market leadership early on to Microsoft and the PC manufacturers. They were not more innovative than Apple, were not first, and were not better, but, through strong leadership and strategic planning, Microsoft became—and has remained—the world's leader in software and computer operating systems. And the PC still dominates.

John Maxwell codified these concepts in his book *The 21 Irrefutable Laws of Leadership*.[8] In Law #2, "The Law of Influence," Maxwell claims, "the true measure of leadership is influence—nothing more, nothing less." Maxwell outlines five myths of leadership:

1. The Management Myth: Management does not equal leadership. Managers maintain direction. Leaders change it.

2. The Entrepreneur Myth: Salesman/entrepreneurs may or may not be leaders.

3. The Knowledge Myth: Knowledge does not equal leadership.

4. The Pioneer Myth: Simply because you're in front doesn't mean you are lead-ing—you must have followers.

5. The Position Myth: "It's not the position that makes the leader, it's the leader that makes the position" said Stanley Huffy from Saatchi Advertising.

What does this have to do with leadership in medicine? It illustrates that personal leadership is not about being most innovative, first, smartest, the best, or otherwise; it is about effectiveness. It is about effectiveness on the organizational level and it is about effectiveness on the personal/individual level. As Stephen Covey has written so eloquently, self-leadership ("Private Victory™") must precede success in our social or work environment ("Public Victory™").[3] For whatever reason, some physicians seem to assume this basic principle has "taken care of itself" by virtue of their having become physicians and being successful, as defined by income, status, and education. Sustained personal success requires paying even closer attention to the Private Victory™ in our daily lives.

Personal leadership in medicine is not about competence alone. Being the Department Chair does not define a leader. Position is not leadership. Being a good man-ager in a clinical department is not leadership. Describing a new technique or procedure is not leadership—it's innovation. All of these things may be a piece of being a good per-sonal leader, but alone they are insufficient. Being a leader isn't about always being right… even in medicine. In fact, one measure of a leader is the maturity to admit when one is wrong. Irwin Federman, a venture capitalist and former CEO of Monolithic Memories has stated: "Leaders listen, take advice, lose arguments, and follow."[9]

Federman's statement is clearly counter to commonly held misconceptions about leadership. What is considered good leadership in business should be no different than that in medicine, because good leadership is about the individual. It is not some grandiose concept that applies to the way "we are out there…in public." It's about understanding ourselves to the very core of our existence. It's about Covey's "Personal Victory."

Kevin Cashman, author of *Leading from the Inside Out,* defines leadership as "authentic self-expression that creates value."[10] "Authentic" as Cashman uses it, means that we are willing to admit—to ourselves and to others—what our strengths and weaknesses are as an individual. He refers to this as doing an "internal 360-degree" evaluation.

"Self-expression" is the concept that we understand and communicate what is important to us as individuals. As an individual, my wife and family (including my dog, Jake, by the way), the qualities of integrity, honesty, and self-discipline, and edu-cation are of central importance to me. As physicians, we also have certain qualities that are important to us: compassion, competence, continuous learning, high-quality delivery of care to patients.

Finally, as Cashman says, this "authentic self-expression" should create "value" for self, family, and community. Obviously, the qualities just mentioned create "value" for patients. But the more basic qualities—integrity, trustworthiness, honor, wisdom—create value for others, such as your family and those you interact with most frequently.

Cashman isn't alone in the promotion of these concepts. Others, most notably Stephen Covey, have promoted similar concepts—in essence that personal mastery of principles is the key to public victory, as he puts it. Covey defines "principles" as truths that are timeless, universal (true in all cultures), and self-evident (they cannot be argued against). Such principles include: integrity, honesty, trustworthiness, patience, humility, temperance, modesty, and living The Golden Rule. Covey has a central theme of individual trustworthiness as the basic principle required for personal leadership—the type of personal leadership that will lead to public victories as well. He defines "trustworthiness" as an individual who is competent and has character. In turn, he defines "competence" as "a person with knowledge and ability in a given area." "Character" is defined as a person who "exhibits integrity, maturity, and an Abundance Mentality™."[†] He points out that, in order to have trust between individuals, each individual must be personally trustworthy. He defines personal leadership, being trustworthy, as the "first level of leadership."[3] Along those lines, Robert Lynch states that "trust is the foundation of all cooperative enterprise, and integrity is the basis of trust."[11] So character, competence, and integrity—congruence between what you say and what you do—are important components of personal leadership.

Kouzes and Posner write, in *The Leadership Challenge,* that leaders have five fundamental practices[12]:

1. Challenge the process

2. Inspire a shared vision

3. Enable others to act

4. Model the way

5. Encourage the heart

They state that leaders must inspire a vision that is viable, valid, and credible. For leaders to "Model the way," and "Encourage the heart," the individual must be a strong personal leader and have a complete understanding of the crucial importance of interpersonal relationships.

Kouzes and Posner polled more than 20,000 workers on four continents (America, Asia, Australia, and Europe) and asked them to rank 20 leadership characteristics, which had been pared down from 225 qualities identified by managers as being important to leaders. The respondents were asked to select seven qualities that they

---

[†]The Abundance Mentality™ is the concept developed by Covey that, in virtually any economic or business situation, there are more than enough monetary resources for anyone involved. The counter concept is the Scarcity Mentality™, which views the world as being one "fixed pie" and each individual tries to get as much as he or she can in direct competition and to the exclusion of others.

"most look for and admire in a leader, someone whose direction they would willingly follow." The results were amazingly consistent between continents, with the top four qualities being:

1. Honest   88%

2. Forward-looking   75%

3. Inspiring   68%

4. Competent   63%

The percentages drop off to 49 percent for fair-mindedness after those four. Note that the principle "honesty," a component of integrity, and competence, both crucial to Covey's definition, are in the top four of this massive data set.

The central theme of most work in the non-medical business literature is that leadership begins with an individual taking personal responsibility for one's self. This would include accepting responsibility for our personal decisions and for behaviors that successful people are prone to develop (arrogance, impatience, stubbornness, single-mindedness, intolerance of even minor errors, etc.), which are not optimal behaviors for a leader. It starts and ends with us as individuals. It is the actions of individuals, as leaders of self, which drive personal *and* business results. They are also what helps successful people become even better and happier. This is true of medicine too.

The fifth point of Kouzes and Posner, "Encourage the heart" is called Law #10—"The Law of Connection"—by John Maxwell.[8] Basically, leaders "touch the heart before asking for the hand." These are very similar premises and are best captured in Daniel Goleman's work on "emotional intelligence."[13] Goleman describes "emotional intelligence" as "the capacity for recognizing our own feelings and those of others, for motivating ourselves, and for managing emotions well in ourselves and in our relationships. It describes abilities distinct from, but complementary to, academic intelligence, the purely cognitive capacities measured by IQ. Many people who are book smart but lack emotional intelligence end up working for people who have lower IQs than they but who excel in emotional intelligence skills."

Goleman carefully lays the groundwork for his theory by utilizing data from multiple large studies in social sciences and psychology. From this work, he has identified five basic emotional and social competencies that dramatically affect one's personal effectiveness in professional life[14] and are reproduced here:

1. "*Self-awareness:* Knowing what we are feeling in the moment, and using those preferences to guide our decision making; having a realistic assessment of our own abilities and a well-grounded sense of self-confidence.

2. "*Self-regulation:* Handling our emotions so that they facilitate rather than interfere with the task at hand; being conscientious and delaying gratification to pursue goals; recovering well from emotional stress.

3. "*Motivation:* Using our deepest preferences to move and guide us toward our goals, to help us take initiative and strive to improve, and to persevere in the face of setbacks and frustrations.

4. "*Empathy:* Sensing what people are feeling, being able to take their perspective, and cultivating rapport and attunement with a broad diversity of people.

5. "*Social skills:* Handling emotions in relationships well and accurately reading social situations and networks; interacting smoothly; using these skills to persuade and lead, negotiate and settle disputes, for cooperation and teamwork."

Goleman has found emotional intelligence to be two-to-four times more important than technical competency in predicting "star performance" of employees.

Why is this relevant here? The concept of emotional intelligence is inseparable from personal leadership and interpersonal skills. The development of these five elements, in addition to living Covey's principles, is essential to the development of personal leadership and interpersonal skills that will result in greater success as a leader in social or work environments, as well as in interactions with loved ones. Where are these skills more important than in the interpersonal relationship between a patient, a physician, and the others involved in the patient's care?

So What Is Leadership?

Trying to define leadership is akin to the well-know comment about art: you know it when you see it. In some cases, good leadership is apparent, especially in public arenas. Although we usually think of a leader as someone in the "public arena," we must realize we are all leaders of ourselves. As Kevin Cashman has said: "We are all the CEOs of our lives."[10] Good leadership results from superb personal leadership—the principled leadership of one's self. The qualities of leadership that are most important are an amalgam of many peoples work, combined into a short list.

Trustworthiness is defined by having high character and competence. Competence is obviously related to one's knowledge and technical skills. Can the person do what he or she is supposed to do and, more often than not, do it well? But, as we have seen, competence alone is not sufficient for leadership. If one is trustworthy, trust can develop between you and other trustworthy individuals. Trust is the most significant predictor of an individual's satisfaction with an organization, according to Kouzes and Posner. Others believe that trust is the "highest form of human motivation."[3] Give someone your trust, and you will be amazed how far they will go for you.

Part of the character piece is, as Covey states, the principle of integrity, congruence between what you say and what you do. But how do we know if we have integrity? We know by constantly monitoring our lack of integrity—where we are able to see when and where our actions have not followed our words.[15] Do we tell our staffs, residents, and students to have compassion for patients and then not show compassion to our staff, residents, or students? Do we talk about how important work-life balance is and then justify missing important family events because "duty calls?" Do we say that our entire motivation and focus is to help our patients and then complain about our incomes? Do we bad-mouth "the suits and bean counters upstairs" for "not taking care of the business," while not being proactive about understanding the business ourselves? Do we want greater physician involvement in the management structure and then not trust the physician in management, who has given up clinical practice to make decisions because he or she "is no longer really a doctor and no longer understands what it is like to be in the trenches?"

The concept of unconditional confidence, defined as the "confidence that we are capable of discarding inaccurate assumptions and ineffective strategies in the midst of ongoing action,"[16] is another concept I believe is important to personal leadership. Robert Quinn has offered a different definition of unconditional confidence. He states that "unconditional confidence" is "confidence that comes from knowing that we can learn our way through virtually any situation."[17] A third potential meaning of "unconditional confidence" is, simply, "trust." If you trust someone, you have unconditional confidence that they will do as they say and act as you expect.[15]

Covey's concept of Abundance Mentality™ is rare in our profession and needs to be developed. An understanding of and belief in the Abundance Mentality™ is important to leadership, especially in succeeding beyond personal leadership and becoming a successful leader of a group or organization. It is crucial in any negotiation process.

Dee Hock, CEO emeritus and founder of VISA, has found a proper conclusion concerning leadership. He feels that the difference between leader and follower is nonexistent, because, in the end, we are all, at the same time, leaders and followers. He points out there is no time when our personal knowledge, wisdom, and judgment are not more valuable than another's. And there is no time when another's knowledge, wisdom, and judgment are not more valuable than ours. That individual, at any time, can be our superior, subordinate, or peer. It doesn't matter.[18]

Hock relates how he likes to ask managers what they consider to be the single most important responsibility of a manager.[19] He states he always gets diverse responses, from managing and selecting employees, to motivating them, training and appraising them, and so on. He notes that the responses all have one thing in common: They are all downward looking, and inevitably have to do with the *exercise of authority*. He goes on to note that anyone who has responsibility for others has four responsibilities. The first responsibility is to manage self—"one's own integrity, character, ethics, knowledge, wisdom, temperament, words, and acts." He goes on to say, "It is a complex, never-ending, incredibly difficult, oft-shunned task." He feels that the management of self should be our focus and take the best of our ability at least 50 percent of the time.

The second responsibility of one with managerial responsibilities is to devote a quarter of his or her time managing those who have "authority over us: bosses, supervisors, directors, regulators, ad infinitum." The third responsibility we have as managers is to spend a fifth of our time managing our peers—"those over whom we have no authority and who have no authority over us—associates, competitors, suppliers, customers." If you do not have their support and trust, they can derail you in anything you are doing. Conversely, they can ensure your success. Finally, our fourth responsibility is to those over whom we have authority. If we have properly managed ourselves, our superiors, and our peers, little time is needed to manage our subordinates. As Hock says: "One need only select decent people, introduce them to the concept [described above], induce them to practice it, and enjoy the process. If those over whom we have authority properly manage themselves, manage us, and manage their peers, and replicate the process with those they employ, what else is there to do except see they are properly recognized, rewarded, and stay out of their way?"

Hock continues: "It is not making better people of others that management is about. It's about making a better person of self. Income, power, and titles have nothing to do with that."

Hock concludes this section of his book by saying it really isn't about management at all. One can't "manage" a boss, peers, or subordinates. One can, however, support them, persuade them, motivate them, and stimulate them. Hock notes: "Eventually the proper word will emerge. Can you lead them? Of course you can, provided you have properly led yourself. There are no rules and regulations so rigorous, no organization so hierarchical, no bosses so abusive that they can prevent us from behaving this way."

This book is entirely about the 50 percent of time we need to spend on ourselves, and how we as individuals—as physicians—can affect our patients, staffs, residents, students, businesses, and even families by a greater focus on our personal leadership and interpersonal skills.

My definition of personal leadership consists of character, competence, and integrity, as these three things seem to embody many of the other principles discussed. These things allow one to have unconditional confidence. And leaders understand they are to serve those around them—not be served by "their people."

A Personal Leadership Focus in Medicine: Commitment to Change

As stated earlier, in doing an extensive review of the literature as it relates to leadership in medicine, it is clear that physicians confuse leadership with many things. "Leadership," in the medical literature, is used to describe, or is even used interchangeably with, terms such as:

- Management

- Intelligence or knowledge

- Technical skills

- Clinical competence

- Innovation

- Chairmanship

Because of his or position, it is assumed that the chair of a clinical department is a "leader"—often called "positional" or "borrowed" leadership. But this really isn't leadership. The process of becoming a physician has, in many cases, resulted in the development of successful people with less-than-optimal personal leadership qualities and interpersonal skills. The education of physicians is completely stacked against the development of leadership qualities needed in today's complex medical environment. Today's reality requires that physicians not only be clinicians, but also live as part of complex organizational and social systems. We have reached this state not because of anything we as individuals have consciously done or failed to do, but rather because (at least in part) the system developed to select and train us operates counter to engendering good personal leadership and interpersonal qualities. We also may have forgotten some important principles we learned earlier in our lives—or perhaps we allowed those qualities to be "trained out of us."

Changing the leadership culture in medicine will have a wide-reaching impact. It will benefit our patients, our office staffs, our practices, our universities and medical schools, and ultimately the profession. Our family lives will improve. Enhancing personal leadership skills of physicians will improve the profession's control of its destiny, as well as personal and organizational bottom lines. Enhancing your personal leadership and interpersonal skills will ultimately put more money in your pockets.

Making a commitment to such change as enhancing one's leadership skills is always a personal choice, and often not an easy one. Viktor Frankl, who wrote *Man's Search for Meaning,* clearly illustrates that man's last freedom is always having the ability to choose one's response to any circumstance.[20] Because Frankl's concepts were developed out of his experience in a Nazi concentration camp, one can hardly ignore his position on personal accountability for one's own decisions. Quinn notes that Frankl's book can be boiled-down to two relevant points:

1. People are always free to choose.

2. A sense of purpose gives one the strength and the capacity to "transcend even very abusive and even life-threatening situations."[15]

This leads to the time of a decision on your part: to continue to explore your personal leadership characteristics (whether you are a physician or not). Ideally, most readers continue to be open to examination and a commitment to changing medicine, or at least to personal improvement. Through your commitment, we can affect medicine and institute occupational rehabilitation, find congruence between the seemingly incongruent goals of good patient care and the business of medicine, and greater peace and job satisfaction for ourselves.

In the end, physicians won't argue about these concepts "not being true."[15] Physicians, especially successful physicians, might say, "it isn't relevant to my world." They might say they "live in the real world," and these principles and concepts don't apply. But recalling Covey's definition of the principles of personal leadership, they are timeless, universal, and self-evident—it cannot be logically argued that they aren't "relevant." Quinn made this point in his book "Change the World," stating what people really mean to say in circumstances where major change is proposed is that this sort of change is "too hard" or requires "too much sacrifice" on their part.[17] The change we are speaking of won't be easy. A quote from Kouzes and Posner's "The Leadership Challenge" seems appropriate at this moment, as it relates to significant change: "Our fear and apprehension are greater barriers to success than the actual difficulties or risk itself."[12]

If, as individuals who have already achieved great success—often with significant sacrifice to ourselves and family— we are brave enough to improve our personal leadership skills, we will enhance the sense of gratification we receive from our work—the nonmonetary value of what we do will become more apparent to us. While a beneficial side-effect of this will be an enhancement of the financial bottom line, it should not be the focus for wanting to improve oneself. The choice is up to each individual and is highly personal; it portends a shift and openness to thinking differently. Acknowledging that one can improve his or her personal leadership does not imply weakness on the individual's part. Quite the contrary, it says to everyone you have the strength and insight to appreciate that—despite being successful—everyone can improve their personal leadership and interpersonal skills.

Having read this far, you now know the tremendous benefit that awaits those in medicine who choose to improve their personal leadership and interpersonal skills. The choice ultimately becomes yours as an individual as to whether you will read on and be open to the concepts and to the possibility of personal change. This brings to mind an excerpt from Parker Palmer's work: "No punishment anyone lays on you could possibly be worse than the punishment you lay on yourself by conspiring in your own diminishment. With that insight comes the ability to open cell doors that were never locked in the first place and to walk into new possibilities that honor the claims of one's heart."[21]

CHAPTER 2 ⌾⌾⌾⌾⌾

Imminent Impact I: Results of Personal Leadership and the Business of Medicine

Although leadership of the American health care enterprise was initially the province of the physician, over the last half century, it has become almost exclusively a nonphysician activity.[22]

The TRIZ Principles—Why Business Leadership Literature Is Relevant to Medicine

One obvious question readers might have is: "What possible relevance does the non-medical business literature have to medicine or the business of medicine?" The answer to this excellent question, at least in part, can be found in the concept of TRIZ (pronounced "trees"). TRIZ is the Russian acronym for "Theory of Inventive Problem Solving," which was developed by a Russian naval officer after World War II to help stimulate innovation in Russia. The officer, named Altshuller, and his staff developed the principles of TRIZ after reviewing more than 2.8 million patents worldwide and studying 21 percent of the world's most innovative patents in an attempt to understand how people and industries solved problems of various types. Recently, Domb has revived the TRIZ concepts and has been promoting the concepts of TRIZ and its application to businesses interested in accelerating innovation. The relevance of TRIZ to the question at hand—"How is nonmedical business literature relevant to medicine and the business of medicine"—lies in the "Three Key Discoveries" of Altshuller's research[23]:

1. Problems and solutions were repeated across industries and sciences.

2. Patterns of technical evolution were repeated across industries and sciences.

3. Innovations used scientific effects outside the field in which they were developed.

A common problem encountered in business is low customer and employee satisfaction. When organizations are faced with such problems, changes in leadership are often instituted with the specific intent of enhancing employee satisfaction and job performance, which subsequently enhances customer satisfaction. In other words, the solution to the business problem of low satisfaction in this example is effective leadership. In the business literature, one can find hundreds of real-life examples of this in the smallest business to the IBMs and GEs of this world. It is no different in medicine. The impact of personal leadership and interpersonal skills that has been documented time and time again in nonmedical businesses, based on the TRIZ principles, will be realized in medicine. Enhancing the personal leadership and interpersonal abilities of individuals in business organizations has been a major strategic focus in business and results in documented enhanced abilities to recruit and retain talent, enhanced employee and customer satisfaction, and ultimately increases in revenue and shareholder value. The first key discovery of Altshuller, "problems and solutions were repeated across industries and sciences," is the key to my point. In medicine, the problem of employee and patient satisfaction—currently at low points that would not be tolerated in any other business—can be addressed by applying the solution of personal leadership.

The second TRIZ point—"Patterns of technical evolution were repeated across industries and science"—is relevant too. Gill, in a review of literature regarding physician leadership found: "To date, the physician leadership literature is based on normative traits of basic responsibilities, rather than on a definitive set of role competencies associated with strict professional entrance requirements. This trait-based description of role responsibilities in the physician leadership literature trails organizational leadership research and trends by almost 20 years, which calls for much more rigorous research about physicians in leadership roles."[2] In other words, a leadership focus now is simply part of the evolution of our profession.

There is no reason to believe that applying the leadership "solutions" developed in business to medicine will not result in the outcomes as defined by the TRIZ principles.

Leadership and Results

Ulrich *et al.* write about effective leaders' having a balance between leadership "attributes" (e.g., integrity, honesty, trustworthiness, character, etc.) and obtaining "results" for the business. They see the balance between attributes and results leading to a cycle of results that ultimately reinforce the leadership attributes.[24] They label this the "virtuous cycle"—in which the leader must have "attributes 'so that' results can be obtained," and "results are obtained 'because of' attributes." In other words, good leadership should lead to results, and results are obtained because of good leadership. (See figure 2-1, page 17.)

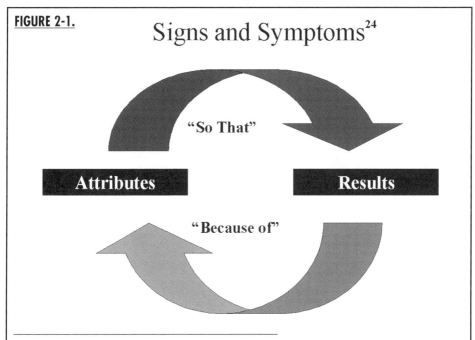

FIGURE 2-1.

Signs and Symptoms[24]

"So That"

Attributes

Results

"Because of"

Good leadership requires a balance between developing leadership "attributes" and obtaining results. Leadership attributes, e.g., integrity, character, honesty, etc., are developed so that results can be attained, while results are obtained because of attributes in this model.

Ulrich *et al.* point out that, in nonmedical businesses over the past decade, there has been tremendous emphasis on the development of the "attributes" part of the leadership equation, often forgetting that leaders are also responsible for obtaining results. They claim leadership development has gone so far toward development of "attributes" that it has almost excluded the reality that leaders are also responsible for obtaining business "results." In medicine, the reverse has occurred. The greatest emphasis of medical training is on obtaining "results," to the virtual exclusion of conscious efforts to develop "attributes," where "results" in this case relate to patient care and outcomes. (See figure 2-2, page 18.)

This assertion is supported by data from the Medical School Graduation Questionnaire, All Schools Report 2000.[25] Of more than 14,400 graduating medical students responding, fully 30 percent said they had "no opinion," "disagreed," or "strongly disagreed" that the "*fundamental* knowledge, skills, *attitudes,* and *values* (emphasis added) that medical students should possess at the time of graduation were made explicitly clear to students." One-third of our medical students don't feel they are taught fundamental attitudes and values important to being physicians.

This unwitting exclusion of conscious discussions concerning personal leadership attributes in medicine can result in an attitude of "the ends justifying the means" as it relates to patient care and a physician's job. This can ultimately lead to the development

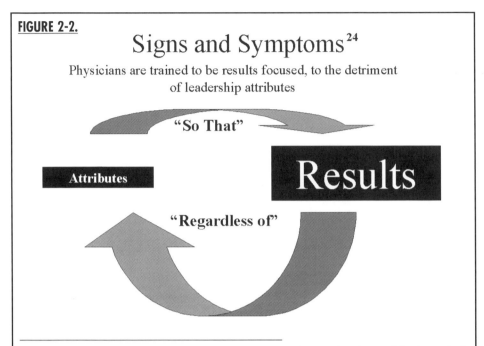

FIGURE 2-2.

Signs and Symptoms[24]

Physicians are trained to be results focused, to the detriment of leadership attributes

"So That"

Attributes

Results

"Regardless of"

In the training of a physician, the focus is on obtaining results, to the virtual exclusion of developing leadership attributes. Little conscious emphasis on attributes can lead to an "ends justifies the means" attitude in obtaining results in patient care, where a physician can justify his or her poor treatment of staff and other behaviors as being for the "greater good of beneficial patient outcome," regardless of attributes.

of behaviors that are not conducive to good interpersonal relationships and that result in suboptimal personal leadership abilities. It can create an attitude that, as long as the patient is cared for, it doesn't matter how it gets accomplished—how nurses are treated, how office staff are handled, can become a secondary consideration, their being used merely as "instruments of patient care."

Results and Value

Result: v. 1. to arise or proceed as a consequence from actions, circumstances, premises, etc.; be the outcome.

Value: n. 1. attributed or relative worth, merit, or usefulness.[26]

Business is all about results and value. The actions of an organization or leader and the circumstances that they create ultimately determine the results obtained by that organization or leader. Results are experienced by a customer, who can be internal or external to the organization and who assigns some value to the results. An important point is that only the customer—the receiver of the results—can determine the value he or she receives from a product or service; the deliverer of the results does not determine value. The deliverer of results may determine the price of a product or service, but this does not mean there is value to the product or service. If customers do not perceive a positive value for a product at its price, they don't buy it. If a can of soda costs $1, but I don't like soda, it has no value to me, even though it has a market value of $1. My dog Jake, while having no monetary value, is incredibly important to me, and hence has tremendous value.

Value is not always determined by some monetary measure. As in the definition given above, the "worth, merit, or usefulness" that one attributes to something is the value, as determined by that individual. Value, then, can differ between individuals for the same product, service, or outcome.

The LECO Principle: The Leader→ Employee→ Customer→ Organization Value Chain

Ulrich *et al.* go on to point out that, especially in business, there are four key stake-holders for which results must be obtained: employees, customers, the organization, and investors. I view this as a "value flow" that begins with the leader, who affects the value employees receive from their jobs. They, in turn, affect the value customers receive from the business. The value that the customers feel they have obtained simultaneously translates into value for the organization. The Woods Development Institute calls the concept The LECO Principle: **L**eader→ **E**mployee→ **C**ustomer→ **O**rganization (figure 2-3, below). In business, investors are part of this equation.

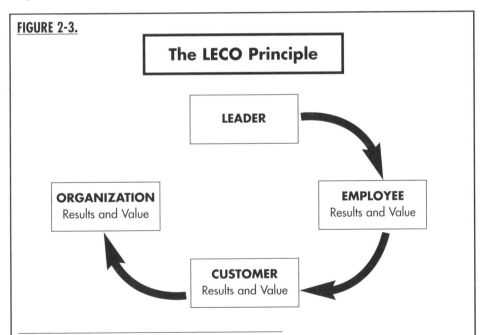

FIGURE 2-3.

The LECO Principle

LEADER

ORGANIZATION
Results and Value

EMPLOYEE
Results and Value

CUSTOMER
Results and Value

The LECO Principle states that the leader of any organization is responsible for the results obtained by each group, as well as for the value that each group perceives they receive. The better the results a leader obtains with the employees and the greater the value employees perceive in their jobs, the better the results and the value the customer perceives, which translates into organizational results and value. Over-focus on one area to the exclusion of another ultimately results in this chain being broken, to the detriment of the entire system.

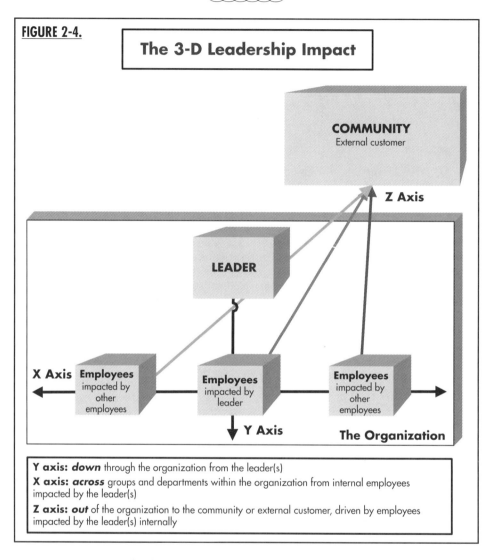

FIGURE 2-4.

The 3-D Leadership Impact

COMMUNITY
External customer

Z Axis

LEADER

X Axis — Employees impacted by other employees

Employees impacted by leader

Employees impacted by other employees

Y Axis

The Organization

Y axis: *down* through the organization from the leader(s)

X axis: *across* groups and departments within the organization from internal employees impacted by the leader(s)

Z axis: *out* of the organization to the community or external customer, driven by employees impacted by the leader(s) internally

Because organizational value is generally predictive of investor value, "investors" have been left out of the equation.

Ulrich *et al.* suggest that, while most businesses seem to be focused on one of these four groups more intently than others, none of these segments can be completely ignored, or the "business system" (basically, a complex ecosystem) will be out of balance.

The 3-D Impact of Effective Leadership

The LECO Principle diagrammatically implies a linear, flat effect of leadership, but, in most businesses, effective leaders can and should have a three-dimensional impact. Effective leaders—whether the CEO as the leader at the top or an employee-leader within the organization—generate results and value across three axes (figure 2-4, above):

- ■ **Y axis:** *Vertically down* from the leader to the employees.

- ■ **X axis:** *Horizontally across* the organization as employees beneficially influenced by the leader affect other employees in the organization (an expanding effect akin to throwing a pebble in quiet water).

- ■ **Z axis:** Depth *penetration into* the community as a result of employees across the organization affecting external customers

This model is mentioned to avoid leaving the reader with the impression that leadership is a linear or two-dimensional, flat world, and to emphasize the interdependent realities of leadership and leaders. While the LECO Principle is simple to remember, it is incomplete without this perspective. This is an important concept for all leaders, and, as we will see, it is especially important for physicians.

Physicians tend to think that the only results that are important are those achieved for the "customer," that is, the patient. Ulrich *et al.* point out that results are not just things like production and sales—or, in medicine's case, the outcome of a particular treatment for a specific patient. The happiness of your office staff, of the OR staff, of the nurses on the floor in the hospital, of your administrative assistant are results that you are responsible for as a leader. Satisfaction is a result, just like the profit you split at the end of the year or the stock you have in your organization. Further, the results one obtains with one's staff are more important and valuable than many people think.

Ulrich points to research that clearly indicates there are lead and lag indicators of results with these four stakeholder groups.[27] He notes that employee results tend to predict customer results, which simultaneously predict organizational result. Improvements in customer and organizational results predict investor results. If employees are happy and well cared for, feel valued, and are rewarded appropriately, they tend to be motivated and will treat customers accordingly. If they are verbally abused, under appreciated, underpaid, and over-worked, results with customers will reflect those employee results. The LECO Principle and 3-D Impact are bi-directional—if the leader acts in a way that results in employee dissatisfaction and unhappiness, customer satisfaction will reflect that dissatisfaction and unhappiness. Leaders cannot decide that employees are receiving "good value," because "value" or "results" can only be defined by the receiver, not the "giver." Likewise, only patients can determine the value they are receiving.

There is a common dictum concerning customer satisfaction that demonstrates the impact that office personnel can have on customers. If an individual has a bad experience in a certain store or a certain office, he or she will, on average, tell 9 people of that bad experience. Each of those 9 people tell 9 more people. Very quickly the bad experience of one person results in communication of that bad experience on a near-logarithmic scale.[28] On the flip side, if an individual has a good experience, outcome, or result, he or she will, on average, tell only two persons.

The Albrect Report Card further substantiates this train of thought. It found that customers leave a business for the following reasons[29]:

- 1% leave through death

- 3% move away

- 5% leave to do business with friends

- 9% prefer the competition's product

- 14% had one bad encounter

- 68% leave because they said the actions of the company showed indifference

The indifferent actions included electronic greetings (voice maze), voice mail, and poor service from a receptionist (an entry-level position). Many companies use voice mail services and the like in order to save money, but, in reality, they cost much more than they save. If more emphasis were placed on training and retaining good people, many employee-based reasons for customer loss would disappear.

There is no reason to believe that the dynamics of customer and employee retention or loss in nonmedical businesses are any different in medical businesses. When nonmedical business organizations invest in people, such as leadership training and behavioral coaching to enhance personal leadership and interpersonal relationships, they experience 60 to 300 percent growth over the competition, a return on investment (ROI) of 150-1000 percent,[30] 200-300 percent return of sales higher than the competition, and 50% higher ratings on service, including quality and customer service. This is important to the business of medicine, which is all about service.

Most resumes focus only on the ability and experience of the candidate for a position and most interviews (unless they are behavioral interviews) fail to pick up on the behavioral traits that indicate a person's likelihood of success in a given organization. This is true in medicine as well. Most job descriptions, even in the medical profession, are task oriented; yet more people fail, not through being unable to do the tasks, but through behavioral style—a lack of fit with the organization, or conflicts with behaviors of specific individuals within an organization. In fact, up to 85 percent of employee turnover is due to behavior incompatibility. In one study of non-licensed employees in a long-term nursing facility, 24.3 percent of resignations were because of personal/staff conflicts—very much a leadership issue.[31] In the health care profession, the national monthly turnover between January and September 1999 was 1.7 percent— one of the highest turnover rates of all industries. By comparison, national monthly turnover in the finance industry was only 1.2% and in manufacturing it was 1%.[32]

When employees leave an organization, it is expensive—perhaps being even more expensive to the organization than customer (or patient) loss. The cost of replacing even an entry-level employee is staggering according to the latest research. Deloitte & Touche reports it spends about $7,000 per hire when it uses traditional search agencies and classified ads.[33] Another report estimates that recruitment and retraining costs to replace a departing employee range from 1.5 to 2 times that employee's annual salary.[34] Others more conservatively estimate the cost to be between 70 and 200 percent of the employee's annual income.[35]

A formula has been developed to help measure the cost of turnover in an organization.[36]

1. *Annual wage: employee's annual salary x 0.25 =* _____

2. *Annual benefits: employee's annual salary x 0.30 =* _____

3. *Total turnover cost per employee (add Lines 1 & 2) =* _____

4. *Total number of employees who left organization =* _____

5. *Total cost of turnover (multiply Lines 3 & 4) =* _____

Let's say you have 15 employees in your small medical office, with an annual turnover of 4 individuals, or 27 percent, which is not an unusual rate of turnover in any medical office or business. And let's say the average income of those leaving was $25,000—a rather modest sum. Applying the above formula, the 15-person organization is losing $55,000 annually because of employee turnover. If you could eliminate the turnover, you could give everyone in your office a $3,000 raise and keep $10,000 for yourself or invest it in the business. Turnover *can* be reduced by enhancing personal leadership and interpersonal skills.

The discussion so far has not considered the cost to the organization when an employee is not getting his or her needs (i.e., results and value) met in the workplace: increased sick days, tardiness, absenteeism, low energy, stress, and bad attitudes are the likely outcome. Even though the cost of turnover and reduced effectiveness don't register on the organization's profit and loss (P&L) summary, the costs to the organization are measurable. In fact, the latest research indicates that decreasing turnover allows an organization to pay more and still drop labor costs. Lowering turnover increases profits, builds better teams, and raises morale. And satisfied employees' lead to satisfied customers. "Turnover in the health care industry is a major detriment to the delivery of cost-efficient, quality care," according to Kiel.[37]

Another study examined the impact of four specific culture elements found in business:

■ *Mission*—the purpose and direction of the organization.

■ *Involvement*—personal engagement of employees by leaders in achieving the mission.

■ *Adaptability*—employees' ability to understand what customers want, change in response to new demands, and learn new skills.

■ *Consistency*—shared values, systems, and processes that support efficiency and effectiveness in reaching goals.

In research on 1,200 companies ranging in size from 10 to 300,000 employees, it was shown that average return on investment was 30 percent for companies showing strength in all four culture traits. Conversely, the study found that in companies with an average ROI of 9 percent or less, the scores in those four business culture traits were low.[38]

The four cultural elements are determined by leaders throughout the organization, not just the CEO. Individual employees play a huge role, and, in the end, it is their personal leadership that gets the job done. It just gets done better if other strong leaders make their job easier. In medical practices every physician plays a leadership role. Every physician determines the culture of their office. Every physician's behavior can either enhance morale or make people miserable. Every physician can help retain employees and patients, or unconsciously drive them away.

The American Management Association (AMA) has calculated that the average middle manager spends 20 percent of his or her time resolving or dealing with conflict within the organization.[39] Imagine a health care organization with 50 middle managers. If the average cost of these individuals is $80,000 per year, the organization is spending $800,000 *annually* in income and benefits resolving conflict. In a smaller office with staffs making an average of $25,000 per year and 15 persons on staff and 3 manager-level people, this correlates to $5000/employee/year or $15,000 annually to resolve conflict in your small office. These numbers, while perhaps not overwhelming in the case of a small office, do not take into account lost productivity of those individuals on staff involved in the conflict that the manager must mediate. The Children's Hospital of Pittsburgh reported it cost $17,486 on average to replace a staff member in its poison control center.[40] The specific costs include advertising/recruiting, $326; interviewing expenses, $360; orientation and training, $9,250; processing, $350; and overtime monies, $7,200. It listed a series of less tangible effects that also cost money, but the dollar figures make the point. If personal leadership training and development enhanced the interpersonal behaviors of individuals within the organization, resulting in higher performance of their managers, more satisfied employees, and a better work environment, it should reduce the time leaders/managers spend dealing with conflict and hence reduce organizational costs. It should also reduce turnover and its attendant costs.

In perhaps the most concrete example of how employee satisfaction can affect customer satisfaction and revenue, Pascale *et al.* present the impact of enhanced employee satisfaction on the large retail store, Sears. They describe an internal study conducted by the then CEO of Sears, Ed Brennan.[41] Under Brennan, it was found that a 5 percent improvement in employee satisfaction, occurring as a result of a leadership initiative, resulted in a 1.3 percent improvement in customer satisfaction. The improvement in customer satisfaction was highly correlated with customer retention and volume, which resulted in a 0.5 percent increase in store revenue. More impressive, this improvement in revenue was seen in just 3 quarters from the initial point of the documented improvement in employee satisfaction.

It doesn't get much more straightforward: Improved employee satisfaction improves customer satisfaction, which improves profits. "Ca-ching!" says the cash register, all because of enhanced employee satisfaction and how it is positively affected by personal leadership. There is no compelling reason to believe that the data discussed thus far are any less valid for medical businesses or practices. It all boils down to the same thing: personal leadership qualities and the relationship the leaders within the organization have with their employees.

The DEPO Principle℠: The Doctor→ Employee→ Patient→ Organization Value Chain

We have seen from TRIZ Principles that problems and solutions to those problems, as well as evolutionary patterns, are similar across industries and sciences and from The LECO Principle that the value and results of personal leadership translate sequentially through to employees, customers, and organizations. Therefore, the same value chain documented to create results in business—beginning with personal leadership—should directly relate to employee and patient satisfaction, financial results, and even malpractice liability in medicine. The Woods Development Institute has adapted The LECO Principle to medicine, calling it The DEPO Principle℠: **D**octor (Leader)→ **E**mployee (Nurses and other staff)→ **P**atients (Customer)→ **O**rganization (figure 2-5, below). The doctor is responsible for the results obtained with other health care employees—whether nurses, nursing assistants, pharmacists, housecleaning staff, or administrators—regardless of whether they are directly employed by the physician (e.g., office employees or hospital-based employees). Doctors are also responsible for results obtained with patients, of course. In medical organizations, patients often have at least as much contact, if not more, with the nursing and housekeeping staff, as they do with physicians. In order to ensure optimal customer (i.e., patient) satisfaction, it is crucial that the doctor, as the leader of the patient care team ("customer-care team")

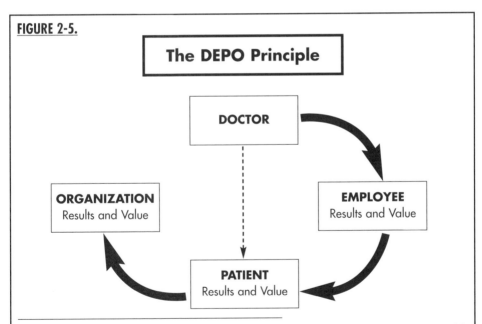

FIGURE 2-5.

The DEPO Principle

The DEPO Principle℠ states that the doctor, the "on-the-ground" leader in medicine, is responsible for the results obtained by each group, as well as the value that each group perceives it receives. In medicine, although the doctor is directly responsible for the patient, the doctor's staff often has a greater amount of contact with the patient and substantially affects results and value obtained with patients. Happy, satisfied staffs are predictive of patient satisfaction; the converse is also true. As with the LECO Principle, over-focus on one area to the exclusion of another—even if that "area" is the patient—ultimately results in this chain's being broken, to the detriment of the entire system.

ensure a happy, satisfied, motivated staff from the time the patient is admitted to the hospital or greeted at the office door to the time the patient leaves the office or is discharged from the hospital.

Patient value and satisfaction translates into organizational value—revenue. If patients are pleased with their care, they reward you by staying with your practice and returning to you. By staying with your practice, they contribute to the organization's bottom line. This is the DEPO Principle[SM] at work: good personal leadership translating into organizational value, simply by taking good care of your employees and what you already do now: take good care of patients.

The 4-D Impact of Effective Physician Leadership

Physicians are in unique roles as "on-the-ground" leaders. Leaders are responsible for obtaining results with employees and for the results the employees obtain with customers. However, individuals in leadership roles in other industries almost never have direct contact with the end customer, as the physician does. For example, I own several computers, but Steve Jobs has never sold, delivered, or fixed any of the items I have purchased from Apple Computer (nor, for the matter, has any of his vice presidents, regional managers, etc.). I have interfaced only with the sales people in the stores. Steve Jobs unquestionably affects Apple employees, and they affect me, as the 3-D model states. Even though I am on the consumer "axis" and outside the Apple organization, the leader is still helping determine how I perceive value in what I am receiving through the employees. This is 3-D impact of the organization's leader.

In medicine, physicians, the "on-the-ground" leaders, have a "4-D" impact (figure 2-6, page 27)

The 1ˢᵗ Dimension- "Y axis": Vertically down from the physician leader to the employees of the health care organization. This includes nurses, aides, housekeeping and transportation staff, technicians, and floor/ward administrators whether or not they are employed directly by the physician. The personal leadership and interpersonal skills—behaviors—of physicians have a direct impact on these individuals. The physician leaders set organizational culture or "tone" through their employees. As mentioned earlier, healthy culture is accomplished via open, effective communication, modeling appropriate behaviors, and ultimately "walking the talk" for all in the organization (and beyond) to witness. Integrity—congruence between what one says and what one does—is critical for physicians. For example, if one preaches about "compassion" for patients while visibly treating clinic or hospital staff without compassion, the message is lost and the individual carries little credibility with the staff. The "walk" doesn't match the "talk." Organizational climate, primarily a reflection of employee attitudes and effectiveness, is determined by physicians as the leaders and is positively correlated with the patient's perception of "service quality."[42]

The 2ⁿᵈ Dimension- "X axis": Horizontally across the organization as employees beneficially influenced by the physician leader affect other employees in the organization, resulting in further enhancement of organizational tone or climate. The better

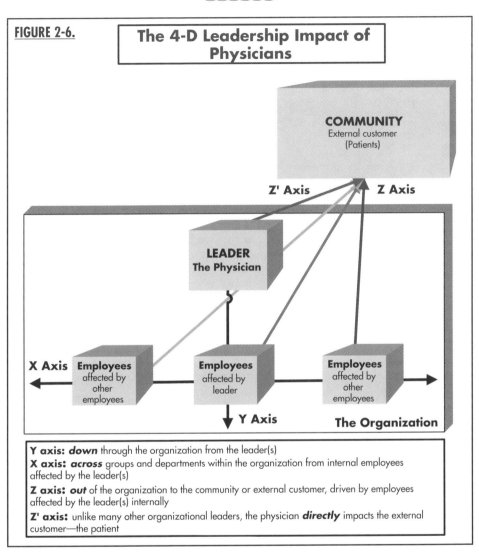

FIGURE 2-6.

The 4-D Leadership Impact of Physicians

COMMUNITY
External customer
(Patients)

Z' Axis   Z Axis

LEADER
The Physician

X Axis   **Employees** affected by other employees

Employees affected by leader

Employees affected by other employees

Y Axis

The Organization

Y axis: *down* through the organization from the leader(s)
X axis: *across* groups and departments within the organization from internal employees affected by the leader(s)
Z axis: *out* of the organization to the community or external customer, driven by employees affected by the leader(s) internally
Z' axis: unlike many other organizational leaders, the physician *directly* impacts the external customer—the patient

the patient's experience of health care service and the better the communication—which begins before and goes well beyond the patient's encounter with the physician—the more likely there will be a good treatment outcome[43] in addition to lowered liability. This is a critical point, as it is clear that employee burnout and stress are positively correlated with patient dissatisfaction[44] and malpractice liability.[45] Physicians can either reduce the amount of stress experienced by health care employees with whom they interact or increase it, depending on the physician's personal leadership and behavioral characteristics.

The 3ʳᵈ Dimension- "Z axis": Penetration into the community as a result of employees across the organization affecting the external customer (the patient). The patient is affected by all individuals in the organization with whom they have contact. It is the responsibility of *all* employees to ensure that patients have experiences that meet their satisfaction, but it is the "on-the-ground" physician leader whose responsibility it is to ensure that employees are delivering value. The impact of a physician's personal leadership and behavior on the patient doesn't begin and end with the face-to-face time between the patient and the doctor; it begins the moment the patient calls for an appointment or walks into the office and lasts until the patient walks out. Enhancing personal leadership and interpersonal skills of physicians will help them to better communicate with, and develop an increased respect for, the office or hospital staff. The result will be increased job satisfaction and effectiveness of the staff and an enhanced organizational climate that is clearly visible to the patient. While this may appear to be an indirect effect through employees, it is a direct result of the leadership of the organization.

The 4ᵗʰ Dimension- "Z' axis" ("Z prime axis): The physician is unique as a leader because he or she not only has responsibility for ensuring that health care employees effectively interface and provide value to the end customer (patients), the physicians also directly interfaces with the end customer and delivers direct added value. This is the most obvious as well as the most publicly apparent aspect of physician leadership. However, despite being the most visible and widely acknowledged person-to-person interface in the health care system, the physician is still only *part* of the interdependent reality of modern health care that determines patient satisfaction.

In health care, to stick with the Apple analogy, the "floor sales people" are the nurses, receptionists, technicians, administrative assistants, etc. The interaction patients have with office or hospital staff is important in setting the tone for the *entire* patient visit, as the employees reflect the overall organizational climate. At some point, of course, the "on-the-ground" physician leader also interacts directly with the patient. This clearly demonstrates that the "on-the-ground" physician leader affects patients—the end-customer—in two dimensions: through his or her direct leadership of office or hospital staff and through direct patient contact. If the encounter does not meet the patient's expectations or is disappointing in some way, patient satisfaction is negatively affected, and the potential for an unhappy, dissatisfied patient is increased. It is a more complex leadership relationship with the end-customer than in virtually any other business. It requires focus on effective personal leadership and interpersonal skills for "on-the-ground" physicians to optimally manage across all four dimensions.

Leiter and colleagues studied nurse job satisfaction and how it affected patient satisfaction.[44] The extent of burnout symptoms (e.g., cynicism, exhaustion, and frustration with working conditions of nurses employed in inpatient units) correlated with patients' reports of dissatisfaction with their treatment while in the hospital. Conversely, as one would expect, the more content nurses are with their jobs, the higher patients rated their hospital experiences.

A separate study by Niedz at St. Joseph's in Paterson, New Jersey, demonstrated that patients' perceptions of service quality were positively correlated to patient satisfaction with nursing care. Patients' perceptions of service quality were also positively correlated with their perceptions of the organizational climate.[42] Again, leaders—in medicine, physicians—determine employee satisfaction and the climate in organizations.?

Jones has reproduced these findings in an indirect way in a study of 12,000 health care workers, examining how stress on the job affects medical malpractice risk.[45] Departments and hospitals in which workers had the greatest number of complaints concerning on-the-job stress had the highest rates of medical malpractice claims against them. Others have corroborated Jones' findings. Bratt *et al.* found significant associations between job stress for nurses and group cohesion, professional job satisfaction, nursing leadership behaviors, organizational work satisfaction, and nurse-physician collaboration.[46] Collaborative decision making with physicians has been strongly related to satisfaction for nurses.[47] Job-related stress, in addition to salary and benefits, convenience, and work schedule, is one of the main reasons for nurses' changing jobs.[48]

The personal leadership of physicians is relevant to these findings, because good leadership can affect many of the things that result in job dissatisfaction and stress of health care employees. Being genuinely appreciative of a nurse's assistance can go a long way in making sure they feel emotionally rewarded—saying "thank you." Treating them fairly and as part of the health care team—as opposed to an "instrument of patient care"—helps them feel connected and supported in their jobs. Even things such as work overload and skimpy financial rewards can be affected by good personal leadership, especially if that leadership is emanating from multiple physicians throughout an organization. Pressure can be brought to bear on the institution's administrators to change such things as benefits. The staff will clearly see and appreciate physician support, reducing their stress and enhancing their satisfaction.

Another thing to consider in the discussion of employee turnover and retention is the dwindling source of talented staff in medicine. The prosperity of a health care organization is contingent on its ability to find, train, and retain a high-quality staff, which obviously includes nurses.[49] With nearly 60 percent of the current nursing force over the age of 40 years, combined with the fact that the number of RNs under the age of 30 years has fallen nearly 40 percent, medical offices and hospitals will have to scramble for a limited talent pool, if they aren't already doing so.[50] It is projected that the total number of RNs will shrink even further after 2010, when a substantial number of the "baby-boomer" nurses retire. This makes the importance of attracting and retaining good people even more critical. Losing individuals because of suboptimal personal leadership and interpersonal skills of physicians would be undesirable, if not disastrous to an organization. Retention of talented health care employees may very well become the decisive strategic goal of medical organizations, determining whether they survive, much less compete.

If the costs related to employee loss presented in the preceding section seems daunting, what hasn't been mentioned is the cost to an organization to replace a physician who leaves. Buchbinder and colleagues[51] studied recruitment and replacement costs associated with the turnover of primary care physicians (PCP) by utilizing data from physician recruiters. They surveyed a cohort of 533 physicians below the age of 45 years who had been in practice for 2–9 years and followed them longitudinally between 1987 and 1991. They estimated that recruitment and replacement costs for individual PCPs were $236,383 for general/family practice physicians, $245,128 for general internal medicine physicians, and $264,383 for pediatricians. Total turnover costs for the 533 physicians in these three PCP groups were $69 million. They concluded, "This turnover has major fiscal implications for PCP employers because loss of PCPs causes health care delivery systems to lose resources that could otherwise be devoted to patient care," or used in enhancing the business infrastructure. It is probably safe to assume that subspecialty physicians, such as surgeons or neurologists, would be even more expensive to replace.

So good personal leadership and interpersonal skills determine employee and patient value, but are personal leadership and interpersonal skills tied to the effectiveness of an individual's performance? The answer is "Yes." Hunter *et al.* have compared the economic value of top performers—those in the highest one percent related to income—to that of average performers across multiple professions.[52] They found that individuals in the top one percent of occupations with high complexity, including physicians, added value that was up to 127 percent more than that of the average performer in the same industry. Personal leadership qualities, such as emotional intelligence, have been directly tied to individuals who are considered "top performers." Goleman[13] and others have found that emotional competencies make up half or more of the ingredients of individuals who are standouts in any profession. Further, he has found and presents a substantial body of data that clearly shows that people who have high degrees of emotional intelligence are able to develop emotional intelligence in their employees, adding tremendous value to an organization's bottom line. Emotional intelligence is a crucial piece of any leader's personal success.

A study done by Levinson and coauthors from the Oregon Heath Sciences University in Portland found that physicians who had good communication and interpersonal skills tended to have a lower liability risk.[53] Further, they found such physicians tended to spend more time per routine patient than did physicians who had been sued. In fact, the length of the patient's visit had an independent effect in predicting claims status. How much extra time was spent with patients by physicians who had not been sued as compared to those who had? Three minutes.

Beckman and associates[54] studied 45 plaintiffs' depositions selected randomly from 67 depositions that were made available from settled malpractice suits filed between the years of 1985 and 1987 in a single large metropolitan medical center. Their basic goal was to ascertain "Why the patient sued the physician." They also sought answers to "Who suggested maloccurrence?" They concluded:

"...the decision to litigate was often associated with a perceived lack of caring and/or collaboration in the delivery of health care. The issues identified included perceived unavailability, discounting patient and/or family concerns, poor delivery of information, and lack of understanding the patient and/or family perspective. Particular attention should be paid to the postadverse-event consultant-patient interaction." This conclusion supports the finding that physicians have lawsuits filed against them largely because of weak interpersonal skills and because of the failure to appreciate the importance of those skills in the physician-patient relationship. Many of these traits are tied directly to emotional intelligence and the principles of personal leadership.

The role of the patient's family in malpractice liability is also important. This conclusion has been driven home by the results of the Adventist Health System, which eliminated family visiting hours throughout its system, including the emergency department. Families can come and go as they please, 24 hours a day. While Adventist has noted that this policy does create some difficulties for the staff, the idea has greatly reduced litigation expense in the hospitals in which it has been instituted. Basically, it is thought that, when things "go wrong," family members are less likely to "point fingers at anonymous health care providers if they were there and know that the doctors and staff did all they could do for the patient."[55] Individual physicians can have the same effects in their practices. It always boils down to the relationship.

A second study supports these findings. Huycke and Huycke, from the University of Oklahoma Health Sciences Center characterized patients who called plaintiff attorneys' offices with claims of malpractice.[56] The researchers were allowed to speak to a cohort of callers *before* the potential plaintiffs were allowed to speak to attorneys. They utilized six law offices in 5 states and spoke with 502 of 730 callers over 10 randomly selected days in 1991. Fully 53 percent of patients' decisions to call a malpractice attorney were due to poor relationships with providers *before* an injury. Other reasons included television advertising by law firms (73 percent) and financial concerns (36 percent had medical bills exceeding 50 percent of their annual income).

It has been shown that patients want physicians to be honest with them concerning medical mistakes. Patients are less likely to sue, even for moderate and severe mistakes, if physicians inform them of the mistakes.[57] In fact, they are about 50 percent less likely to sue if informed by the physician. The bottom line concerning malpractice is summed-up well by Robin *et al.* "In modern culture, the malpractice lawsuit is the most accessible vehicle for the expression of vengeance or 'getting even.' Patients who feel ignored or rejected by their physicians are more likely to consider a lawsuit as a way of forcing physicians to share the responsibility for the outcome and the patients' experience of suffering."[58]

Communication skills are critical to any effective interpersonal relationship, including those in business. And in what business is the interpersonal relationship between the customer and "business personnel" more important than in medicine? Recalling Goleman's concepts of emotional intelligence,[13] personal leadership, empathy, and other social skills are required to maximize one's effectiveness in interpersonal relations. The physician-patient interaction is an interpersonal relationship that requires—in fact, mandates—such skills.

Even the amount of money earned by a practitioner can be substantially affected by personal leadership skills. A personal friend of mine works as a nurse practitioner in a large city on the east coast. Her story is very telling as to the value of good personal leadership and interpersonal behaviors in medical practice:

"Laboring under mandates demanding higher revenue generation set by an inner-city primary care network, I decided to focus on the patient rather than on the organizational directives. Although I was busy, I tried to make each patient feel secure in his or her time with me. My strategy was successful, in that I became "over-productive," resulting in an increase in the number of patients coming to the clinic to see me. As patient numbers increased because of my efforts, the entire office was affected. The medical assistants, front desk staff, and referral clerk were inundated with extra work. Because the budget would not allow for additional hiring, I began to do what I could to help my coworkers, such as checking weights and blood pressures on my patients, making triage calls, and completing the entire referral form rather than just the name and birth date. The most important action I took was to thank everyone I worked with at the end of every day for their service and to make sure that they knew that we providers could not function without them.

"For the year 2000, I brought in four times my salary and helped to boost the visit volume for the entire office. I am cautiously pleased with this success. My doctor colleagues have adopted much of the same behaviors to increase their productivity. I unknowingly assumed a leadership role."

This is a clear example of The DEPO Principle℠ at work; as word got out about this individual and her patient focus, the number of patients coming to the clinic increased. The story illustrates some great personal leadership qualities; such as showing others you will lend a hand at work that "isn't yours." Her willingness to help others was a huge morale booster to the other nonphysician staff, leading to increased effectiveness throughout the clinic. Her behavior—focusing on the patient instead of the "efficiency mandate"—affected the entire organization, resulting in more patients and happier, more motivated staff. Ultimately her personal leadership and interpersonal skills—simply focusing on the patient—resulted in an increase in the bottom line.

While The DEPO Principle℠ and the 4-D model illustrate the impact of personal leadership on the tangible, economic aspects of medicine and individual physician practices, it is also relevant to the flow of intangible value. While the financial upside to enhanced patient and employee satisfaction has been detailed, what has not been discussed a great deal in this chapter is something one might assume would be obvious: enhancing patient and employee satisfaction is, by itself, a worthy result. Enhancing the reputation of your practice or your organization as being "patient-focused" is an intangible result with intangible value. If your organization is known as "a great place to work," it results in intangible value—and one that will have an ever-increasing impact on an organization as the race for talent accelerates in health care. An institution that is visibly dedicated to enhancing the personal leadership and interpersonal skills of physicians, one that understands the tangible and intangible values of The DEPO Principle℠ and what it returns to the organization through "on-the-ground" leaders, will have a competitive edge. And it will be an organization full of motivated, happy, satisfied, and fulfilled patients, employees, and physicians.

CHAPTER 3 ⬭⬭⬭⬭⬭

Step One Toward Fulfillment— Temporizing the Paradox: The Bottom Line versus the Hippocratic Oath

Again, you simply can't think efficiency with people. You think effectiveness with people and efficiency with things. I've tried to be "efficient" with a disagreeing or disagreeable person and it simply doesn't work. I've tried to give ten minutes of "quality time" to a child or employee to solve a problem, only to discover such "efficiency" creates new problems and seldom resolves the deepest concern.[3]

The Fallacy of Increased Efficiency as a Business Strategy in Medicine

I have a friend who is a partner in a large multispecialty clinic in a western state. This clinic had the highest patient satisfaction ratings in the state, based on independent surveys of patients. In the past year, however, it has begun to see a steady decrease in patient satisfaction. This, due to The DEPO Principle℠, has resulted in patient loss and decreasing income to the clinic.

Like many organizations, the clinic decided to hire some external consultants to "help" the clinic deal with this downward spiral of patient satisfaction. The consultants decided the clinic physicians and staff needed to become "more efficient," so, of course, a focus on efficiency was initiated.

I asked my friend, "How do they expect to help the clinic become more efficient?"

He said, "They think we'll be okay if the primary care guys just see more patients. I don't know how they are going to be able to do that though, because they are already complaining they are too busy—and they are. They don't even have time for new patients."

This is a classic story. Our income is dropping so "we need to do more." "We need to see more patients." Whether due to managed care or simply because of continually decreasing reimbursement, doing more has only one sure outcome: increased fatigue and the frustration of not having the intended effect, as this approach comes with no guarantee of increased income.

"Increasing our efficiency" in medicine can't result in much enhancement of the bottom line when people are already seeing a full schedule of patients. In an environment in which patient satisfaction is already decreasing, I can virtually guarantee that patient satisfaction will either fail to improve or will get worse. Patient satisfaction is correlated with physicians who are patient-centered; physicians who are not seen by patients as being "patient-centered" have less satisfied patients.[59] In attempts to "increase efficiency," basically to see more patients in a given time, the likelihood of a physician being regarded as "patient-centered" decreases. In chapter 2, we saw that a patient-centered approach in an inner-city primary care clinic culminated in enhanced revenue through a word-of-mouth reputation for "patient-centeredness."

In my assessment of such problems as patient satisfaction, efficiency does not seem to be the answer to the problem of decreasing profits in medicine. As Covey emphasizes, one is efficient with things, but effective with people.[3] If this is the case, where does one concentrate efforts to maintain or even to grow profits? There are three areas that are under-appreciated as potential or untapped revenue sources in medical organizations:

- Increased patient (customer) retention and attraction
- Reduced employee turnover
- Reduced malpractice liability (and the possibility of reduced malpractice premiums as a group)

All else being equal, if an organization is able to do these things, it will make more money. The way to realize them is through enhancing personal leadership and the interpersonal skills of the "leaders-on-the-ground"—physicians. By enhancing our effectiveness with our employees and patients—by becoming more focused on the individual—we will realize benefits usually attributed to increased "efficiency" in more linear businesses.

An efficiency focus in medicine has other, perhaps worse, problems. First is the implicit message we send to the patient. In attempting to become "more efficient," the focus is financial, *not* enhanced care. Hilfiker notes about efficiency: "Even beyond these two more or less practical factors of busyness and money, efficiency and productivity seem to have acquired a sort of independent life and value all their own in the world of doctoring. In our training, the surgeon who could perform an appendectomy in twenty minutes rather than forty became, in our minds, the better surgeon; the intern who could keep up with the steady flow of patients in the emergency room came to seem better than the slower, perhaps more careful one. Thus efficiency and productivity became a yardstick for measuring oneself as a competent physician.

"On a different level, the perceived need to be efficient and productive gave us physicians a large measure of control over others. The rest of the office staff clearly had to structure itself to maintain the doctor's highest efficiency....All of this made sense, of course, but it also served to cement the hierarchy, to place me firmly in control. Patients, too, could be manipulated by my need to be efficient. Practically any interchange could be cut short on the basis of busyness. All I had to do was stand up, and patients knew they had only a little time left."[60]

Some, perhaps many, who read this passage will feel the same pang of guilt I did when I first read it. I can clearly remember instances where I would stand up to send the message "I was finished," even when—perhaps especially when—I knew the patient was not finished with me. Even though I was perhaps thinking I "needed to stay on my schedule" (again, efficiency), more often than not my standing up was due to my discomfort with having to "deal" with things I didn't want to have to "deal with," personal or emotional issues tied, however loosely, to the topic at hand. In short, efficiency is never the answer when dealing with human beings.

There are clearly ways for physicians to enhance the amount of time they do have to spend with patients. One is to hire nurse clinicians or physician assistants to handle tasks that can free the physician's time. Berwick notes: "When patients need information, they need information, not appointments. When they need medication, they need medication, not visits."[61] In other words, a physician's response to a patient who has called the office to ask a question or get a medication refill is often to instruct the nurse to "Have them come in," despite the fact that it could have been taken care of over the phone. Such practices have at least three consequences that are to no one's advantage: 1) the patient must take time off to come to the physician's office, when a 5-minute telephone conversation might have been all that is required; 2) it takes the physician's time as well, which might better be spent increasing the face time with other patients; and 3) it costs the health care system money. Basically, this is an expensive practice that is not respectful of the time of patients. This approach, of course, presumes that the physician has previously established a healthy personal relationship with the patient.

The Inseparability of the Practice of Medicine and the Business of Medicine

The Nalle Clinic: A Case Study in the Failure to Appreciate Leadership and the Business Aspects of Medicine

Little did we realize that there were almost no issues that were either purely practice or business. Rather, every medical decision impacted the business, and every business decision affected the practice of medicine.[62]

Holleman carefully documents the weaknesses of the clinic that led to the steep downward spiral and ultimately to closing the doors of this prestigious, Charlotte, NC-based medical organization after 79 years of continuous operation. He discusses the same generic but nonetheless pervasive issues with which many health care organizations are struggling, such as increased expenses, decreased reimbursement, and increasing regulatory oversight. But he drills down deeper into the organization's problems, and uncovers the key weaknesses of the Nalle Clinic that resulted in its ultimate failure.

He writes:

"Like many large medical clinics, we suffered from a disconnect between a physician's actions and the consequences of those actions."[60] He goes on to describe a compensation system that was an economically unsustainable model. "The dynamics of the income distribution plan were such that the impact of a physician's performance—whether he or she worked particularly hard or had a more leisurely pace—tended to be spread throughout the entire group.

"If physicians felt they were underpaid, for example, they focused on the [compensation] formula, or what was the "clinic" doing about it, rather than looking at the processes, expenses, or productivity of their practice….Similarly, physicians did not benefit from sacrificing for expense reductions or suffer from excessive expenses."[60]

A huge problem for the clinic was a lack of valid feedback mechanisms for the evaluation of physician performance, leading to an inability to tell an individual how he or she stood compared to peers and partners. "No one felt they needed to improve their performance, which blunted the incentive to move to a more uncomfortable, but possibly better 'new way.' This is 'the way we have always done it' was the overwhelming attitude."[62]

Attempts to "change course" were needed if the clinic was to be salvaged, and Holleman acknowledged it "needed a culture shift" if it was to survive. He soon realized that a "culture shift" was not straightforward in the face of declining profitability, especially when increased productivity (again, "efficiency" = increased physician productivity) was only part of the solution. He noted: "But gaining significant changes in behavior would be time-consuming and would require one-on-one coaching with the staff."

Because one-on-one coaching would take "too long" (even though it does result in sustained changes in behavior, as you will see in chapter 10), the Nalle Clinic decided to pursue a "quick fix" to its problem by seeking a "hospital deal." The "quick-fix" solution seemed to be a better way for the clinic, considering its limited resources. Ultimately, due to several *clinic-induced* delays of the "hospital deal," the clinic failed because of two consecutive poor revenue months and massive resignation of physicians. The number one error that "sealed the fate of the Nalle Clinic" was "lack of leadership."

The Nalle Clinic failure can be lumped in a general conclusion applicable to medicine in general: There is a generalized lack of understanding and appreciation by physicians that medicine, even though it prides itself on ethics and morals, is still a business. To expect to practice medicine while ignoring economic realities—whether it is an economically unsustainable income plan, lack of physician accountability or myriad other problems that affect the business—will result in failure and hence inability to deliver care. The medical profession needs to understand and accept this reality in order to maintain personal and professional integrity and to survive.

Personal and Professional Integrity: Admitting to Ourselves that Medicine Is a Business

In chapter 1, "integrity" was described as "congruence between what we say we will do, and what we do." Another way to say it is "congruence between what we say and the way we act." There is a theory that, in our professional lives, a type of personal hypocrisy is at play. Argyris states that we have an "espoused theory" (how we claim to behave) and a "theory in action" (how we actually behave—what people actually see).[62] To others, this can appear as a lack of integrity. Argyris contends that we are not merely unaware of this discrepancy in our daily lives, but, "In fact, we are sure it does not exist."[63]

Subsequent work in this area by Argyris[64] led to the development of an understanding that there are universal patterns in our professional lives, regardless of occupation, based on four core values. Argyris contends that individuals strive to:

1. Remain in control

2. Win

3. Suppress negative feelings

4. Pursue rational objectives[64]

He argues that these are values that we all hold in our professional lives and that any suggestion of failure feels like a threat. We avoid threats because of the negative feelings they create for us, and we "dissociate" or separate ourselves from anything that will make us feel as if we are "losing" or not fulfilling our professional duties. As Quinn states, "Ironically, we shut down at the exact moment we most need to be open to learning. In doing so, we begin the process of stagnation or slow death" in our professional lives.[17]

Most physicians will recognize (but will probably associate with "someone else") an example from medicine. Think of the last patient you treated who did not improve with your prescribed treatment. The patient returns to the office several weeks after the therapy was initiated but is no better. It feels as if we are not in control of the situation because there has been no response to our recommended treatment. We like to "win" but we subconsciously view the failure of the patient to improve as a "loss," again because the expectation was the patient would improve with our recommendation. Because we "strive to suppress negative feelings," we pursue a rationalization to suppress the feeling of "losing" and think to ourselves that the reason the patient didn't improve is he or she probably did not comply with our recommendations. Of course there are other possibilities that we may not want to explore, may not appreciate, or may not even consider as a possibility, such as the fact that we might have missed the diagnosis or prescribed the wrong medicine. Further, our reaction in such a situation may result in losing the patient's respect, with subsequent loss of the patient from our practice. In other words, this line of thinking can affect our business negatively. As in the Nalle Clinic example, sometimes we don't see how our actions in practice affect the business and vice versa. As Argyris said, it isn't that we don't see that we are acting this way when it occurs; it is that we "know it isn't true."[64]

I like to remain in control as much as anyone. While I was in practice, I never really felt like I had control of the business aspects of medicine, much less understood them. Declining reimbursement from insurance companies and Medicare decreased my income about 5-7 percent annually for several years. I like to win, and so I worked even harder (again "efficiency"), accepting more referrals and doing more cases, only to see my income continue to drop and becoming more physically and emotionally tired. Telling myself I was in medicine to help patients and society, not to make money was of little comfort and was not entirely truthful at that point in my career, even though that is what we are taught to believe in our training. This disconnect led me to feel that I was losing not only money, but control of and connection to what I was supposed to be in the eyes of others. In order to suppress these negative feelings, I began to rationalize that the insurance companies and government were "doing this to me." If insurance companies and the federal government are responsible, I was absolved of the responsibility of understanding and taking care of the business of my own office and profession. I failed to address the situation in more effective ways, such as finding ways to affect the bottom line through increasing patient or employee retention in the organization.

A few observations illustrate these disconnects, where individuals claim or hope to be one way, while visibly, perhaps unintentionally, acting another. Many of us have seen physicians who claim to "do what they do" for the sake of human kind or their patients and then threaten some form of dramatic action or retaliation ("I'll go somewhere else to practice!") if their income doesn't reflect what they "think they deserve." This incongruence—a form of hypocrisy, whether recognized or not—damages personal and professional integrity. To maintain the personal leadership quality of integrity, we would be better off admitting we all are in the business of medicine. We take care of people because we want to, but we acknowledge it makes us money.

Part of the difficulty lies in our ability to reconcile the apparent disconnect between the moral and ethical aspects of being caring physicians, the delivery of health care, and the practical reality of generating income—the business of medicine. Simply being aware that these disparate issues co-exist and are inseparable assists one in moving forward in good conscience (or at least better conscience), and with transparency to the people we serve. We need transparency—i.e., to admit we are in business—for the public we serve because they are our customers and we should be honest with them, in part because they have contributed to the ethical, moral, and quality demands of the profession. We need to admit to ourselves and become comfortable with the fact that while we take care of people because we like to do it—it is stimulating, interesting, and gratifying—there is still a bottom line. We all have to eat. But let's admit we have to eat, and let's admit we like to eat well. There is no shame in the incomes of physicians, if their hearts are in the right place and they don't base decisions to treat or not treat someone on the basis of ability to pay.

Aligning Our Financial Expectations with the Economic Realities of the Current and Future Medical Environment

We need to begin to shift the mindset of our medical students and residents to acceptance of the inseparability of medical practice and business. We also need to begin to teach them that the financial rewards will not be as great as they have been in the past and that these rewards will probably continue to decrease for some time. This is the perfect opportunity to begin to shift the focus of those in training back to the non-monetary rewards in medicine. While acknowledging the fact that we have an often high level of earnings, we simultaneously need to eliminate compensation as the primary motivating factor for becoming a physician or for improving productivity.

Few medical school applicants are ignorant of the earning potential of physicians. They see physicians driving Porsches, buying $800,000 homes, wearing new Rolex watches, and other things the "average" American does not have the financial capability to do. This expectation creates a mindset—as early as pre-med and medical school—an expectation about what one "deserves" upon entering practice. Despite all of the talk in medical school about helping humanity and the high ideals, the financial aspects are often in the back of students' minds. Further, students hear attendings complaining about their declining incomes, reimbursement, insurance payments and the like. The message is that money is an important motivator of physicians. This conclusion has been supported by the findings of Leitch and Walker.[65] They found that financial rewards ranked as the highest motivational factor for surgeons. (I am confident that repeating this study in other specialties medicine would result in the same findings.)

Such financial expectations result in dissatisfaction and disappointment once one becomes a physician. To cure this malady, we need to close the gap between the financial expectations we (and students) have and the reality of the current medical business environment. The earlier in training this starts, the sooner medicine will have a generation of physicians with expectations aligned with the realities of the evolving medical business climate. Our medical students' and residents' focus will be maintained more intently on the patient if they have clear expectations about future compensation. (The issue of medical student educational debt cannot be ignored in this discussion, but it is addressed in subsequent sections.)

Along the way to attaining this goal, the mindset of practicing physicians also must be reset. We need to relearn the concept that not everything of value in our profession can be monetized, nor does everything we do need to be paid for. In many ways, the US health care system has "conspired" to support, even force, this type of professional hypocrisy. Ultimately, however, how one behaves in any circumstance is still a personal choice. This type of behavioral reinforcement has actually been described in a classic management article.[66] Kerr states that "reward systems are fouled up in that the types of behavior rewarded are those which the rewarder is trying to discourage, while the behavior desired is not being rewarded at all." Society—patients—would like to pay for physicians to be compassionate, kind, and completely focused on them during a visit, but physicians are financially rewarded by patient volume—how many patients they can see in an hour, for example. HMOs want patient to be happy, but they also want physicians to see one patient every six minutes (in some organizations). These are competing and contradictory goals, and we see the results in patient satisfaction surveys. (See chapter 5.)

While the system is set up to encourage certain behaviors (i.e. "efficiency") to "obtain the reward," this behavior is still a choice made by the physician. There is a tendency for physicians to abdicate responsibility for their decisions. Our vocabulary is filled with what Covey calls "reactive language" that absolves us of responsibility.[3] "That's me. That's just the way I am." (I am determined. There's nothing I can do about it.) "If only my partners were more patient." (Someone else's behavior is limiting my effectiveness.) "I can't do that. I just don't have the time." (Something outside of me—limited time—is controlling me.) "I have to do it." (Circumstances or other people are forcing me to do what I do. I am not free to choose my own actions.) Covey notes, "the whole spirit of it is the transfer of responsibility" from the individual using such language. Ultimately we are accountable for our behavior as individuals. The choice (decision) becomes a trade-off, as all choices (decisions) are: do I see one patient every six minutes and maintain my income, or do I focus on ensuring I address the entire patient—medically and emotionally? An attempt to argue otherwise does not demonstrate personal and professional integrity; we cannot abdicate such responsibilities.

A Holistic Approach to Business in Medicine

The business aspects of medicine and patient care should not be covert. We should begin to openly discuss this topic among ourselves, with the public, and with our pre-med and medical students and residents. People understand that any business must make a profit to survive. The business summary of this concept is "no margin, no mission." In medicine, this logic leads to debates—in fact arguments—about cost and quality. If "no margin, no mission" is a truism, for medicine doesn't that translate to "no patients, no margin?"

A recent article points out: "As long as we continue to try to maximize one objective over another, we will never escape the limitations of linear logic. What's more important to a plant: sun, air, water, or soil? We would probably say, "They are all equally important." And so it is with the multiple objectives of all health care organizations and other types of businesses. The trap is to say that one is more important than another and then try to maximize that objective. If we maximize water for the plant, we'll drown it. Sun, we'll burn it. All must be maximized relative to each other—or optimized."[67]

The authors go further with the plant analogy and "change" the model to represent a health care organization with the objectives of "financial health" and "patient care." Some individuals will propose to maximize "financial health" while others may want to maximize "patient care." In the end, either of these choices in isolation "will be dysfunctional for the organization in the long term."

As mentioned above, any organization has multiple components, and employees are one component that must be taken into account. In this model, employees must be cared for by the organization and, one might argue, should be cared for well. But this doesn't imply that financial rewards are the only way to do this; good leadership, respect, and interesting and satisfying work go a long way. Of course, we could not say our employees are more important than our patients or there would be no margin.

Finally, no organization stands alone, outside the community in which it resides. "Peter Drucker and others might argue that the business of a corporation must transcend its community....Any health care organization must make a deep and continuing commitment to its geographical community, because, again, it is an interdependent reality."[67] Investment in the community should be viewed as an investment in the health care organization's future.

So, any healthy health care organization should attend to its financial needs and to the needs of its patients, its employees, and the community in which it resides. The DEPO Principle[SM] essentially encompasses these things. "This philosophy leads an organization to attend in equal measure to the welfare of its patients, its financial health, the well-being of employees, and the building of its community. An organization that we might call "The Optimal Organization." There will be those who say, 'fine, noble ideas, but the reality is....' Their doubts and caution are real and must be respected. But if we can help them see that economic and institutional realities are not fixed constraints, and that they, as individuals are not victims of a reality, but the creators of it, together we can help to create a new reality for health care organizations."[67]

Doing this would eliminate some of the personal and professional integrity gaps related to our views on medicine and business. Even this, however, should be viewed as just the first step in the process of trying to find a more permanent solution to the seeming incongruence between business and medicine—The Bottom Line vs. the Hippocratic Oath. Chapter 7 will look at this issue in greater depth.

Individuals and their perceptions of their occupations within health care need to change from a linear focus on their niche within the system to an understanding that health care is a complex adaptive system. A complex adaptive system is defined as "a system of independent agents that can act in parallel, develop 'models' as to how things work in their environment, and, most importantly, refine those models through learning and adaptation.[68] Pascale *et al.* present a "new model" for businesses based on the current thinking of complex adaptive systems and the science of complexity. Their work led to the development of four, bedrock principles, which are "inherently and powerfully applicable to the living system called a business."[69] These four principles are directly relevant to the health care industry.

1. Equilibrium is a precursor to death. When a living system is in a state of equilibrium, it is less responsive to changes occurring around it. This places it at maximum risk.

2. In the face of threat, or when galvanized by a compelling opportunity, living things move toward the edge of chaos. This condition evokes higher levels of mutation and experimentation, and fresh new solutions are more likely to be found.

3. When this excitation takes place, the components of living systems self-organize and new forms and repertoires emerge from the turmoil.

4. Living systems cannot be directed along a linear path. Unforeseen consequences are inevitable. The challenge is to disturb them in a manner that approximates the desired outcome.

For this discussion, chaos is defined as an unlikely event or occurrence in which patterns cannot be found or interrelationships understood within the system. The examples the authors give of this sort of behavior include the swarming of bees or ants that take over a picnic. While their activity may seem chaotic, they are actually behaving as a complex adaptive system, moving toward a common goal. The economy is another example of a complex adaptive system. No matter how hard economists try to "boil it down" into predictable pieces defined by mathematical equations, they will never be able to predict what will happen. Further, the authors state: "'Living systems' isn't a metaphor for how human institutions operate. It's the way it is.[69]"

An illustration of these four laws can be seen in the Nalle Clinic's failure. The compensation structure set up in the clinic is an example of equilibrium. The attitude of "This is the way it has been, and it's always worked before," is a classic attempt to maintain equilibrium. It is a red flag that unequivocally demonstrates personal or organizational stagnation. Pascale *et al.* note that, for individuals "immersed in equilibrium," it is difficult to recognize the stability as a threat because "it often wears the disguise of an advantage." They state that equilibrium is "concealed inside strong values, or a coherent and close-knit social system, or a well-synchronized operating model."[70]

Certain features embraced by organizations can actually serve as "equilibrium enforcers," things that promote equilibrium, even when it becomes clear to some individuals that equilibrium is leading them down a path of certain doom. Curiously, "equilibrium enforcers" tend to be admired most in some companies, even though functionally they result in thwarting the sought-after advantages of diversity. "Equilibrium enforcers" include:

■ Persistent social norms (e.g., a compensation system or the inability or unwillingness to address physician performance measures).

■ Corporate values (e.g., mission statements that are used to "justify" behaviors that reinforce equilibrium).

■ Orthodox beliefs about the business (e.g., "we can't do that because….").

"Equilibrium enforcers" can be used as excuses as to why something "can't be done" or is "not in alignment with the mission statement," or is "unethical."

The other three principles were also violated in the Nalle Clinic example:

■ Nalle Clinic physicians did not respond to the threat of failure, and resisted moving to the edge of chaos and opportunity. They did not respond with meaningful experimentation or solutions. This has as much to do with the leadership of the "on-the-ground" physicians as it did with upper management's ability to lead a response.

■ Nalle Clinic physicians did not self-organize and no new forms and repertoires emerged from the turmoil. This requires not only strong leadership, but also strong and willing followership—relinquishing the autonomy that, more often than not, hamstrings physicians in the making of good group decisions. This will be discussed later in greater detail.

■ The decisions and direction the Nalle Clinic was attempting were relatively linear and directed. In the end, unforeseen consequences (e.g., the hospital deal failing, with no back-up plan) related to this path were the death knell of the organization.

The problems facing the practice of medicine and the business challenges associated with these problems cannot be solved with "business-as-usual" approaches. Linear and "that's the way we have always done it" thinking will lead more organizations down the Nalle Clinic path. The sooner physicians appreciate the complex adaptive nature of health care and their role as "on-the-ground" leaders, the more quickly the problems facing the industry will be solved in an optimal manner.

Section Two

Personal Leadership and Interpersonal Derailments

CHAPTER 4 ⟨◯◯◯◯◯⟩

*The Seven Common Leadership Missteps*ᔆᴹ *of Physicians*

The Seven Common Leadership Missteps*ˢᴹ* of Physicians explain, at least partially, leadership behaviors seen in medicine today. Missteps are defined as inappropriate behaviors or attitudes developed, manifested, and maintained by physicians—consciously or unconsciously—because of their education and/or personal, professional, or societal expectations. Some of these behaviors have developed in response to the public or their perception of physicians and medicine. These missteps can make the development and maintenance of good personal leadership qualities difficult and in some cases may actually form barriers to personal leadership. Some of the missteps are distinct, while others are clearly intertwined with one or more of the others.

When I started thinking about leadership in medicine, I asked myself: "Why do physicians, despite being successful people, seem to have sub-optimal personal leadership and interpersonal skills?" I wrote a list of 20 behavioral/attitudinal faux pas that I had witnessed or personally experienced in my training and career and explored each in detail. (See Appendix, page 181.) From this list of 20 "mini" missteps, common themes emerged, allowing grouping of the missteps into seven general categories. Each of the categories represents a common stumbling block for physicians related to personal leadership and interpersonal skills.

Each of the Seven Common Leadership Missteps*ˢᴹ* is made up of one or more of the original 20 missteps listed in Appendix One. When one of the original 20 missteps is first introduced as a component of one of The Seven Common Leadership Missteps[SM] it appears under that misstep's heading, highlighted in bold print.

Clearly, the behaviors and attitudes one observes in daily life may not fall neatly into just one of these seven general categories. The missteps aren't black and white. If one is arrogant, it could simultaneously fall under Misstep #2, Failure to Consistently Demonstrate Respect for Individuals, and Misstep #3, Lack of Personal Leadership. If one lacks integrity—says one thing and acts in a contrary manner—it reflects more than the misstep of Lack of Personal Leadership. It is the concept of each misstep and an ability to recognized when one is succumbing to a misstep that is important. It is not important to be able to diagnose and pigeonhole every single behavior of a human into one of the seven missteps. After all human behavior is not linear.

The Seven Common Leadership Missteps[SM] of Physicians
Misstep #1. Failure to Seek Win-Win Solutions

"Win-Win" does not mean we kick their butts twice.[11]

A nice lead-in to this misstep is provided by Hilfiker: "Doctors are selected and trained to be competitive, and I am no exception. One has to be competitive to survive the premedical winnowing process and make it into medical school, competing very successfully in college to qualify (and then half the qualified applicants are denied entrance because of lack of space). Once one is admitted, the struggle only continues, partly because the selection process ensures a class full of competitors, partly because there is constant vying for desirable residencies, partly because the best grades and the rewards go to the student who can, on his own, come up with the right answers. Cooperation seems almost like cheating."[71]

Win-Lose Paradigm and "Win-Lose" Education—Competition

Trying to do well and trying to beat others are two different things. Excellence and victory are conceptually distinct…and are experienced differently.[72]

The most destructive things to the development of personal leadership skills in the medical profession begin and end with how we train doctors. In fact, many of the sections that follow can ultimately be linked back to our education as physicians. The entire educational process of a physician is a competitive game with other students, residents, and fellows. Once a physician is in practice, competition continues with one's partners and with other groups in a hospital or community, only now the competition is for patients, income, and prestige. Shell and Klasko note: "Many doctors can recall being warned during their first premed orientation session to: 'Look to your right and look to your left—only one of you will make it into medical school.' This message to "look out for yourself" because medical training is a dog-eat-dog world is reinforced at many stages of the educational cycle. Some premed schools accept hundreds of students when only 20 or 30 slots may be available in a medical school program, setting off a competitive frenzy among students."[73]

Because of the way we are selected and educated, we end up seeing everything as "win-lose." We compete in college with our classmates to get into medical school. If you get in, you "win." Someone else loses, but you have gotten what you wanted. In medical school, we compete for ranking in the class so we can get the best residency. You win—someone else—usually faceless to us—loses. In residency, we compete for fellowship: win-lose. From fellowship we compete for the best jobs: win-lose. In practice we compete with other groups or physicians in the same city for patients and for health care contracts: win-lose. While you may be thinking, "I never thought about someone else being a loser," the reality is that the mindset created by this training is very much win-lose. Win-lose competitive selection and thinking does not promote respect for the other individuals involved in the competition or negotiation.

Without question, changing the educational system and eliminating this attitude of "win-lose" would benefit all those involved in health care—physician, employee, and patient alike. It is impossible to lead if one thinks he or she must always win.

The Media—"Best Doctors List"

The media contribute to the medical professions' "win-lose" attitude. The ranking of doctors and hospitals is misguided and creates an illusion of value. Unfortunately, this is something that physicians and hospitals have taken up with the gusto akin to a starving dog in a garbage dumpster, now using such misleading rankings in advertisements for themselves or the institution.

US News and World Report does one such ranking annually, in an article entitled "America's Best Hospitals."[74] It acknowledges in the article that "These days, even average hometown hospitals offer sophisticated medical care." They go on, however, to say, "But the institutions cited in the 12th annual edition of 'America's Best Hospitals' provide a degree of specialized care few community hospitals can match." What they fail to note, however, is that their methodology is suspect (flawed) and most people don't require "specialized care." Ranking increases the competition between the ranked institutions, especially academic centers, which are bastions of "win-lose" thinking in medical education. Our focus should be on a "win-win" solution—how to improve all of health care delivery in all geographic areas with the available funds, instead of worrying about "who is best." Ultimately, trying to define "who is best" is counterproductive, inducing even more unhealthy competition in medicine, and is, in the end, meaningless. The practice of ranking only serves two purposes: it gives institutions and physicians inappropriate and unhealthy advertising ammunition, and stimulates competition, potentially resulting in hospitals adding services simply in the interest of economics—to compete with the hospital down the street. Both of these outcomes increase health care cost and does so probably without substantial benefit to patients.

Leaders and institutions don't need to beat anybody. They just need to be the *best they can be.*

Inability to Negotiate

Negotiation to most physicians means getting what they want—winning. The process often takes the form of overpowering the opposition through professorial proclamations of position or facts, with little appreciation or regard for the other party or his or her position, assuming the other party is even heard. Listening to the other party is not a major concern of physicians and is often just "something one has to endure while waiting to get what we want." While some physician-negotiators are clearly very skilled, the profession in general has much to learn about the skills of listening and negotiating and the concept of "win-win."

Shell and Klasko outline some of the same principles in the 20 original missteps in physician leadership.[73] They describe "biases physicians bring to the table" of any negotiation process as "barriers" to physicians being effective negotiators. While the authors focus on the physician executive operating in a provider organization or managed care environment, their comments are applicable to physicians in virtually any setting.

The biases that they say physicians bring to the negotiation table are:

- The competitive us-versus-us bias
- The autonomy bias
- The hierarchy bias

The competitive "us-versus-us bias" is highlighted by an example of the difference between business school students and physicians, each given exactly the same negotiation problem to solve. The goal of the exercise is for each group to find the "hidden solution," demonstrating their ability to find and exploit shared "win-win" interests. Coming up with the solution in the exercise actually doubles the amount of money both parties can make from the transaction. About 8 of 10 MBA students or business executives will eventually find the "win-win" solution. When physicians are given this same problem, almost none of them are able to solve the problem. "…the physicians seem hesitant to risk cooperation, fearing a win/lose result that might make them look bad. Indeed, in debriefing the case, doctors sometimes express the feeling that they would rather have everyone lose than give anyone else a chance to get more than his or her fair share. Finally, the worst solutions come from mixed groups of physicians, i.e. attendings, residents, and medical students. These groups find it almost impossible to cooperate."

The authors note, as this book has, that medical education is responsible, at least in part, for this finding. Covey refers to this type of negotiation outcome as the "Scarcity Mentality™," in which negotiators believe they need to get as much of a fixed pie as they can, to the exclusion of others, and before anyone else can get more than they.[3] The situation described above is, in fact, the ultimate illustration of the Scarcity Mentality™. In order to lead, one must be able, and have the desire, to find the "win-win" solution more often than not.

Misstep #2. Failure to Consistently Demonstrate Respect for Individuals

"All day long I was being asked for advice. All day long I was considered indispensable. Even outside the office I was treated with deference. It was only too easy to perceive myself as inherently more important than others."[75]

Respect for individuals can be violated in many ways, some so subtle that we many not even appreciate it when we do it. Of the original missteps identified, the "Perfectionist mentality," "Physician self-deception: 'The God Complex,'" and "Failure to appreciate the importance of interpersonal relationships" clearly relate to respecting people and their thoughts and acknowledging and being understanding of human fallibility. The concept of the "Captive Audience Phenomenon" is also introduced in this Misstep. If one ponders the material of this section as it relates to our patients, much of what is really being discussed revolves, essentially, around the misguided and oft-abused—in fact, ridiculous—concept of "clinical detachment."

The Physician Hierarchy—The Frozen Bureaucracy

Hierarchy can violate respect for the individual, when it is used in a superior-subordinate fashion. I witnessed an example of hierarchical structure at a major annual medical meeting in Chicago. (This same hierarchical dance can be viewed annually at any number of national medical meetings.) Individual attendees were categorized into groups, based on their roles, using different colored badges. All MD fellows had yellow badges, while "Allied Health" professionals wore blue badges. Exhibitors wore red badges. This immediately allows an individual to classify an individual into a certain hierarchical "category" merely by looking at the nametag color. While some may argue this serves some purpose, I'm unclear what that purpose would be. After all, anyone who has a badge has obviously paid, in whatever capacity, to attend. (In fact, exhibitors often pay huge sums to offset the cost of the convention.) My impression is that this practice basically allows one to distinguish between physician and nonphysician, which is clearly a "superior-subordinate" hierarchical mentality.

I witnessed behavior during the meeting that suggests this is at least a partially accurate view. It was not uncommon to see a person with a yellow badge address only an individual with a yellow badge (a physician), even though there was a third or fourth person with a blue (allied health) or red badge (exhibitor) standing along side the "yellow badge person."

It could be argued that such a hierarchical arrangement is merely an unattractive aspect of the profession, but it is much more damaging than that, especially to our relationships with employees and patients. The authority of physicians can clearly be an inhibition to optimal interpersonal relationships and respect for the individual. A physician is given a tremendous amount of respect, and a great amount of credence is given to his or her opinions on matters not only of medicine, but of all things. Often this "respect" is given without any question or without any previous demonstration that such "respect" is deserved.

Hilfiker observes: "As a new physician fresh from my internship, I was amazed at the considerable authority invested in me, not only in my consulting rooms but also among office and hospital staff and even within the general community. My patients to a large extent obeyed me, the staff deferred to my decisions, the community respected my opinions even in nonmedical matters. My position as physician automatically conferred upon me an authority that was independent of my abilities."[76]

Many young physicians finishing training expect this sort of reception and, more often than not, receive it. This can certainly lead to a self-perpetuating hubris that few other professions can afford (or get away with).

This type of unearned respect, the near deification of the physician—whether just out of training, or in the 25th year of practice—is damaging to the patient, health care employees, and the physician. It can lead to the physician's developing a damaging sense of indispensability and results in a chasm between the physician and patient.

"Such an authoritarian relationship created a nearly impassable gulf between my patients and me. Since I was the expert, authority, decision-maker, the one to be obeyed, the relationship could not be an equal one. Whether the patient accepted it (thus legitimizing the distance between us) or fought against it (thus creating an adversarial situation), each of us was separated from the other, unable to solve our mutual problem. In addition, relationships of this sort gave me an exaggerated sense of my own importance. All day long I was being asked for advice. All day long I was considered indispensable. Even outside the office I was treated with deference. It was only too easy to perceive myself as inherently more important than others.

"The prestige and authority that accompanied my position as physician seemed initially very attractive, almost adequate rewards in themselves for all the other pressures of the job. In the end, however, they helped to isolate me from the healing relationships with my patients that might have allowed me to handle the stresses of the job in a more balanced way over a longer period of time."[75]

Avoiding the misstep of Failure to Consistently Demonstrate Respect for the Individual will require one to relinquish this destructive, misplaced and unearned authority—and begin to comprehend that such authority, and clinging to it, prevents us from having healing relationships with our patients.

Hierarchy is also a potent "equilibrium enforcer." Recall in Chapter 3 the discussion of equilibrium as being the "precursor to death." The medical hierarchy is on a slow downward spiral to death as we speak. The hierarchies in medicine (especially within universities) are often the drivers of the "persistent social norms, corporate values, and orthodox beliefs about the business,"[77] as well as medical education. This type of equilibrium can result in a failure to respect individuals who are trying to push the organization to the edge of chaos and drive beneficial change throughout the system. Hierarchies are antithetical to complex adaptive systems.

The Perfectionist Mentality

Perfection is apparently not what life is about at all, since perfection is nonexistent. Since we are not perfect, we have to be accountable.[78]

The "Perfectionist Mentality" is another pervasive concept in medical training. It is the idea that physician should make error-free decisions—that mistakes are intolerable and unacceptable. Unfortunately, such an attitude only creates unrealistic expectations that can be fulfilled by no one and that create guilt in all. Further, it probably prevents people from achieving their best. In a "no-mistakes" environment, no matter how unrealistic, avoiding failure becomes more important than solving problems, and is a surefire way of avoiding success.[79]

This type of training—expecting perfection—can lead to physicians not respecting individuals. As physicians expect themselves to be error-free, they become intolerant of others who make errors—even minor errors. The "perfectionist mentality" has also created problems for medicine in the legal arena. Even the public now expects physicians to be perfect, and the malpractice attorneys have gladly carried this banner high. Souba writes, "Time, energy, and resources will have to be invested in the leadership development process: role models will be vital, broad-based empowerment will be essential, and the notion that failure is unacceptable will have to be eliminated."[5]

Hock probably summarized this concept best, even though he was speaking about society in general, when he said: "We need the legitimization of doubt....[A]dmitting the possibility that we don't know all the answers is the difference between hubris and humility."[18] It is okay to not know the answer to everything—and in fact, be willing to openly admit it. There is a humorous ridiculousness to the concept that physicians—or anyone for that matter—should make error-free decisions when dealing with human beings. Think of it in this way: It has been estimated that the number of possible moves in the game of chess is 10^{120}. This number of possibilities exceeds the number of milliseconds since the Big Bang creating our Universe. It exceeds the number of elementary particles in the observable universe.[80] Or consider the even more impressive fact that, in an organism with a mere 1,000 pairs of genes, there are 10^{300} possible genetic combinations—which makes the number of possible chess moves seem miniscule.[81]

With this much possibility, with so many dynamic combinations in all systems—let alone the human system, which has a thousand times as many genes as the organism mentioned above—doesn't it seem outrageous, in fact laughable, to think we always should "know the answer?" Doesn't it seem misguided to expect perfection in decisions about diagnosis and treatments in the face of essentially limitless diversity and potential for response?

Think of this in terms of a patient with a bacterial infection. You, as the physician, prescribe one of many possible antibiotics to treat this infection. Basically, this situation represents two exceedingly complex systems (the patient and the bacteria) with virtually an infinite number of possible responses and combination of responses within each system, with the added variable of treatment with an antibiotic. The human has the potential ability to respond to the infection and the antibiotic with virtually unlimited combinations (1000×10^{300}). The individual bacterium has a virtually limitless potential to respond to the human and the antibiotic. The total number of combined potential interactions between human, bacterium, and antibiotic makes the fact that we ever accurately predict the outcome seem like a miracle! It is a wonder we are ever right. To get away from this "Perfectionist Mentality" is a step in the right direction of not only respecting individuals, but also learning about compromise and listening to and respecting alternative points of view.

The "Captive Audience Phenomenon"

Not only is medical training a "win-lose" series of educational steps, but one of the few professions that, if you don't like the program you are in, you have two choices:

suck it up and put up with it, or quit. The likelihood of a medical student or resident actually being able to transfer into another training program is essentially nil. They are, in effect, within an "organizational concentration camp." Because medical students and residents have developed the "win-lose" mentality through the training they have endured, to quit is a double-whammy; not only will they not get another chance, they "lose." Because of this system, medical students and residents are a "captive audience," serving at the pleasure of the medical school and attending staff.

Physicians might want to consider the following question: Were you treated with the same degree of compassion and consideration during training that your attendings' professed to have for their patients? Were you were treated as well as your attendings claimed to treat their own families? What message does it send to a resident when he or she is verbally or mentally abused, and in the next breath told to have compassion for patients? It tells me there is a disconnect between the attending's words and actions—in other words, a lack of personal integrity. It is an issue of personal respect for the individual.

"Induced behavior is the essence of leadership, no matter how modest. Compelled behavior is the essence of tyranny, no matter how benevolent," Hock says.[18] Note that he probably does not mean "inducing" behavior through intentional instillation of guilt in people, as so often occurs in medical training.

The underlying premise of such a teaching approach is the misconception that one can't be compassionate and considerate of residents and medical students and still be demanding as to the quality of their performance. One can be both.

Why don't we let residents transfer to other programs at will, and force institutions to compete to keep the best people, just as other knowledge-based industries do? This would provide incentives for attendings to treat residents respectfully, and it would promote more humane design of training programs to retain residents. This sort of approach—competition for the best talent—has resulted in remarkable things in the high-tech industry. Remember TRIZ?

Another group that is a "captive audience," albeit not as fixed as residents or medical students, is the office staff of physicians, as well as hospital staffs. Consider the experience of a nurse practitioner whom I spoke to recently.

"Nurse practitioners work in collaboration with physicians in varied roles throughout the health care system. Within the medical arena, patients consider them as physician colleagues, and they are expected to function independently. However, in reality, we are still seen as merely "nurses" by physicians, in a subordinate role...not as a partner in patient care.

"My experience has been limited to primary care. Regardless of the experience—or inexperience—of the physician, doctors have always occupied the "lead provider" roles. A nurse practitioner in the "lead provider" role, defining the expected numbers and generated income for the doctors would be heresy, even though it is reality in many cases."

This individual provides substantial support to the office she works in (both financially and personally), reduces the burden of the physicians she works with, and still feels like and is treated as a "subordinate." Again, a lack of respect for the individual and the value the individual brings to the practice is demonstrated.

In some ways, the problem with our office and hospital staff may be worse than with our medical students and residents. "As I made my way through the years of medical training, I was often astounded by the rigidity of the medical hierarchy. Attending physicians were on top, followed by residents and interns. Even the residents had to be careful not to step on the toes of the attending physicians, but it was the gap between physicians and the rest of the hospital staff that was the widest. Physicians made their evaluations and wrote their orders in almost complete isolation from the observations and opinions of the nurses who were in charge of the patients' care on a day-to-day basis; and physicians never even talked to the aides and orderlies, who had the most intimate and prolonged contact with patients."[82]

The "captive audience phenomenon" is really just a piece of the hierarchy built around and serving at "the pleasure" of the physician. Hilfiker goes on to note that, while some aspects of hierarchy are helpful in promoting efficient functioning, hierarchy and how physicians utilize it can also result in inappropriate expectations or behaviors by physicians. "However, what may be a legitimate way of organizing a group of people can very quickly degenerate into authoritarianism. In medical jargon, physicians 'order' a nurse to administer medications, implying a relationship between doctors and other staff members which may never be appropriate. Certainly, it leaves little room for the kind of cooperation that is basic to a supportive workplace or good medical care. (In addition, it's only a small step for the physician to start ordering his cup of coffee from the same nurse.)"[82]

The "captive audience" phenomenon isn't merely a concept. It's real. Physicians need to learn the concept that non-medical businesses have developed that one should be treating employees as best customers or, in fact, volunteers. Physicians should learn to treat their staff, residents, and medical students as they would their most important patients. In the end, the concept of "you can buy their hands, but not their hearts. You can buy their backs, but not their brains" should stimulate us to win our medical students, residents, and staffs' hearts and brains. If we do that, their hands and backs will willingly follow. In general, the statement that "people do not care how much you know, until they know how much you care" is a truism.

Physician Self-Deception

Physicians are often taught they "have the most noble and important job in the world." To have an attitude that one's job is "the most important" results in disrespect of other's work and occupations. It is a form of self-deception. We in medicine are just part of the social fabric and the overall economy. We have an important job, but we need to respect what others do as being just as important to society as what we do. It is an interdependent reality. If all physicians decided to "strike," the effect on society would be minimal. Only the sick would particularly care; all others would simply be mad at us. Few individuals are going to have empathy for a strike of a profession for which the average income puts most individuals in the 90-95th percentile of all workers in the world.

How many times have you seen a city brought to its knees because of a sanitation workers strike? How many times have you seen a significant portion of the country paralyzed by an airline pilot's strike? What about a teachers strike? Public transportation? Quite frankly, a hospital nurses' strike would have a greater impact on society than a physician strike. Who would take the "orders?" It would be akin to every soldier below the rank of general deciding not to go to the war. How effective would such an army be?

Many of the concepts related thus far, including self-deception, result in physicians' having a divorce rate higher than many other professions. Even marital problems can start with or result from the educational process in medicine. I recall interviewing for a particular surgery residency where I was told, "if you are married when you come, you will leave single. We have a 100% divorce rate among our surgical residents." Worse, this was stated proudly, as if it was a "badge of worthiness" and that the people accepted were "so dedicated to medicine" that they sacrificed all else just to come to the program.

Finally, for this misstep, we return to the concept of "efficiency" and relationships with people, in this case our patients. As Covey has stated, we are efficient with things and effective with people,[3] and physicians often forget this. That we are doing our best for our patients simply because we are efficient is a form of self-deception. The concept of "efficiency in medicine" is not novel. Hilfiker succinctly captures the problems with failing to understand the difference, and what "efficiency" in a doctor-patient relationship can result in: "As with clinical detachment, then, the attempt to respond to the pressures of medicine by becoming more efficient inevitably damages both the physician-patient relationship and the physician's own concept of self. Yet the issue is a subtle one. It is simply not possible to refuse to consider the demands to be productive and efficient, for they are important issues in our task of caring for patients—especially since physicians are still in short supply. Yet these values have such a profound effect on the practice of medicine that the physician needs to remain constantly aware of the trade-off between efficiency and deeper personal relationship, between productivity and medicine as an art. When the physician finds that he is not taking the needed time for reflective meditation upon the meaning of his job, when he finds he is using laboratory tests and x-ray studies instead of in-depth interviews, when he is giving pills instead of counseling or explanation, when he himself is not getting his needed sleep; at these points the physician needs to ask himself whether the values of efficiency and productivity have not in fact gained the upper hand, submerging other important medical and human values. Has productivity become a goal in itself. Has the attempt to meet more and more patient needs ultimately turned into its opposite? Has the physician become a servant, not of his patients, but of productivity and efficiency themselves?"[83]

Efficiency seen in this light begins to lose its luster. We don't need more efficiency in medicine; we need more effectiveness. Hilfiker addresses this topic head-on: "The unintended consequence is that the person tends to disappear and the patient becomes an object, a thing upon which the physician acts. It is no accident that the talk of medical personnel is filled with references to people as if they were diseases or parts of the body. 'Dr. Hilfiker, there's a broken leg in the ER' may sound humorous out of context, but it reflects the reality of medical detachment.[84]

Leaders respect all individuals at all times and in all situations, regardless of status and title. They treat people by the same principles, whether they are patients, families, residents, or nurses.

Misstep #3. Lack of Personal Leadership

Most powerful is he who has himself in his power.—Lucius Annaeus Seneca

This misstep might be a "super-category" that incorporates the other six. So many things affect the ability of one to lead, but Hock has noted, it basically comes down to spending a lot of time working on oneself.[18]

This misstep is composed of at least three of the original 20, and includes "Chairman's Syndrome," "The Captive Audience Syndrome," and "Over-focus on technical or intellectual ability as a proxy for leadership." It goes without saying that "The God Complex" heavily influences this misstep.

The Chairman's Syndrome

The attitude a chair should try to cultivate may charitably be called self-delusion or, uncharitably, arrogance.[85]

Collins writes that "executives need to accept the fact that the exercise of leadership is inversely proportional to the exercise of power."[86] He goes on to explain that many business executives confuse leadership with power, and that "older executives" complain of the "lack of loyalty" in the younger generation. However, he points out that there is no less loyalty in the younger generation. They are simply less willing to grant power to a single organization or person, are less subservient, and ultimately have more degrees of freedom. He concludes that "the most productive relationships are, in their essence, mutual partnerships rooted in a freedom of choice vested in both parties to participate only in that which is mutually beneficial and uplifting."[86]

Substitute the word "chairman" or, even more generically, "attending physician" for "older executive" and "medical student," "resident," "fellow" or "office staff" for "younger generation" in the preceding paragraph and it paints a picture that looks pretty similar to medical education today. The major difference is med students, residents, and fellows don't have the flexible options that those in the business world have, as they are essentially a "captive audience."

We have discussed the "win-lose" aspects of medical training. Now we are concerned with the "pecking order" that is so often reinforced—consciously or not—in medical training. "More than most professions, a medical title carries expectations as to how those above and below that status will be treated. Age, merit, and value often take a back seat to professional status and academic rank. In an almost militaristic order, medical faculty line up in front, while attendings, residents, interns, students, nurses, and other staff fall into place behind them.[73]

Unfortunately, this truth can carry over to patient care, as it relates to an individual's opinion about a treatment or intervention. We have all heard a medical student make a suggestion about the treatment of a patient that is better than the regimen planned by more "superior" personnel, only to be squelched by a resident or attending in order to keep the superior-subordinate roles intact. The "Chairman's Syndrome" is about the concept of "positional" or "borrowed" leadership; that is, an attitude that, because of one's position, one should automatically be deferred to and that this translates into leadership. Margaret Thatcher, former Prime Minister of Great Britain, once said: "Being in power is like being a lady. If you have to tell someone you are, you aren't."

In general, individuals who practice such forms of "leadership" create low-trust environments and really aren't in power; they just control. It is a failure of personal leadership and lack of understanding of the importance of interpersonal relationships all rolled into one. If you think you are leading but no one is behind you, you are just going for a walk. If such practices dominate the environment, from the chairman down, it is destructive and is neither useful nor helpful in building working relationships between peers, residents, or students. Further, because the teaching staff is the model for the trainees, the behavior is learned and perpetuated downward by those in training. Residents treat medical students in this fashion when that is all they have seen in their own training programs.

Lest some physicians dismiss this concept of "captive audience" and "physician hierarchy" as hogwash, let's look at some exceedingly powerful data from more than 14,000 medical students providing input into the 2000 Medical School Graduation Questionnaire, All Schools Report from the Division of Medical Education at the Association of American Medical Colleges.[25]

- 84 percent of medical students reported being "publicly belittled or humiliated at least once."

- 57.6 percent of medical students reported being "publicly belittled or humiliated occasionally or frequently."

- 26.4 percent of medical students reported being "subjected to offensive sexist remarks/names" at least once (16.9 percent occasionally or more often).

- 20.9 percent of medical students reported being "required to perform personal services (e.g., shopping, babysitting)" at least once (11.1 percent occasionally or more often).

We may quibble about "what do they mean by 'humiliated?'" but if being "required to perform personal services" does not imply a "captive audience," i.e., individuals afraid to *not* comply with their "superior's" request for personal services, what else is the data telling us? Any one of the bullet points above should embarrass our profession and our medical educational system. And who is ultimately responsible for these results? The leaders in medicine.

Kanter points out that the individuals most likely to "act in an autocratic fashion toward those below them in the hierarchy" are most likely to be individuals "who are restricted and controlled themselves."[87] The source of mistreatment of the medical students above was clinical faculty 50 percent of the time and residents 50 percent of the time.[25] This begs the obvious question: "Where are residents learning such behavior?" The answer is equally obvious: they are learning from their teachers. If they aren't learning this from their teachers, the follow-up question becomes: "Why isn't such behavior being corrected?" (Of course this presumes there is a mechanism by which the behaviors could be identified. The report suggests that such measures are, in fact, essentially non-existent.[25])

The manner in which residents and medical students are treated in the name of "education" must be changed if we are to change the personal leadership and interpersonal skill so individuals in the profession of medicine.

While we have data on medical students, we don't have data about what office staff is asked or expected to do. I do have a story, however, that highlights a similar sort of abuse of office staff. A close family friend used to be the office manager for a very large, successful physician group in a major city. One of the physicians' wives had gone on a shopping spree the day before and had decided it would be a good idea to purchase 50 pairs of shoes. The next day this woman decided she "didn't like some of them" and decided to return all 50 pair. Only she didn't want have to return them personally, so she asked her husband if my friend, the office manager, could return the shoes. He obliged his wife and asked my friend if she "would mind returning the shoes." The only comforting thing about this story is the fact that, apparently, the husband and wife must have gotten along well, having the same degree of impairment in judgment and what constitutes reasonableness related to wardrobe and expectations of employees. My friend said "No."

Physician Self-Deception

Physicians have an amazing ability to deceive themselves. "Physician Self-Deception" is sometimes manifested as the "I have the most important job in the world" attitude, reflecting an under-appreciation of the fact that they are just one cog in the wheel of an interdependent world.

The Arbinger Institute has published details on the phenomenon of self-deception as it relates to personal leadership.[88] It uses a story about a husband and wife who have a small baby to illustrate its main point. In the story, a husband and wife are sleeping, when the husband hears their infant start to cry. His first thought is to get up and go take care of the baby and let his exhausted wife sleep. But then he begins to think to himself along the lines: "Hey, I work hard and bring home the bacon. And I have an early meeting tomorrow. Why can't she see that I have responsibilities and get up and take care of her kid." In other words, he begins to *manufacture* reasons why his rest is more important than his wife's. In other words, the husband "self-betrays," because he suppresses his initial impulse to be helpful, which he knows is the higher road.

The Arbinger authors make the point that, just before we "self-betray," we usually have just seen something "we should do or be." When we enter self-betrayal, we "enter a box" and begin to see people as objects—because it is easier to deal with "objects," as opposed to people who have the same desires and needs as we. Basically, it is a violation of personal integrity and respect for the individual.

Another example illustrated in the Arbinger book is the case of waiting for an elevator, which is just opening, and noticing a person down the hall who you know will need the elevator. Your initial thought is usually to hold the elevator, but, in the general hurry of the day, you simply jump on, and the doors close just before the person arrives. You have self-betrayed your original impulse to be kind and helpful.

The Arbinger book points out four key items about the self-deception of self-betrayal.[87] When we are self-deceiving, we:

1. Inflate other's faults

2. Inflate our own virtue

3. Inflate the value of things that justify our self-betrayal

4. Blame

Some of us have developed the art of self-deception to its highest form. We are able to justify shirking all types of responsibilities, using our jobs as doctors as a basis for such an attitude. How many readers know someone who successfully avoided jury duty because they were "on call" or any other of a hundred excuses. Of the four components of self-deception list above, I know I have called on "inflation of my own virtue" and "inflated the value of what I do" to avoid more than one obligation, whether to society at large or in my personal life. My attitude was, "I am more helpful to society by being a physician than by sitting on a jury." Even blame comes into the picture: "I shouldn't have to serve jury duty anyway—that criminal would not have committed the crime if he or she were a responsible person." Of course, how much income I might lose if I sat on a jury for a week came into my thinking.

Think of a patient who has failed to respond to prescribed therapy. If we assume the patient was noncompliant, we are inflating their faults, while simultaneously inflating our own virtue by suppressing the possibility we made the wrong diagnosis or gave the wrong medicine. Because the treatment failure "couldn't possibly be our fault," and the patient's "noncompliance" explains the failure, we have justified our self-betrayal, and the blame is on the patient. This demonstrates a failure of personal leadership and integrity on our part and a lack of respect for the patient.

Over-Focus on Technical or Intellectual Ability as a Proxy for Leadership

Cohn provides a wonderful example of misunderstanding what it takes to be a leader, and confusing leadership with technical ability and knowledge. "Surgeons make excellent leaders because of the complex logistics of operations that they must organize virtually every day and the requirement for decisiveness in every operation."[89]

The fact that medical training is so competitive, so difficult, and so long, requiring both technical and intellectual prowess, often leads to the assumption that we are "leaders" simply because we survived and are successful in practice, that we can successfully complete an operation. Simply being able to take out someone's colon or lung cancer or diagnose their hypertension and treat it effectively does not mean you are a leader. Competent maybe, but not a leader.

Your technical skill and knowledge are not sufficient for you to consider yourself a leader, any more than becoming the chairman of a department makes you a leader in anything other than title. Covey often describes individuals as being "trustworthy" because of "character and competence." He defines "character" as exhibiting "integrity, maturity, and an Abundance Mentality™." "Competence" is defined as an individual who has "knowledge and ability in a given area." Neither alone is sufficient to be trustworthy. Both are required for leadership—personal leadership—because you can't be a leader unless you are trusted, and being trusted requires you to be trustworthy.[3]

Covey uses an example of physicians in his lectures. He asks, "Would you trust a surgeon who is competent, but has no character? How would you be able to trust that you really need the operation if he or she doesn't have character? Would you trust a surgeon who has high character, but is not competent?" Too often, physicians would retort, "I would rather sacrifice character and be competent, than have all the character in the world and be incompetent." This is an abdication of responsibility for oneself and an "end justifies the means" attitude.

Failure to Appreciate the Importance of Interpersonal Relationships

The original misstep, called "Failure to appreciate the importance of interpersonal relationships," is critical in the current misstep. If one of the original 20 missteps had to be selected as being the most important, this would probably be it.

The ability to work within an organization is crucial in medicine. Even in a solo practice, one must interact with hospital personnel, patients, and office staff. Interpersonal effectiveness requires personal effectiveness, that is, personal leadership and interpersonal skills. We don't work with hospitals; we work with the individuals in hospitals.

McCall has identified "ten deadly flaws of physician managers"[90] that apply to all physicians:

1. Insensitivity and arrogance
2. Inability to choose staff
3. Over-managing (inability to delegate)
4. Inability to adapt to a boss
5. Fighting the wrong battles
6. Being seen as untrustworthy (having questionable motives)
7. Failing to develop a strategic vision

8. Being overwhelmed by the job

9. Lacking specific skills or knowledge

10. Lacking commitment to the job

McCall quotes a senior physician executive who noted that, concerning the failure of physician executives, "It's almost always people management that does them in." This too, applies to all physicians, because whether we are formally managing people or not, we all must interact with our staffs, our patients, and others. Earlier we learned that interpersonal skills such as those listed above are highly correlated to malpractice liability risk. At least six of them (numbers 1, 5, 6, 8, 9, and 10) are important components of personal leadership and can affect any individual's ability to have successful interpersonal relationships.

Leaders understand that people don't care how much you know until they know how much you care. The development of interpersonal and personal leadership skills allows you to show others how much you care first. Only then will a leader be able ask for their help.

The misstep of failure to demonstrate personal leadership can lose business for a physician, and embarrass our profession. I have a friend who found out, using a home pregnancy test, that she was expecting a baby. Her doctor confirmed this with a serum pregnancy test. She went to see her OB/GYN for her first ultrasound to check the baby, at which time the physician informed her the baby was dead as there was no heart beat. She was scheduled for a return appointment to prepare her for a D&C to evacuate the dead fetus.

She returned for the appointment and a repeat ultrasound was done to see if she had passed the fetus spontaneously. The physician performed the ultrasound himself. She had not passed the fetus and was told to return home and wait for a call. A few hours later, she received a telephone call from the physician's office nurse, who stated that the physician had made a mistake. She was still pregnant, and the baby had a heart beat! Not only did the physician not tell my friend at the time of the ultrasound that she had a viable baby, he did not even have the personal integrity and courtesy to call her himself.

My friend informed the nurse to have her chart ready in an hour so she could pick it up and find another OB/GYN. This is a clear illustration of the impact of not appreciating (or in this case, being completely devoid of) personal leadership and interpersonal skills.

Our goal in medicine should be to be quintessential examples of character and competence, to personally lead ourselves the best we can—not because of what we do but because of what we are as individuals and what we are supposed to represent to the people we serve.

Misstep #4. Lack of Flexibility

The old guard in any society resents new methods, for old guards wear the decorations and medals won by waging battle in the accepted manner.—Martin Luther King Jr.

Of the original missteps, four apply here: "The Physician Hierarchy—the 'frozen bureaucracy,'" "Quick-fix attitude," "Time," and "Skepticism of 'softer sciences.'" Flexibility is not one of the hallmarks of a bureaucracy. The less time an individual has, the less likely he or she is to be flexible, especially when there are expectations about a certain outcome. Skepticism of new approaches and of "soft data"—such as when data are from a living system with complex emotions and feelings (i.e., a human) that do not conform to linear Newtonian science—results in inflexibility in one's thinking. Always wanting to wage "battle in the accepted manner" ultimately leads to defeat.

The Physician Hierarchy—the Frozen Bureaucracy

Hock has referred to the university system as one of the worst forms of Newtonian Age command-and-control hierarchies still in existence. He writes that universities are "of a 400-year-old age rattling in its deathbed as another is struggling to be born—a transformation of consciousness, culture, society and institutions such as the world has never experienced."[91] Part of his institutional focus is directly on the university system.

Hierarchies are not intrinsically bad. They can provide control, stability, pre-dictability, and efficiency when they are properly constituted, and when such qualities are useful and helpful.[17] However, hierarchical systems are *always* based on historical solutions to problems previously encountered. Hierarchies fail when individuals within them fail to confront redundancy or incompetence. This results in things with which we can all identify: turf protection; departmental money battles; arguments over "autonomy"; retention of incompetent, inappropriate, or stagnant personnel or physicians; and so on. Inflexible maintenance of hierarchy—the kind that exists in medicine and some businesses—often leads to a kind of "'abused/abuser' relationship between those in lower and higher positions that is self-perpetuating and mutually destructive."[17] The inflexibility of a hierarchical system and those within it ultimately leads to its destruction, or, at the very least, to near-complete ineffectiveness in accomplishing the organization's mission.

The shortcomings of hierarchies are transparent to most, with the possible exception of those at the top. Yet few seem bold enough to take on those at the top. How many times have you known of situations in which redundancy within the system is ignored, because to eliminate it would have encroached on someone's turf or appeared to be a politically sensitive action, no matter how justified? Worse, especially in medicine, is ignoring incompetence. I'm not talking about the mistakes that we all make—the occasional lack of judgment or technical error. I'm talking about the people who are overtly incompetent, that we have had enough interaction with to not be comfortable with them taking care of one of our family members. The unspoken "blue wall of silence" that police officers are so often accused of exists in medicine because of our training and because of our unwillingness as a profession to address incompetence and redundancy within the hierarchy. While incompetence in medicine is not common, more effective self-policing could substantially elevate the standing of physicians in the eyes of the public. It would also have an impact on liability by creating transparency with the public and beginning to shift the public's expectations away from perfection. The inflexibility of hierarchies can contribute to a leader's difficulties in moving forward. However, just because an organization chooses inflexibility does not mean the leader must.

The "Chairman's Syndrome"

The "Chairman's Syndrome," or top-down mentality, also results in inflexibility. We have all witnessed an attending physician stifling conversations or discussions with residents or medical students with the comment, "That is the way I learned it, and that's the way we are going to do it," or "That's the way I've always done it." These demonstrate clear inflexibility. Recall the earlier discussion concerning complexity of systems and the game of chess? There is no one "right" answer. Also recall the Nalle Clinic story, and Holleman's comment: "No one felt they needed to improve their performance, which blunted the incentive to move to a more uncomfortable, but possibly better 'new way.' This is 'the way we have always done it' was the overwhelming attitude."[62]

Kouzes and Posner found that managers (or in this case, physicians) with the highest control scores—again, a manifestation of inflexibility—have the lowest scores in personal credibility.[12] One can hear the responses of some physicians now: "This isn't a popularity contest." No, it isn't, but all things being equal, people work harder for people they like. Being a leader is more than a title. Paul Hawken stated: "We lead by being human. We do not lead by being corporate, by being professional, or by being institutional."[92] This should be expanded by saying; we do not lead because we are physicians, chairs, or attendings. In medicine, perhaps more than any other profession, we should lead by first being human, flattening our organizational hierarchies, and developing more flexible thinking.

The "Quick-Fix Attitude"

The "quick-fix attitude" is prevalent in medicine and results in inflexibility in problem-solving and in the consideration of new or unique solutions. Physicians are trained in acute intervention to correct acute problems. They often receive the immediate gratification of seeing tangible results. While acute intervention may work in the medical arena, it often does not translate to other aspects of one's life. There are no "quick fixes" for a bad relationship with a spouse, parents, or children.

There are also no "quick fixes" of our current leadership practice in medicine, or lack thereof. It's not like diagnosing and treating strep throat—where a quick course of penicillin will cure the problem. There are techniques that might allow one to temporarily improve some outwardly visible "leadership qualities"—but, as with giving antibiotics to someone with appendicitis, it helps for only a while. In the long term, a more permanent solution must be applied if one is to get better, and one must be flexible enough to understand the need and make a long-term commitment when that is required.

The "quick fix" mentality leads to individuals in the profession getting used to seeing immediate results of the interventions they prescribe, or, at the latest, within weeks. It leads to the inflexible and unrealistic expectation that everything in the world of medicine happens quickly; physicians then begin to transfer this expectation to the rest of their lives. In the hospital, they give orders to nurses, and it is done. In the office, they ask, they get. What does this lead physicians to expect at home? In a restaurant? At a car dealership?

This line of thinking can also lead to different and perhaps more destructive expectations than those already suggested. It can contribute to physicians' having an attitude of being "the great healer." Worse, for patients, is the response of some physicians when they (patients) fail to get better after prescribed treatments. Physicians can adopt an attitude of "If I can't fix it, it either isn't broken or can't be fixed." This is an inflexible, destructive mindset. Anything less than this expected outcome is an inconvenience to the physician's schedule—not conforming to our carefully devised plan and paradigm of diagnosis-treatment-cure. This type of reaction and attitude is destructive to the physician-patient relationship and is one reason patients increasingly seek alternative forms of health care, not for diagnosis and treatment but for someone to genuinely listen and care.

This inflexible mindset is a completely unrealistic expectation outside the acute care medical arena, yet it is the dominant paradigm of medical training and medical practice today. Patience is a virtue that physicians are lacking in many cases. Reducing service personnel to tears is not something that one with high personal integrity does—in medicine or in life.

The "Quick-Fix Attitude"—Time

The statement "I don't have time" is heard on a routine basis. This attitude is illustrated by conversations I have had with physicians who have reviewed the LeadeRx℠ Personal Development Program. Far and away the most common concern was, "This seems awfully long for physicians to take the time to complete." It takes less than 90 minutes to assign raters and complete the survey! This amount of time seems quite reasonable as the first step on a journey of potentially life-long self-learning and improvement. One cannot expect to be able to memorize a few "concepts" and have a sustained life-changing experience. This is a classic "quick-fix" comment, illustrating not seeing the value of the long-term investment because of inflexibility in thinking: "I know this is important but I don't have the time."

The "quick-fix" mentality can make it difficult for physicians to make a long-term investment of time. With such intense focus on acute intervention and rapid correction of patient problems, seeing the benefits of interventions requiring an investment of time can be difficult. Not everything can be remedied with a one-week course of antibiotics. Enhancing personal leadership skills can't be done in one week either; it requires commitment and flexibility in one's schedule. Reading a book or attending a weekend seminar will not result in sustainable personal leadership and interpersonal skills. This isn't a "crash course." It's a "life course." It is a process that takes months to see change, especially if the changes are to be sustained. Flexibility allows us to control our schedules and commit to things that are important to us.

Skepticism of the "Softer Sciences"

Sometimes what counts can't be counted, and what can be counted doesn't count.—Albert Einstein

Another contributor to physician inflexibility is a pervasive negative attitude about the "softer sciences" upon which much of the best leadership principles are based: sociology, social science, social psychology, management science, organizational behavior, and so on. Scientifically trained physicians are skeptical of such soft approaches to defining one's world. Gill points out: "Nevertheless, understanding the applied scientific underpinnings of individual, group, organizational, and system behavior and of change management provides an excellent foundation for physician managers to develop their leadership skills."[93]

When Gill speaks of "scientific," she is speaking of the softer sciences, such as sociology and psychology of individuals and organizations (groups), not the "hard sciences," such as physics, chemistry, and anatomy. Her statement applies to all physicians, not just those in management roles.

In medicine, measurement (data) is the altar at which we worship and the trough at which we feed. But measurement can, in some cases, be merely idolatry and leave our plate, if not our souls, bare. Many believe that medicine has come as far as hard science will bring us, from the standpoint of evolution as a profession. Newtonian linear science will only explain the scientific-technical aspects of medicine—perhaps incompletely in the end. It completely ignores the human-interpersonal aspects where linear models do not apply, and usually serves to minimize the human element. In medicine, we have the tendency to want to boil everything down to its most elemental parts; in the process, we forget about the person. Philip Anderson, the 1977 Nobel Prize winner in physics—perhaps the most stringent of sciences and with the greatest propensity for breaking things down into their elemental components—notes: "The ability to reduce everything to simple fundamental laws does not imply the ability to start from those laws and reconstruct the universe. In fact, the more the elementary particle physicists tell us about the nature of the fundamental laws, the less relevance they seem to have to the very real problems of the rest of science, much less society."[94]

Some within our own profession are beginning to see, understand, and promote such concepts. Berger notes: "Change is not a logical, linear, or intellectual process. It operates on various emotional and interpersonal dimensions that are essential to mastering change. It challenges long-held assumptions and encourages non-traditional thinking."[4] In other words, we need to be flexible in our thinking. If we are to take the medical profession to the "next level," we must re-define leadership in medicine, what it means in interpersonal terms, and dedicate ourselves to that vision. The practicing physician of today, and those training to become physicians, will have to un-learn the sterile, linear-reductionist approaches of the past and embrace current personal leadership concepts. Teaching personal leadership in medical school is completely congruent with medical education, despite the impression that it is based on "softer science." We should go so far as to select pre-med students who have documented good personal leadership habits, and we should build leadership succession planning into the medical schools and our profession.

Leadership attributes are soft. Integrity, honesty, character, and trustworthiness cannot be measured like blood pressure or cholesterol. While we can't measure such qualities, we can measure their effect. In order for leadership in medicine to move forward, there must be a willingness to accept that some things simply can't be boiled-down to a number and printed on a lab report or an x-ray report form. We can't send a requisition down to the pharmacy for a STAT infusion of "leadership and interpersonal skills."

Shifting how we think and make decisions in medicine to a perspective of being able to make sound scientific judgments while remaining sensitive to the patient and the interpersonal aspects of the relationship is difficult—but fundamental. Armstrong noted the difficulties of appreciating the perspective of the softer sciences from the "modern perspective" of society today: "It is a perspective that is difficult for us to appreciate in the modern world, because it cannot be proved empirically and lacks the rational underpinnings which we regard as essential to truth."[95]

The medical profession must become more aware of the personal aspects of human relationships and be sensitive to how we affect those around us. This is not contrary to knowing and applying the science of medicine; to the contrary, such skills are tantamount to respecting and treating all individuals in a manner becoming of the profession.

If we cannot grasp such soft concepts, how do we ever know a patient actually improves, in the absence of a lab test, x-ray, or other hard data proving they are better? If a patient says his or her pain is better, do we believe them? It has gotten to the point that some physicians have difficulty believing patients are improved without some "objective measure." I presented some data at a large national medical meeting on the topic of constipation. Part of my presentation concentrated on a patient-based measure of "satisfaction with treatment." I showed how strongly correlated a single question was to predicting patient satisfaction. One of the panel members asked: "But do you have data to actually demonstrate they were improved?" In this example, he wanted to see an x-ray test "proving" their constipation was better—a patient responding affirmatively to a simple question, saying he or she felt better, was not good enough. This person all but ignored the fact that these patients said they were improved. A leader understands that interpersonal relationships cannot be dealt with in terms of hard science and measurements, but require open-mindedness and flexibility.

Misstep #5. Inability to Be a Team Player

I think we as doctors have to recognize that we are not omnipotent. We have to be part of a health care team, particularly when it comes to more complicated types of care. There are many other ancillary health professionals—nurses, occupational therapists, physical therapists—that are truly critical parts of the team in terms of delivery of care to the American people.[96]

This misstep can be the downfall of any individual hoping to be successful in a business that deals with people, including colleagues or subordinates. Of the original 20 missteps, four are relevant to the concept of being a "team player." They include: "Win-Lose Education," "Physicians are Autonomous," "Reluctance to Trust," and "The Challenge Syndrome." In some respects, the "Captive Audience Phenomenon" also contributes to this misstep too, although a bit indirectly.

There are increasing calls for more physicians to obtain MBAs and gain other business experience in order to enhance "leadership in medicine." A recent article proclaims: "It is my firm belief that this sort of program [additional business and management training for select physicians] will become even more essential in medicine as the transformation to the corporate model becomes ever more prevalent....It is not our moral superiority but our commitment to the core missions of our profession, based on the priority of patient care, that make us [physicians] more suited for leadership in medicine."[97]

The core problem related to leadership in medicine is not that there are not good leaders at the top (although one can always be a more effective leader). The core problem is that, because physicians are poor team players, the leaders have no willing physician followers except in the direst of circumstances. Physicians often have difficulty in selecting leaders because they are usually unwilling followers. "On-the-ground" leaders must appreciate the power of trusting their leaders and good "followership." Good followership, after all, is what high-functioning teams are all about. Paradoxically perhaps, a physician wishing to become a good leader and to be truly effective must understand how to be an effective and willing follower.

Win-Lose Education

The "win-lose" training that we endure is the antithesis of what it requires to be a good team player. Everything related to a medical education from pre-med right on through to practice is a race to be first and best. Hilfiker addresses this: "One would think, though, that once we physicians have passed beyond our training, the overwhelming amount of knowledge and expertise required would ensure cooperative relationships among us; but we inhibit ourselves from entering into those relationships because of the habits of our training, and the stresses of our work. The pressure to perform, to be the best, continues and undermines the attempts to cooperate closely."[71]

Cooperation and teamwork are inseparable. A team whose members don't cooperate is not functioning as a team, and a team member who isn't a team player is not really part of the team. Yet medical education is set-up in a competitive student-eat-student structure. Shell and Klasko note: "Many schools advise premed students to take only courses that narrowly focus on their ability to excel in medical school, ignoring courses on personal development and communication that might, in the long run, open students' eyes to the gains possible from cooperation."[73]

It is clear that such competition is destructive to developing an interest or willingness or ability to participate in a cooperative team environment. Not only does this narrow, competitive "me-me-me" focus hurt one's ability to function on a team, it encourages behaviors counterproductive to what we hope for in a profession that espouses compassion, caring, consideration, and thoughtfulness as core personal values and beliefs.

Shell and Klasko aren't the only researchers to have found such educational systems to be counterproductive to developing individuals into team players. Kohn writes about the win-lose aspects of education too, and describes the medical training system perfectly: "Of all the ways by which people are led to seek rewards, I believe the most destructive possible arrangement is to limit the number that are available [e.g., limited medical school or residency slots]. To do so is to replace the possibility that people will try to assist each other with the near certainty that they will try to defeat each other. But whether it is permitted by a standard individual incentive system or required by a race for rewards, contests are destructive for several reasons beyond the fact that they preclude the sort of teamwork that leads to success."[98]

Kohn brings up the issue of rewards and teamwork several other times in the context of education. He points out that grades and the competition for class rank create destructive behaviors. "The surest way to destroy teamwork, and therefore organizational excellence, is to make rewards scarce—that is, make people compete."[99]

Yet the medical training system persists in ranking students, and using such ranks as a basis for selecting individuals for residency. The data examining this practice clearly suggest it does not engender cooperation or teamwork. "It is never a good idea to praise someone by comparing her to someone else. Phrases like 'You're the best in the class' (or for adults 'in this department') ought to be struck from our vocabulary. The research is quite clear that such comments undermine intrinsic motivation, but their most pernicious effects are subtler: they encourage a view of others as rivals rather than as potential collaborators."[100]

The way in which physicians are trained actually encourages the development of behaviors that are not conducive to collaboration, cooperation, or being part of a team. It is not hard to see how this type of training contributes to the sense that one should be "autonomous." When medical students and residents hear attendings speak about "autonomy," it just makes things worse.

Physicians Are Autonomous—A Persistent Fallacy

Competition almost never results in synergy or the best performance. Pursuing excellence is a collaborator's game. Competition is about making someone else inferior; collaboration is about accomplishing something superior.[12] Likewise, individual autonomy is conceptually counter to synergy and collaboration, both implying the willing participation of more than one party. Autonomy assumes that, in every case, the individual knows the right answers or, at the very least, can act without any controls. Knowing "all the right answers" or attempting to maintain an environment in which we are in complete control—or even thinking we do and are— can lead one to challenge everything. Challenging everything communicates that we mistrust others involved in the discussion (whether this is true or not), especially when they are subject to a constant barrage of challenges. Collaboration requires trust, and teams must collaborate to be effective.

Even our customers, our patients, understand the need for teamwork and want it from their health care providers. The Picker Institute notes, "Patients strongly desire a system in which health care professionals work together effectively, follow a coherent plan of care, and demonstrate familiarity with their unique needs and circumstances. Instead, patients interface with numerous health care staff—specialists, consultants, interns, residents, nurses, and therapists—and have, at best, a fuzzy understanding of titles, roles, and patterns of authority. The resulting confusion is not insubstantial. Patients are asked the same questions over and over again, have multiple visits scheduled to accommodate provider schedules, and are given vague and sometimes conflicting messages from clinicians."[101]

Research supports the contention that lack of coordination of patient care affects patient outcomes and increases the chance of complications.[101,102] Coordination of patient care when multiple physicians are involved provides a wonderful opportunity for a unified team approach, yet physicians, wanting to "keep control of their schedules," become obstacles to such possibilities.

Physicians "cling stubbornly to their independence in part because their professional credentials are often purchased at such high personal and emotional cost. Nevertheless, physicians' natural preference for working as 'lone rangers' creates a significant obstacle to their effectiveness in negotiation."[73]

The physician's tendency to fall back on "autonomy," especially when confronted with external change or pressure, can be used as a cloak, a self-protective form of self-deception, making it appear that physicians are focusing on "what's in it for me?" The quest to maintain autonomy can lead to failure to appreciate the interdependence of oneself with other components of the health care system and of society at large. A more fruitful approach, not only in the current business-focused health care environment but also for our patients, would be for physicians to see themselves as partners with all parties involved in patient care or their business, and to seek win-win solutions framed by the attitude of "what's in it for all of us?"

As Shell and Klasko point out, "autonomy is a poor fit for complex business environments, such as health care today."[73] Physicians can keep insisting on remaining autonomous, but only at ever-increasing costs—emotionally and financially—to themselves.

A physician's expertise and the authority he or she is able to leverage because of that expertise can be an incredibly damaging combination as it relates to being a team player. "The physician's high level of expertise also contributes to this attitude [of autonomy]. There is often the unspoken assumption that he knows the job of each team member better than the team member himself. (If this assumption was ever true, it has certainly long been invalidated by the high levels of training given to most nurses, technicians, pharmacists, and therapists today.)"[103]

I recall my own experience with this very issue. I enjoyed doing critical care while I was in training and in practice, so I tended to have many patients on respirators. Early in my career, I used to become offended and defensive when the respiratory therapist would make suggestions or inquire about my orders for the ventilator settings. I learned several important lessons from such experiences: one is how much more these "support staff" actually knew compared to myself. Two is how much more motivated they were when I began to treat them with the respect they deserved as people, let alone as professionals. Three is how trusting them to do their job substantially freed me from doing things I didn't need to be doing. Giving up my false sense of autonomy and realizing that these individuals were valuable team members made all the difference in the world.

It is not necessary for a leader to know how to do everything. It is necessary for him or her to know which team member is best suited for the job and how to empower the person to do it without jealousy or micromanaging.

Reluctance to Trust

Despite wanting autonomy as individual practitioners, physicians share an almost supernatural degree of trust in the opinions of a medical colleague as it relates to the care of a single patient and other clinical matters. Cummings writes: "All of us, having gone through the same rigors of academic competition—physical, mental, and emotional challenges—automatically have significant understanding of the price our peers have paid and something about their personalities and the motivations that have sustained them. But realize that intense isolation evolves as a consequence of the above. This sometimes limits our perspective and makes us distrustful of nonpeers and of other roles and things we do not understand. Additionally, physicians are taught to challenge everything for the good of the patient. This easily evolves into challenging everything, period. Therefore, it is predictable that physicians will challenge even one of their own if he or she assumes a different role than theirs that may significantly affect, modify, or limit their own prerogatives."[104]

In other words, the autonomous attitude of physicians, again as a result of training, leads to difficulty not only in following and being part of a team, but even in trusting someone to lead them.

This reminds me of a conversation I had with a physician executive of one of the largest HMO health plans in the country. I asked him what he thought of leadership in medicine in general. He rattled off about five or six things without even having to pause to think about it. One of his responses was that "physicians need to learn how to choose a leader. But they can't and don't because doctors hate being part of a team and can't function within teams. I know a guy at the AMA who says that 'trying to get doctors to follow a leader is like trying to get eagles to fly in formation.'"

His conclusion was that physicians basically don't trust anyone other than themselves to lead them. Recalling the "win-lose" paradigm and the inability to negotiate, where physicians just wanted to make sure "no one got more than they did," reinforces this gentleman's statement. Not only do physicians' not select leaders; physicians are unwilling to be led. In other words, physicians don't follow either.

Leaders not only create, but also thrive in environments of trust in their organizations. They know that, without trust, not only are effective teams not possible, nothing is possible. Leaders appreciate that their most important responsibility is to others and that they are just one part of an interdependent reality.

The Challenge Syndrome

The Challenge Syndrome emanates from the fact that we are taught to challenge everything for the good of the patient. Unfortunately, this too easily evolves into behavior that leads us to challenge everything, period.

My father, a physician, wrote me a letter shortly after I was graduated from medical school, full of his considerable wisdom, that warned me of this very mindset. He said, "Becoming a physician will allow you to be an expert in medicine, if you work hard. It does not mean you are an expert in anything else."

His statement has a great deal to do with being part of a team, listening to and relying on others who know more than we do. If we voice opinions about things in which we are clearly not expert—and voice them with such conviction that those around us do not question us—it is another form of "win-lose" thinking. It is a reflection of a less-than-optimal ability to listen and hear others.

I have a friend who makes his living as a certified financial planner. He claims that his most difficult clients, beyond question, are physicians, and theirs is the occupation least likely to follow his advice. They are also the most likely to get into financial trouble from their own financial decisions. I subsequently asked my own financial planner about my friend's opinion. He heartily concurred, adding, "Physicians are notorious in the financial community for not taking advice and making very costly decisions."

This is basically a form of arrogance. Asking a question is not a bad thing; persisting to "push one's point" in an area where one has essentially no experience is what I am talking about. It is not a good trait for a team member.

Failure to Appreciate the Importance of Interpersonal Relationships

How many physicians allow their residents or office staff to call them by their first names. I know of very few; I allowed my office staff to call me "Mike" when I was in practice. It does wonders for interpersonal relationships in the office and helps morale immensely. The staff feels more respected, more connected, and part of a close-knit team.

Physicians use the manner in which they are addressed and how they address others, whether consciously or unconsciously, as another mechanism to maintain authority over "their world." It is an example of a difference of respect, no matter how subtle. "What we call each other is symbolic. Too often the physician remains "Dr. Hilfiker" long after the nurse has become "Annette." Physicians usually perceive themselves as bosses, even though they are often not the staff's actual employer.[105]

The concept of treating one's employees with dignity and with the same respect they have for you isn't something I thought up. Drucker is on record as saying that the single biggest competitive edge in business the next 25 years is "knowing people's strengths" and "treating them as associates."[106] He added that "exposing them to challenges" and "placing them in the place where they can make the greatest contributions" are two other concepts that will confer competitive advantage.

Leaders know they don't know it all and rely on and empower—trust—those on the team who do know the answers. They are not intimidated by what they don't know, and they welcome the knowledge and contributions of others. Leaders realize they are not experts in everything. Real leaders know that's why they have a team to rely on.

Misstep #6. Failure to Develop Others

There may be some confusion as to why this is a misstep for physicians. After all, physicians train medical students and residents. However, training someone in technical skills or imparting knowledge is not the same as helping them to develop as a person. The original concept of "Difficulty in providing behavioral feedback to others" is the relevant concept here, with some elements of "Perfectionist mentality." Helping a person develop better personal leadership and interpersonal skills requires careful observation of behaviors and constructive, routine feedback.

The Perfectionist Mentality

Trying not to fail is, of course, very different from trying to succeed. One's efforts in the former case are geared at doing damage control, minimizing risks, getting by.[107]

We need to ensure that we begin to shift from training people in the mindset of "perfection" to the Army's mindset of "becoming the best you can be." In medicine, we need to change the way we respond to mistakes—even critical errors—shifting from blaming, belittling, and other punitive actions to explanation, responsibility, accountability, and ensuring that individuals learn how to become better from errors that are made. We need to establish nonpunitive systems of reporting errors and get away from the perfectionist focus.

This reminds me of two concepts regarding "mistakes." Covey has said "The way we respond to a mistake effects the quality of our next moment."[3] Have you ever snapped at your office staff after you have made a mistake? They had no clue as to "what they did to cause" your reaction.

Cashman has stated, "Failure is a subjective label we apply to unintended or unexpected experiences."[108] What if we began to think about (at least some) "mistakes" in medicine as "performance enhancers" or "educational opportunities." I recall one episode in my training when I was assisting in the heart bypass operation of a man who had undergone a heart bypass years earlier. In the process of opening his chest to expose the heart for the operation, I felt a thin band of tissue against the backside of his breastbone. I "broke" this band with my finger using what surgeons call "blunt dissection," a technique that can be used in a variety of situations—except cardiac surgery. My maneuver tore a small (but significant) hole in the right atrium of the patient's heart and resulted in substantial blood loss. After the situation was under control, the cardiac surgeon had a fairly frank discussion with me about technique. This particular surgeon was very good with interpersonal relationships. I felt awful, but it never happened again. While this was a mistake, it was also a very important and memorable "educational opportunity." The surgeon used this event to help me develop as a surgeon and as a person by his response. The guilt I felt was my own.

Helping individuals to develop without resorting to unconstructive criticism or belittlement is an art we should all seek to learn or improve. Further, such approaches don't just teach the medical lesson, they also teach important interpersonal skills.

Difficulty in Providing Behavioral Feedback to Other Physicians

The rest of the staff will meekly submit to a lecture about an alleged mistake on their part, whereas they must find some discreet way to bring the physician's mistakes to his attention so as not to offend him. Serious mistakes on the part of the physician are not talked about except, perhaps, behind his back.[105]

In the nonmedical business world, giving feedback as it relates to behavior is generally not considered offensive. It is not considered bad and is often welcome. Entire training programs in nonmedical businesses are focused on coaching for enhanced behaviors. In medicine, however, because the profession is steeped in the "win-lose" paradigm, virtually any criticism can be considered offensive. Much like the "challenge syndrome," when one's behavior is questioned, the response by physicians is often defensive in nature. Or worse, the self-deceiving fallback of "I was only trying to take care of my patient," a.k.a. "the ends justifies the means," is used.

This misstep is a two-way street: the likelihood of a defensive response from the physician with the behavioral problem and the unwillingness of the observing physician to point out the unacceptable behavior. It is collusion in inappropriate behavior without knowledge of how it really affects both individuals.

In this case, the responsibility lies with the individual observing the behavior. If one's internal sense of principle is in order, tactfully pointing out your observation should not be an overwhelming task. Even in the most extreme responses, your security is based within yourself, and not rocked by an insecure person lashing back.

It should be pointed out that behavior such as yelling at a nurse or another staff member is a basic failure of personal leadership, a failure to respect other people, to treat them as a person and not as a "tool" of patient care, not as an object. Not only does this behavior not help people to develop, it also sends the message that such behavior is acceptable, leading others to emulate it, to the detriment of the entire organization.

Another reason physicians have difficulty accepting feedback in a medical environment relates to direct patient care. No physician makes a decision about a patient flippantly. If any behavioral feedback given to a physician is even remotely connected to an interaction with a patient, this will likely set off a fire-storm of emotion. Physicians like to think they are right—all the time—as it relates to their patients.

Berger states that he feels physicians are suffering from the "Piñata Syndrome," which he describes as "everyone is taking a whack at me."[4] This is essentially a form of paranoid mistrust, which he says is manifest by the symptoms of "physician lounge grumbling and griping, sniping at medical and administrative leaders, resistance to examining best practices, and a refusal to hold colleagues responsible for their behavior."

Finally, data support the existence of this misstep. Fully 41.7 percent of more than 14,000 medical students either "disagreed" or "strongly disagreed" with the statement, "Students were given timely feedback on performance in clerkships."[25] This number is unchanged from the 1998 and 1999 medical school graduating classes.

Leaders understand the importance of giving honest, timely feedback in a compassionate way.

Misstep #7. Lack of Openness

The eyes are of little use if the mind be blind.—Arab proverb

Our ability to develop and grow as individuals, that is, beyond our medical interests, ideally should be viewed as a fun and exciting personal challenge. Unfortunately for many physicians, this ability is inhibited by a lack of openness—openness to change, openness to feedback, and openness to personal development and the time required to achieve it.

This misstep is an amalgam of "The Physician Hierarchy," "Inability to Self-Assess," and "Information Overload." These apply here for different reasons. You should already appreciate that hierarchical structures are often not open or innovative, or particularly concerned about development and growth of individuals. Lack of openness contributes to the inability of physicians to assess themselves and makes developing self-growth programs somewhat difficult. Finally, information overload is relevant on two levels. First, we have limited time and spend much of that time wading through reams of medical literature in an effort to "stay current." Second, perhaps we are not open to reading nonmedical material and don't develop and grow as individuals because we read too much medicine and not enough newspapers, other literature, and self-growth or self-improvement material.

Inability to Self-Assess

Marshall Goldsmith, founding director of Keilty, Goldsmith & Company, states that, of all professional groups with which he has worked, physicians are the one group that consistently self-rates their personal leadership and technical skills higher than peers or subordinates rate them.[109] He claims 80-90 percent of physicians rank their skills and abilities in the top 10 percent of the profession. Airline pilots apparently fall just below physicians, and athletic coaches just below pilots. Only 60-70 percent of attorneys self-assess their abilities higher than peers or subordinates rate them.

Goleman's work suggests that self-awareness is crucial to developing emotional intelligence.[13] If one is to commit to change, one must be able to see one's strengths and developmental needs; one must be open to self-evaluation or assessment and change. "We can't solve problems until we realize we have a problem of not seeing the problem."[88]

Physicians' have problems self-assessing because they are generally successful individuals and are unable to see the need for change. Goldsmith has stated that it is easier for successful people to change because they are usually good at setting and achieving their goals. It is harder because they are successful and may not see the need for change, or if they do see the need, they may be reluctant to change the behaviors they see as having "made" them successful in the first place. Generally, successful people can't see that they are successful *in spite of* less-than-optimal personal leadership and interpersonal skills.[109]

If individuals are not open and do not see their behavioral shortcomings, and do not see the "pain" these shortcomings cause themselves or others, they have no motivation to change. If they are unwilling to admit they have a problem, unwilling to ask for help, or too proud to believe they can do anything wrong, there is no use in even trying to give them feedback. This profile is clearly not one of an individual who is open. The purpose of a 360-degree feedback program* is to assist individuals in seeing and understanding areas for improvement, and developing a personal growth program.

While the focus here has been on physicians, it is clear that overestimation of ability is not uncommon. Kruger and Dunning[110] state that three points may be made about an individual's competence in the various "domains of life," in which we all operate on a daily basis:

1. Success and satisfaction depend on knowledge, wisdom, or savvy in knowing which rules to follow and which strategies to pursue.

2. People differ widely in the knowledge and strategies they apply in these domains, with varying levels of success.

3. When people are incompetent in the strategies they adopt to achieve success and satisfaction, they suffer a dual burden: Not only do they reach erroneous conclusions and make unfortunate choices, but their incompetence robs them of the ability to realize it.

Kruger and Dunning say that "the skills that engender competence in a particular domain are often the very same skills necessary to evaluate competence in that domain—one's own or anyone else's."[110] Experts on this topic consider incompetent people to lack *metacognition,* or *self-monitoring skills.*

These two investigators subsequently set-up a series of four studies to demonstrate their points. One of their predictions was that incompetent people, paradoxically, would be able to gain insights about their shortcomings if they were made more competent through training and thus were provided with the self-monitoring skills required to be able to realize their performance had been substandard. The key findings of their work were:

1. The demonstration of incompetence depends on the domain at hand; one may be competent in one area and not another (e.g., language skills vs. social skills).

2. In order for the incompetent to overestimate themselves, they must have some "minimal threshold of knowledge, theory, or experience to suggest to themselves that they can generate correct answers."

3. "Those who performed particularly poorly relative to their peers were utterly unaware of this fact."

---

*A 360-degree feedback program examines the discrepancy between the manner in which an individual self-assesses him- or herself and the manner in which those around them perceive them to behave or act. See chapter 10.

4. Finally, as they predicted, improving the skills of participants and thus enhancing their self-monitoring skills helped them to recognize the limitations of their abilities.

These statements are not meant to imply that physicians are incompetent, at least as related to providing patient care. However, it is entirely possible that we have difficulties in recognizing our ability in the domains of personal leadership and interpersonal skills. It is undoubtedly possible that we have developed, in our years of training, a minimal threshold of knowledge, theory, or experience to suggest to ourselves that we can generate correct answers related to our personal leadership and interpersonal skills. It is also entirely possible that those who have suboptimal personal leadership and interpersonal skills are utterly unaware of this fact. It is also likely, in fact highly probable, that greater insight into our strengths and deficiencies would give us a greater ability to self-monitor our personal leadership and interpersonal skills, ultimately helping us to become better, more effective individuals. In fact, it could be argued that all of these things are true, and that even those who are not incompetent are not as good as they could be, in part because of all of their training and the impact of the other missteps operating in their daily lives.

"Captive Audience Phenomenon"

The "captive audience" effect carries over to physicians and to their practices. Physicians are, as a group, risk-averse as related compared to other professions—not just as it relates to patient care, but also in the openness or willingness to move to other practices or to other cities, to try new methods of generating business or new business models, or to quit practice and try something else. Compared to the rest of the working world, physicians have a greater likelihood of simply "parking" for their career, with perhaps one practice change along the way.

Information Overload

Hock says, "We are educated beyond our ability to understand."[18] He was talking about the rate of information change in society in general. In medicine, it is much worse. The explosion of medical literature has virtually buried the physician who has any interest in staying abreast of "current thought" in his or her field. The burden is exacerbated by having to wade through tons of nearly worthless published information.

The emphasis on "being current" is important, but a legitimate question is, "What must be done to stay current?" Realistically, only several articles per month are of value. Finding those articles is the difficult part. We would be better off as a profession if we targeted those few valuable pieces of information and then opened ourselves to reading nonmedical material, including leadership development literature found in the nonmedical business world. Focusing on the medical literature results in a form of "forced illiteracy"[3] or closed-mindedness. Openness will lead to development and growth in our personal lives.

We have also allowed our premed students to become focused on science to the exclusion of a liberal arts education. Forty percent of medical students graduating in the year 2000 thought humanities "other than English" were either only "slightly important" or "not important" at all in preparing them for medical school.[25] Implicit in the way the question was answered is an underlying belief by the students that courses not explicitly "preparing" one for medical school are not important. Worse is the implication that medical students fail to understand how other courses (for example, ethics, sociology, theology, even accounting) might benefit their careers and broaden their thinking, especially as it relates to the humanistic focus of medicine.

Leaders understand that they need to develop all aspects of their lives, balancing their work and personal lives. By being more complete individuals, we will better serve our employees, patients, and families.

The Seven Common Leadership Missteps[SM] of Physicians are real. At some level, and in some capacity, they act in every physician's life on a daily basis. The toll it takes on our personal gratification, our fulfillment, and our happiness, at work and at home, cannot be underestimated. The degree to which they operate, however, is something in which we clearly have a choice. "These responses—clinical detachment, efficiency and productivity, prestige and authority, hierarchy, and wealth—are not intrinsic to the practice of medicine. Although the structure of modern medical practice may encourage them, we physicians also choose to endorse and accept them, in part as a way to relieve the inordinate pressure on our work. They seem to offer a kind of escape. Unfortunately, the escape is only illusory."[111]

Physicians, can choose a different path—a different way to be. We can choose to make a concerted effort to improve ourselves. My father gave me all of the information about the missteps and advice on how to avoid them in a letter he wrote to me less than a month after I graduated from medical school.

Dear Mike,

The main reason for writing is to put down a few thoughts which, in all the hubbub of graduation weekend, couldn't be said. I'm certain you know that we are all very proud of your accomplishments, and we know you have had to work long and hard to obtain them. I fear, however, that your hard work is only now beginning. You are bound to become very, very fatigued, both physically and emotionally, as your training advances. This can easily reach the point that you become cynical and incompassionate or even lead to your becoming depressed. There's no secret manner by which these can be avoided that I know, but simply being aware that they can occur gives you a leg up in handling them. Don't be too proud to seek help if these become more than moderate severity. Try and remember that physical rest is important, so "cool it" when you get a chance. Physical workouts may temporarily help the emotional stress, but not the physical exhaustion.

As you get further along, I suspect you will see people, possibly many of them, who get to feeling that they are owed and deserve a six-figure income and unquestioned respect from every facet of society. This attitude only produces disgruntlement and I hope it doesn't befall you. I hope you are doing this because it is what you want to do and that it is a noble and honorable profession. If you do your best, you will obtain a decent and comfortable income and will earn the respect of your patients and colleagues. But these must be earned, they can't be demanded. Try and never flaunt your degree or specialty. Remember that out of your field, you have no more expertise than anyone else and having an MD doesn't make you an expert in education, foreign policy, or politics, or any field.

I wish I had some trench coat advice for you about getting along with your chief and other staff. I guess you just wing it, ask your predecessors and watch and see what works (or does-n't work). Most people always learn more with their mouths closed than with them open. I would urge you to avoid getting the reputation of being a chronic whiner, both among your peers and senior staff. There is always something to complain about and always shall be until perfection arrives. If you must complain, be certain of your ground, present it in a coherent manner, offer what you think is a good alternative and, above all, don't get mad. If you don't prevail, accept your defeat gracefully and don't hold a grudge. A good sense of humor, which you fortunately have, will be one of your greatest friends, so keep in close touch with it....

Many young professionals feel that their position requires that they manifest their success with flashy cars, clothes, etc. To me, this is unseemly and makes them look ludicrous. I think understatement makes a much more favorable impression in the long run.

Keep smiling.

All my love,

HJW

Side-Stepping the Seven Common Leadership Missteps[SM] of Physicians

Why should we be interested in enhancing our personal leadership behaviors? The main reason is to become better people, to become a better brother or sister, mother or father. It will enhance your satisfaction, gratification, and fulfillment in your job and with your loved ones.

There are business reasons too. In the nonmedical business world, leadership qualities and the impact that leadership has on employee moral, effectiveness, and retention are apparent, yet this is a concept often lost in the medical business world. In looking at results, whether good or bad, there is a value chain connected to the four types of stakeholders in business systems. The four stakeholders in business have been described using The LECO Principle. In medicine it is The DEPO Principle[SM], which states that the "value chain" is that the doctor—the "on-the-ground" leader—determines employee results and perceived value, which predict patient results and perceived value, which predicts organizational results.[27]

As we saw from the application of the TRIZ Principles, this value chain also functions in medicine: A physician's leadership skills will be translated down into and throughout the employees of the organization and out through the patients seeking care within the organization. When speaking of leadership, it is not only the physician executive at the top, but also every physician at every level throughout the organization. In the quest for positive leadership results, it is more crucial to ensure that "on-the-ground" physicians have leadership skills (and leadership training) than those at the top, because they and their staffs are the ones taking care of patients. If an organization accomplishes this, it will, as a beneficial side-effect, gain "built-in leadership succession planning" and an unbroken string of effective leaders throughout the organization and ultimately throughout the profession of medicine.

Section Three

Hard Data on Soft Things

CHAPTER 5 ⬭⬭⬭⬭⬭

The Customers:
Where Did All the Patients Go?

Perhaps nowhere is the alignment between customer expectations and the actual service experience more out of whack than in the health care industry. Prison inmates and hospital patients have a lot in common. Both are subject to excessive questioning; stripped of their usual clothing and possessions; placed in a subservient, dependent relationship, and allowed visitors only during certain hours.[55]

Patient Satisfaction

The Picker Institute surveyed more than 350,000 patients in the past 10 years, focusing on what they value in their health care. The Institute has identified eight dimensions of care that patients value and seek from physicians and the health care system:[112]

1. Respecting a patient's values, preferences, and expressed needs

2. Access to care

3. Emotional support

4. Information and education

5. Coordination of care

6. Physical comfort

7. Involvement of family and friends

8. Continuity and transition

Physicians can directly affect all of these dimensions as they care for and interact with patients and employees, yet many of these things are clearly counter to reality, as noted in the quote from Hamel leading this chapter. Note in the Picker data that "Access to care," "Coordination of care," and "Continuity and transition" are directly related to or have a component of timeliness and/or customer convenience. Each of these things is adversely affected by an "efficiency focus."

The Picker Institute has also found that results concerning patient "satisfaction" per se are misleading. Many "fixed-response" patient satisfaction surveys obtain results suggesting patient satisfaction is quite high, with as many as 73 percent of patients rating their overall care as "very good" or "excellent." But, Picker notes, this is in sharp contrast to what patients say when they either speak or write about their experiences. The Picker group notes: "The people who participated in the AHA focus groups, regardless of their education or income, geographic location, or ethnicity, are deeply troubled about the changes they see taking place throughout the health care system: they talk about reduced access to care and higher out-of-pocket costs; they are doubtful about the quality of the care they are getting and about the competence of their caregivers; they see an increasing trend toward care that is cold and impersonal; and they don't fee l things are being done in their best interests."[113]

This may reflect the disconnect between what patients *actually* care about the most and what health care providers *think* they care about. The American Hospital Association conducted a national focus group to examine the public's perception of health care.[114] It found that "people do not believe that there is a system in health care, suggesting a belief that the U.S. health care system is 'fragmented and disorganized.'" The participants in the focus group suggested that, if there actually is a health care "system," it is "one designed to block access, reduce quality, and limit spending for care at the expense of patients." Such statements are not made by "sensational media accounts or the scare campaigns of special interest lobbying groups, but largely from personal experience. Patient after patient tells stories of their struggles to get past the many "gatekeepers" in the system or to get insurance or managed care approval for the care they and their doctors think they need. They talk about how assertive they must be to get answers and the frustrations of trying to coordinate care among many different specialists—and many of them worry about what will happen if and when they are too sick to manage such things on their own behalf. And they describe a feeling of being abandoned when they are released from the hospital—like "jumping off into nowhere," as one patient described it."[113]

With this impression in the general public, it is no wonder that patient satisfaction and trust of the health care system in this country is so low. "Imagine arriving at the airport and being invited to board an airplane that is little more than a horse-and-buggy with jet engines attached. Yet that is what we ask our patients to do every day—put their lives in the hands of a health care system built in the 19th Century for the solo practice doctor with a black bag and trust it to support teams of doctors and other professionals using 21ˢᵗ Century technology."[115]

Kasteler *et al.* found that 48 percent of upper-income and 37 percent of lower-income families who had seen physicians for illness episodes within a one-year period had changed doctors because of dissatisfaction with some aspect of their care, including a lack of confidence in a doctor's competence, unwillingness of the physician to spend time talking with them, and unfavorable attitudes toward doctors' personal qualities.[116] Note that many of these issues—driving greater than one-third to nearly one-half of the patients away—are interpersonal in nature.

More recently, Carlson and coworkers, in a cross-sectional telephone survey of 7,983 New Jersey HMO participants, found that socioeconomically advantaged individuals demonstrated substantial dissatisfaction with their health care. This equilibrated after 5 years of enrollment, when the lower socioeconomic groups were significantly dissatisfied—to an even greater extent than their higher socioeconomic group counterparts.[117] In other words, patient dissatisfaction with health care cuts across all socioeconomic groups.

Hulka and others found in a survey of 1,713 adults in 1,112 households particularly negative attitudes expressed toward the personal qualities of physicians, especially by African-Americans, with cost, accessibility, and convenience also being poorly regarded.[118]

Whether physicians recognize it or not, we have helped create many of the problems in health care we are dealing with today. In a panel discussion with members of the National Committee for Quality Assurance (NCQA),[96] the question was asked: "Trust has always been an essential element of the doctor/patient relationship. Has this changed in recent years?" Thomas R. Reardon, MD, replied: "I think there has been an erosion of trust. The patients aren't sure whether their doctor is working for the health plan or working for the patient. They wonder whether they're going to get necessary care when they need it because of all the media coverage about utilization controls and denials of care by health plans."

Michael Wolk, MD, another panel member in the NCQA discussion, had a little different take on the trust issue: "I think some of the trust has broken down because of valid criticism of physicians on issues that need to be appropriately responded to by physicians. One example is the variation in care we give patients. In cardiology, for example, you might find that there are 15 times more 'caths' per thousand patients in one part of the country than another, and that bypass surgery costs a Volkswagen in Virginia and a Cadillac in New York. We as a society of physicians need to work on our guidelines so that we can narrow the variation in the provision of services, not only to provide better value for the patient, but also to control some of the cost. This has to be addressed if we want patients to trust us."

Trust is purely an interpersonal issue, and the only way to develop trust is to establish a relationship with patients. This can't be done in 6-10- minute visit.

Developing and maintaining trust is one thing, but what about more pragmatic things, such as how long a patient must wait to get an appointment in your office? It should be no surprise that delays are expensive to everyone. They are expensive in direct costs to you, but also in terms of the potential cost in terms of patient satisfaction. The Picker Institute has found that patients who were dissatisfied because of delays in being seen are:

- Less likely to recommend the physician.

- More likely to disenroll from a managed care plan.

- More likely to fail to keep an appointment or cancel, creating unused office time.[119]

On the flip side, patients who receive an appointment in your office quickly are more likely to recommend you to others than a patient who experiences a delay (77 percent versus 49 percent).[120]

Once a patient manages to get an appointment in the physician's office, the issues become quite different. There is probably no other industry that has such low regard for the client's convenience than medicine. In complete alignment with the opening quote of this chapter, Herzlinger has noted: "…the inconvenience of our health care system packs a deadly double punch. Not only does it rob people of their time, it prevents them from obtaining important preventive medical care. Inconvenience, in fact, substantially reduces people's health status and needlessly inflates costs."[121]

What is worse, she notes, is that physicians seem "oblivious to the convenience revolution" that took place between 1983 and 1991. While other industries were intensely focused on enhancing customer convenience during these years, the waiting time for an appointment with a physician increased by 40 percent. This does not even factor in the amount of time wasted by patients navigating the health care insurance system, where "Finding the right person to respond to an inquiry requires yeoman labor."[122]

I used to complain about patients who would show up in the ER for largely routine care. It never occurred to me that many of these individuals had jobs and that their physicians did not have office hours in the evening. Some might think "They should take some time off work during the day and come in." This perspective is one of an individual (i.e., a physician) who is usually in complete control of his or her schedule, who is at a socioeconomic level foreign to most, and who can essentially take time whenever chosen, with little possibility for fallout from a "boss." What other industry has the hubris to expect clients to tailor their schedules to someone they are trying to pay for service? How many of us would go out to dinner at a restaurant that quit taking orders after 5:30 p.m.? The owner of such a restaurant might have the attitude that "If they want dinner, they will just have to arrange their schedules to get here at 4 p.m." Few would agree that this is a very consumer-oriented restaurant, yet this is exactly the way we run our offices in the medical profession. There are, thankfully, an increasing number of providers who are beginning to appreciate the need to have a broader range of operating hours.

Physicians are also largely oblivious to the cumulative impact of patient waiting time on society and societal productivity. In 1990, according to one study, there were 704 million physician visits. If one assumes the required wait per patient was "only" 30 minutes, the loss to the U.S. economy was 14.67 million days of productive work. They additionally estimated that at a conservative value of $20,000 per year of lost time, doctors' waiting rooms calculates out to *$804 million in annual lost productivity.*[123] (A flaw of this study, of course, is it assumes all patients were employed, which is probably not the case. But it is the point that is important; even if only half were employed the numbers are still staggering.) I have heard all the arguments from physicians, including the most popular one: "My time is worth more than theirs on a relative scale." Physicians who use this "rationale" fail to understand that patients are already paying for their time; having unreasonable waiting times make them pay twice—one fee to the physician (a copayment and the cost of insurance) and one fee to the employer for the personal income loss associated with waiting. Such attitudes represent a chasm between the life experiences and expectations of various socioeconomic groups. They clearly are not respectful of the individual and result in difficulty in communication between patient and physicians.[124] Physicians need to step back from their own life experiences (and socioeconomic group) and step into the shoes of their patients to understand their perspective and the ramifications of the situation on their lives.

Herzlinger isn't the only critic of the current health care system as it relates to an unfriendly consumer focus. Hamel speaks of the "orthodoxies in the American health care system." "The sick are considered patients, not consumers. Health care providers dispatch cases, they don't build relationships. The goal is to cure illnesses rather than promote wellness (you don't get reimbursed for wellness). Insurers are in the business of dodging risks rather than improving the health of a population. The entire industry has been organized from the payer backwards rather than from the consumer forward.

"...Whether we ever get a real revolution in health care will depend on whether anyone ever succeeds in taking a wrecking ball to the edifice of industry orthodoxy."[125]

Understanding the cumulative effect of patient wait times on society gives additional insight that emphasizes the interconnectedness of our profession with societal productivity. It makes our time seem less important and patients' time more important. We need to remember that patients choose us; we serve them. To ignore this fact is disrespectful to our patients as individuals.

Trying to hurry patients out of the hospital also hurts us. It surprises no one that hospital stays are being shortened. What may be news to some, however, is that patients are reporting significant dissatisfaction with the discharge process. The Picker Institute has found that patients often leave the hospital without a clear understanding of their medications or the side effects to watch for, with inadequate knowledge of what post-discharge complications they might encounter, or without knowing when to resume their normal activities.[126] Reiley *et al.* found that being discharged from a hospital may be as scary to a patient as it is to be admitted to a hospital.[127] Another study documented that a patient's discharge experience is improved "by clarifying who is responsible for making the decisions about discharge and follow-up."[128]

Communication and Patient Satisfaction

The playwright George Bernard Shaw once quipped that "a profession is a conspiracy against the laity," meaning that its clients are vulnerable despite the fact that they are buyers. In addition, faith and trust play a substantial part in working with someone who provides basically advisory services. Moreover, because of the nature of the problem—health, justice, safety—clients need to have confidence in the professionals in whose hands they literally place their lives and sometimes their fortunes.[129]

Tucker found, in a study examining patient satisfaction, that "access, communication, outcomes, and quality" were the major predictors of patient satisfaction scores in military health care facilities.[130] Waitzkin has outlined the relationship of different social backgrounds and significant problems with doctor-patient communication: "Social structural barriers impede effective communication, however, and information giving remains problematic. Doctors tend to underestimate patients' desire for information and to misperceive the process of information giving. The transmission of information is related to characteristics of patients (sex, education, social class, and prognosis), doctors (social class background, income, and perception of patients' desire for information), and the clinical situation (number of patients seen). Doctors' nonverbal communication abilities are associated with outcomes of medical care such as satisfaction and compliance. Regarding the sociolinguistic structure of communication, doctors often maintain a style of high control, which involves many doctor-initiated questions, interruptions, and neglect of patients' 'life world.'"[124]

Stewart and colleagues[43] describe the "lessons learned from studies about patient's satisfaction or dissatisfactions." They report that the majority of complaints about doctors are usually due to communication problems, not technical competency issues. They also point out the assumption, on behalf of physicians, that effective communication is inefficient. The authors acknowledge that effective communication is a "complex and very interesting issue," but that it is not necessarily true that it must always be "inefficient." Stewart and colleagues also provide strong evidence that communication affects patient adherence to the treatment plan recommended by the doctor. If the communication is clear and effective, the likelihood for the success of any one treatment is enhanced.

Physician/patient rapport is a marker of effective communication between individuals—rapport is a form of, or at least requires, trust. Rapport is central to the doctor-patient relationship. In a survey of 588 hospital administrators concerning their institutions' emergency department physicians,[131] 40 percent stated they had "concerns regarding physician's rapport with patients." Fully 10 percent of the administrators said they would not choose to go to their own hospital's emergency department if they were seriously injured, which was consistent with the 20 percent who said they had "concerns about professional competence" in their emergency departments. Does a lack of communication skill on the part of physicians result in the perception of incompetence or lack of competence on the part of patients? Do physicians who "maintain a style of high control, which involves many doctor-initiated questions, interruptions, and neglect of patients 'life world,'" demonstrate a lack of interpersonal skill? Absolutely. Is it possible that a patient can perceive a physician's inability to explain a condition or treatment to them in an understandable way—in "their language"—as a reflection of technical incompetence on the part of the physician? Does this put patients "on guard" for even the smallest mistakes, increasing liability risk? Perhaps.

Physicians do, of course, have some legitimate concerns relative to physician-patient communication. With patients taking an increasingly active role in seeking information concerning their health care, it takes more of a physician's time to help them understand the information. Yaremchuk states: "It takes time to talk about where patients can get their care, or to help them understand the article they've gotten off the Internet. But time is one thing we have less of because we have to increase our volume. We're always being told to work more efficiently, but there is a limit to how efficient we can be in communicating with patients."[96]

This can clearly be a problem, along the lines of "the folly of hoping for A while rewarding for B." We can't expect physicians to act one way when we pay them for being another way. It is unrealistic to increase our "efficiency" and see six patients per hour and expect high levels of patient satisfaction.

The Information Age and Patients

In Chapter Four, we saw how physicians can manifest "The Challenge Syndrome." As a reminder, physicians are often taught to challenge everything related to patient care, but this can spill-over into other aspects of a physician's life, leading them to challenge everything, period. What I did not point out, however, is that challenging a physician can be a rather dicey proposition, as many physicians have an intense dislike for being questioned as to their knowledge, diagnoses, and treatment recommendations.

An informed patient can lead to substantial tension between the patient and physician. I recall being upset (more than once) when patients whipped-out medical journal articles they had obtained about their conditions. I would rationalize my discomfort with my staff by saying something like "I don't mind their questions, it just takes so much time." In reality, I interpreted this as a challenge to my authority and knowledge.

The internet has made information and data commodities, and this includes medicine. Anyone with a computer and a telephone line has access to virtually limitless amounts of information. Consider these facts (which will be old by the time you read this):

- 60% of Americans use the internet
- 52% of American households have PCs
- 68% of all adults turn to the internet for health advice
- Over 50% of all queries on the internet are health-related[132]

After an individual visits an internet health site:

- 54% were stimulated to ask their physicians about prescriptions
- 50% urged friend/family to see a doctor
- 46% altered their diet or exercise habits
- 45% made treatment decisions
- 41% visited a doctors[132]

In other words, information about health care is easy to get, and it generates patient questions and alters patient behaviors—and questions can be interpreted by some individuals as challenges to their authority or knowledge.

Basically what is happening in health care is that the distance between a patient's knowledge and the physician's knowledge is decreasing because of an increasingly informed populace and free and easily obtained information. This "flattening of the hierarchy" is very intimidating to some physicians, but it will continue. James has clearly described the dynamics of what is happening in health care: "There are radical shifts in power in health care. The flattened hierarchy has dramatically changed the sense of leadership in medicine. Where you create nurse specialists, when you create physician assistants, when you have informed consumers, you begin to flatten the hierarchy. This makes extraordinary changes in leadership style. When the peasants begin to read, the King begins to look stupid. The American Revolution was built on that. If the King couldn't prove he was smart, it was real hard to get Americans to go along with it. Now you have Americans who own defibrillators….Now, if you have this consumer who is increasingly able to get information, the ability to control data is just out the window. You have to prove competency in this flattened hierarchy."[133]

In other words, it isn't enough to have an "MD" behind your name anymore, and it is going to be a long time to retirement for those physicians who can't figure out how to deal with the increasingly informed consumer. The current health care environment is one of revolution, being driven by freely available information and consumers who are more than happy to take responsibility for their health care. James actually went on to say that, in the history of the world, no group has lost so much power so quickly as physicians.

Even with all of the information people can get off of the internet, when individuals who have been looking for information on the internet are asked where they want to get their information, the majority (62 percent) still say their "own doctor." This almost begs the question of whether so many patients would feel compelled to search the internet for health information if their physicians were good communicators and were providing them with the appropriate amount of information. As mentioned earlier, insufficient communication may be construed by patients as caregiver incompetence, and this can lead to, among other things (e.g., lawsuits), a patient's feeling as if they need additional information.

The Patient Satisfaction Survey:
The Instrument and Results Concerning Their Physician and Their Physician's Office

In customer surveys of nonmedical businesses, a rating by the customer of less than 90 percent being at least "somewhat satisfied" is considered unacceptable, or at minimum an area needing significant improvement.[134] This reflects the finding that, especially in industries with a primary focus on customers (as medicine is), not more than 10 percent of individuals will claim to be dissatisfied. A "somewhat satisfied" implies there is room for improvement, because inherent in such a response is "latent dissatisfaction." All responses that fall into the "Somewhat dissatisfied," "Dissatisfied" or "Highly dissatisfied" categories would be considered areas where substantial improvement is needed.

A typical response scale in such surveys gives a customer six choices of "satisfaction" or "agreement" (depending on the question):

- Highly satisfied or strongly agree

- Satisfied or agree

- Somewhat satisfied or somewhat agree

- Somewhat dissatisfied or somewhat disagree

- Dissatisfied or disagree

- Highly dissatisfied or highly disagree

The following statements were listed in two separate sections—one ascertaining satisfaction and one ascertaining agreement—of an internet-based patient satisfaction survey conducted by the author. The objective of the survey was to ascertain how patients' currently view their physician's office and staff and their physician's behaviors related to their personal health care.

The Office (Scale: Satisfaction)
- The greeting you received when you entered the office (Greeting)

- The ease of the sign-in process (Sign-in)

- The length of time you had to wait to see the physician (Wait time)

- The service provided by the physician's office staff (Service)

- The thoroughness of the physician (Thoroughness)

- Your overall satisfaction with this experience (Overall sat.)

The Physician (Scale: Agreement)
- The physician treated me with respect (Rx w/Respect)

- The physician really listened to me (Listened)

■ The physician asked really good questions to diagnose my problem (Good ?s)

■ I felt that I had been heard (I was Heard)

■ The physician treated other staff members in a professional and respectful way (Staff Rx)

■ I generally felt cared for on this visit (Cared For)

■ The physician treated me as an equal (Rx Equal)

■ If I were a doctor, I think I would enjoy working with this physician (MD Work w/MD)

■ If I were in the medical field, I think I would enjoy working in this physician's office (Work for MD)

■ I would recommend this physician to others (Recommend MD)

A summary score is calculated for each section and is represented by "All" in the figures. The description in parentheses following each bullet above is the label on each figure for the respective question.

Results: General Demographic Data

The survey was conducted via the internet between October 11 and October 31, 2000. There were 78 respondents to 161 surveys (51 percent response rate). Gender breakdown of those responding was 36 percent males and 55 percent females, with the gender of 9 percent of individuals not being known; these percentages are consistent with the total number of surveys sent to males and females (39 percent of the 161 surveys were sent to males and 61 percent to females). The higher response rate in females is not unusual for surveys, as women tend to have a higher response rate than men. The age range of the respondents was 25-74 years. While the specific ethnic breakdown is not known in detail, African-Americans, Asians, Hispanics, and Caucasians participated, largely skewed toward Caucasian. This response rate, relative to ethnicity, is also a typical pattern for surveys. Educational backgrounds ranged from high school to PhD/MD degrees.

About the Graphs: The "zero" point of the graphs in figures 5-1 and 5-2, page 93, correlates with the "Highly Dissatisfied" or "Strongly Disagree" end of the scales, while the Highly Satisfied" or "Strongly Agree" end of the scales are at the 100 percent point.

An asterisk denotes a category in which the total number of respondents who were "somewhat dissatisfied" or worse exceeded 10 percent (the lower acceptable limit in nonmedical business). A double asterisk denotes a category in which the total number of respondents who were "somewhat dissatisfied" or worse exceeded 20 percent—double what is considered the lower limit of normal in nonmedical business—and three asterisks denotes dissatisfaction in greater than 30 percent of respondents.

FIGURE 5-1.

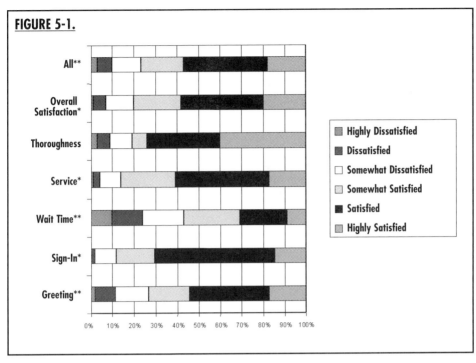

FIGURE 5-2.

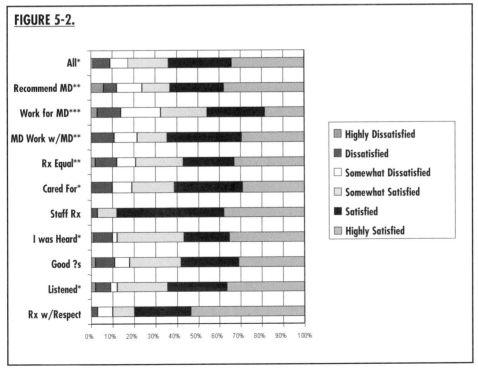

Discussion and Impact

Of the 18 questions on the patient survey, only one had fewer than 10 percent responding "somewhat dissatisfied/disagree." This was the question "The physician treated other staff members in a professional and respectful way." For 17 of the questions, 10 percent or more responded "somewhat dissatisfied/disagree" or worse regarding their impressions of their physicians and their physicians' offices. For 8 of the questions, 20 percent of responses fell into the "somewhat dissatisfied/disagree" or lower categories—double the upper limit of what would be considered acceptable in consumer-focused industries.

Questions with Greater than 20 Percent "Somewhat Dissatisfied/Disagree" Among Respondents

For the office assessment, the overall summary was 23 percent of individuals were "somewhat dissatisfied" or worse. Several single items had even worse scores and should clearly get the attention of practitioners, but an overall rating of 23 percent is more than two times what would be considered acceptable in other businesses.

The fact that 28 percent of patients were "somewhat dissatisfied" with the way they were greeted in the physicians' offices is worrying. Recalling what we know of the "lead indicators of customer satisfaction"—the DEPO Principle^SM—front office personnel and their impact on customer satisfaction, these survey results reflect on the leaders, in this case physicians. The DEPO Principle^SM does not just predict the economic results obtained with patients and employees; it is also reflects personal leadership effectiveness with patients and employees.

Forty-three percent of patients responding stated they were "somewhat dissatisfied" or worse regarding the length of time they had to wait to see physicians. This is supported by data from the Picker Institute, which found that 18 percent of patients reported difficulty in getting appointments and 30 percent reported long waits to see the doctor.[112] One can interpret this in several different ways: One interpretation is physicians are truly giving each and every patient the amount of time needed to resolve the issues at hand. The other, which is virtually guaranteed to occur in some patients' minds, is, "Why does this doctor always overbook?" These delays affect patients' likelihood of recommending you, increases the likelihood they will quit the health care plan you are participating in, and increases the likelihood they will cancel their appointment with you.

In response to the statement "The physician treated me as an equal," 21 percent responded "somewhat disagree" or worse, indicating they felt, in some way, "beneath" the physician. Although physicians may think this isn't important or that patients are being unrealistic, it is still the patient's impression, is still valid, and must be respected and dealt with appropriately.

Another 21 percent "somewhat disagree" or worse with the statement "If I were a doctor, I think I would enjoy working with this physician." They either don't like the physician very much or do not think they could get along with them in some professional capacity, based on their experience as a patient.

In response to a related question, "If I were in the medical field, I think I would enjoy working in this physician's office," 32 percent marked "somewhat disagree" or worse, indicating a perception by the patient that there were "environmental factors" that were perceived by the patient as less than optimal.

Finally, and worst of all for physicians, 24 percent—nearly a quarter—of all respondents said they "somewhat disagree" or worse with the statement, "I would recommend this physician to others." Clearly this sort of response should concern us as a profession and sharpen our focus on patient retention. A greater customer focus—on both patients *and* employees— by increasing personal leadership effectiveness, as the DEPO Principle[SM] states, will have a dramatic impact on your personal practice; as more physicians begin to appreciate this, it will affect all of health care.

Questions with between 10 and 20 Percent "Somewhat Dissatisfied/Disagree" among Respondents

In consumer-focused businesses, any category scoring over 10 percent in the "somewhat dissatisfied/disagree" categories would be an area needing improvement. The questions and the percentage of individuals responding "somewhat dissatisfied/disagree" or worse to the item are listed below:

The Physician's Office

- The ease of the sign-in process   12%
- The service provided by the physician's office staff   14%
- The thoroughness of the physician   19%

The Physician

- Summary of physician   17%
- The physician treated me with respect   10%
- The physician REALLY listened to me   12%
- The physician asked really good questions to diagnose my problem   18%
- I felt that I had been heard   13%
- I generally felt cared for on this visit   19%

In summary, the data suggest substantial customer (i.e., patient) dissatisfaction with medicine and the mechanics of the offices involved in health care delivery. Again, some of these numbers are consistent with the Picker Institute numbers, which found 21 percent of office patients and 36 percent of hospital patients were not as involved with decisions about their care as they wanted to be.[113] Recalling The DEPO Principle[SM], where the physician is the leader personally responsible for the results obtained with employees, patients, and the organization, accountability for obtaining these results lies with the physician. It is the leaders of an organization that determine the culture and affect the attitudes of the employees, not the other way around. This being the case, each physician is responsible for the "front office" results obtained in their practices—the interface between staff and patients. We are each responsible for the impressions patients take away from our offices, in the way they perceive they are treated, and the way they perceive us treating our employees. The more we enhance our personal leadership qualities, the better our interpersonal relationships will be in the office, and this will translate into satisfied patients. I can virtually guarantee you also will be happier as an individual.

One of the problems with medical care today is the ease with which physicians discount patient perceptions in the absence of "hard" data. Refer back to chapter 4 and how "skepticism" hurts us, especially in interpersonal relationships. Be careful about discounting patient satisfaction information because of "small sample size," "non-randomized samples," "an unblinded study," or any other valid *but irrelevant* reason. Perceptions are perceptions. Second, there are many publications that support these data, and articles that are consistent with these findings. It is, therefore, important for the reader to avoid rationalizing the results of this data set away. They are, as this section is titled, "hard data on soft things," and they have face validity.

Enhancing our personal leadership skills and interpersonal skills and embracing the DEPO Principle[SM] will go a long way in helping us to improve patients' satisfaction in our offices and hospitals.

CHAPTER 6 ⬭⬭⬭⬭⬭

The Employees:
Brain-Drained and Disgruntled

The most abundant, least expensive, most underutilized, and constantly abused resource in the world is human ingenuity.[19]

Data from our patient survey and in the literature from thousands of patients have established that there are substantial issues related to patient satisfaction. As we have seen from The DEPO Principle[SM] and 4-D leadership impact, the doctor determines the results with the patient and the value they perceive, in no small part because of the results obtained with employees and the value they perceive in their jobs. The issues of patient and employee satisfaction are inseparable from physician leadership, because physicians are the "on-the-ground" leaders.

Employees as Customers

One of the "customer groups" of physicians, as "on-the-ground" leaders, are our employees, whether in our offices or in the hospitals in which we work. Physicians are the leaders of employees in health care whether they directly employ the employees or not. Their motivation and satisfaction are results for which we are responsible. The Picker Institute has held nationwide focus groups with hospital employees to determine the factors that employees felt affected the quality of patient care in their hospitals. The Institute unveiled three factors[135]:

1. The external environment in which health care organizations operate

2. The organization's structure and culture

3. The division of labor and job design of health care providers

Physicians can directly affect at least two of these factors—the organization's structure and culture and the division of labor and job design.

The employees in our offices and hospitals—who in fact *are* our offices and hospitals—walk out the door at the end of every workday. Our major asset—those helping us carry out our business on a daily basis—are not something we own. Ulrich *et al.* comment: "As business becomes increasingly knowledge and service driven, employee results will continue to become more, not less important. Leaders must recognize and foster the link between successful employee results and the process of building human capital."[136]

Clearly this underscores the critical need for organizations to *retain* the staff they have and create organizations to attract new talent. The authors go on to define "human capital" as "what is inside the heads and hearts of the people who work in an organization." They put a formula to this concept:

Human capital = employee capability x employee commitment[137]

The point they make in their discussion of this formula has powerful implications: high levels of employee capability do not guarantee a high level of human capital. Furthermore, high levels of employee capability will not guarantee business or project success. Without commitment, human capability is not sufficient for organizational success. Covey states this another way: "You can buy a person's hand, but you can't buy his heart. His heart is where his enthusiasm, his loyalty is. You can buy his back, but you can't buy his brain. That's where his creativity is, his ingenuity, his resourcefulness."[138]

This theme is the basis for Maxwell's "The Law of Connection." His basic premise is, "Leaders touch a heart before they ask for a hand."

"You can't move people to action unless you first move them with emotion. The heart comes before the head.

"The stronger the relationship and connection between the individuals, the more likely the follower will want to help the leader.

"It's the leader's job to initiate connection with the people.

"It may sound corny, but it's really true: People don't care how much you know until they know how much you care.

"To lead yourself, use your head; to lead others, use your heart." [139]

Ulrich *et al.* note that companies fail to realize this and subsequently rarely invest in employees whose "human capital" has the most direct effect on customers.[140] In medicine, physicians and their employees have the most direct effect on their customer, the patient. Yet how often has a hospital or clinic encouraged, or in fact paid for a personal effectiveness or leadership course for their physicians or employees? The DEPO Principle℠ suggests this should be a strategic, long-term capital investment for medical organizations.

Do You Hear What I Hear? Signs of Dissatisfaction

The ability of physicians and nurses to communicate and collaborate has been demonstrated to improve patient outcomes and job satisfaction. A study was done to examine the communication that occurred between physicians and nurses in a large medical center. Each subject (both physicians and nurses) completed a written questionnaire and underwent a structured interview with trained social linguistics personnel. Physicians and nurses shared the same perceptions about their roles with regard to the communication process. Basically, they understood their respective roles in giving and taking orders, asking for information, and asking for and giving opinions. However, they significantly differed in their perceptions about their roles relative to giving information or providing education. Physicians thought nurses did not initiate certain types of communication as often as the nurses thought they did. Nurses were particularly interested in having more interaction with physicians, and also expressed the need to be listened to or respected more by physicians. Finally, the nurses were more likely to express interest in having interactions with house staff than with attending physicians, implying some inhibition or intimidation by the latter related to communications.[141]

In our patient survey, 28 percent of the respondents said they were "somewhat dissatisfied" or worse with the manner in which they were greeted in their physicians' offices. Because we know that employees are the interface with our customers—in this case, patients—there is an implication (at the very least) of dissatisfaction among the employees in these physicians' offices.

Twenty-one percent of patients "somewhat disagreed" or worse that physicians treated them as equals. If we are not treating our customer, the patient, as an equal— or even better—how are we treating our staffs? What would our staff say if asked this same question?

A third of patients in the survey "somewhat disagreed" or worse with the statement, "If I were a doctor, I think I would enjoy working with this physician." Does it not bode poorly for us if the impression of our patients is that physicians would not be good team players?

Some of the other results from the patient questionnaire are in alignment with these suggested interpretations, including: 14 percent of patients were "somewhat dissatisfied" or worse with the service provided by office staff, 10 percent were "somewhat disagreeing" or worse with the statement "The physician treated me with respect," and 19 percent were "somewhat disagreeing" or worse with the statement "I really felt cared for on this visit." All of these findings, either directly or indirectly, reflect a degree of employee dissatisfaction in those offices.

Another measure of employee dissatisfaction is revealed by employee turnover in the health care industry. Turnover was explored in chapter 2 as it relates to how leaders are, in part, responsible for turnover of their staffs. The monthly turnover of employees in health care was 1.7 percent between January and September 1999 and was greater that the turnover in the finance industry (1.2 percent) and manufacturing (1 percent).[32] This is a 30 percent higher rate of turnover than in the finance industry during the same period. There is a possibility that a portion of this number may not be due to employee dissatisfaction with employers. For example, some of the dissatisfaction may be due to the rapidly changing medical environment in general. However, as physicians and on-the-ground leaders of health care, we are at least partially responsible.

While there are multiple reasons one might leave a job, the culture of the organization is almost always a factor. Leaders determine the culture and are therefore responsible for employee turnover and for attempting to reduce it.

Organizational Surveys of Employee Satisfaction

The importance of obtaining employees' opinions concerning their work environment cannot be underestimated. An "Organizational Survey" to assess employee perceptions about the organization in which they work can be helpful in understanding such questions. In such surveys, one can assess employee morale, their perceptions of teamwork and the organization's leadership, the likelihood of employees' staying in the organization, and employees' impressions of what patients think of the organization and its physician leaders.

These organizational culture or vitality surveys are great predictors of employee turnover. Additionally, such a survey can show employees that the organization cares about them and is interested in their feedback. Research has shown that allowing health care staff members to participate in decision making contributes to positive job attitudes and helps improve patient outcomes.[135]

Surveys are also great diagnostic tools. The positive things one finds are organizational morale boosters—hidden strengths. The negative things one finds are cancers that can destroy organizational morale and sap the company of the vitality and energy required to effectively compete. The findings of such surveys must be made broadly available in the organization to leverage the positive findings and make the employees aware of where improvements are needed. It is in the best interests of medical organizations to understand and reinforce their strengths, while trying to identify the "cancers" at a curable stage and without resorting to radical surgery.

CHAPTER 7 ⫷⫷⫸⫸

The Physicians:
Step Two Toward Fulfillment—If I'm So Successful, Why Am I Unhappy?

I'll say that if you listen to doctors—maybe I go to too many meetings—there is so much complaining and frustration, doctors who are walking away from the profession because they can't take it anymore.[95]

Is Success Enough?

Physicians are successful by virtually any measure that society might want to apply to us as a profession. We make significant incomes, especially compared to the average income of any other worker; we have a relatively high social status; we are generally respected; and we are highly educated. But if this is the case, why is there so much dissatisfaction among physicians? It is because, in part, success is not the same as satisfaction. Success is not the same as happiness. And success is not the same as fulfillment.

Physician Satisfaction: The Data

Multiple studies have examined physician satisfaction. A recent study was designed to look at the relationship between the satisfaction of general internists and their patients.[142] Eleven academically affiliated general internal medicine practices in the greater Boston area participated in the study, in which the measures were patients' overall satisfaction with their health care and their satisfaction with their most recent physician visit. More than 2,600 patients were surveyed, and 166 physicians participated. The conclusion of the study was that the patients of physicians who had rated themselves to be very or extremely satisfied with their work as doctors had higher scores for overall satisfaction with their health care and for satisfaction with their most recent physician visit.

The Department of Veteran Affairs has examined burnout among its physicians.[143] A longitudinal study from 1989 to 1997 was designed to analyze which demographic and behavioral variables were associated with the intensity of burnout. Eighty-three Medical Center Directors, Associate Directors, and Chiefs of Staff responded to questionnaires sent in 1989, 1992, and 1997. The findings demonstrated that burnout rose from 25.3 percent in 1989 to 38.1 percent in 1997 and was inversely related to the respondent's age. Not surprisingly, the burnout phase in 1997 was inversely related to job satisfaction and resource availability.

Linzer and colleagues studied 5,704 primary care and specialty physicians in the United States, using a survey with 150 items reflecting 10 components of satisfaction, including global satisfaction with one's current job, one's career, and one's specialty.[144] More than 2,300 physicians responded to the questionnaire. HMO physicians had lower satisfaction with resources and relationships with staff and community compared to physicians in other practice settings, such as private or academic practices. Small and large group practice and academic physicians had higher global job satisfaction than HMO physicians. Private practice physicians had 25-50 percent lower odds of intending to leave their current practices within 2 years. "Time pressure" detracted from satisfaction in 7 of 10 satisfaction components, including job, career, and specialty satisfaction. While 83 percent of family physicians in HMOs felt they needed more time than allotted for new patients, 54 percent of family physicians in small group practices also felt they needed more time. This again illustrates the pressure on physicians related to patient volume ("efficiency") and highlights not only how patient satisfaction is lowered by such pressures but also that time pressures negatively affect physician satisfaction.

Frank *et al.* have looked at career satisfaction in women physicians by surveying a nationally representative sample of 4,501 female physicians (59 percent response rate).[145] Thirty-one percent of the female physicians would maybe, probably, or definitely not choose to be a physician again. Thirty-eight percent would maybe, probably, or definitely prefer to change their specialty. The independent predictors by logistic regression analysis of these outcomes were the woman's age, the woman's having a sense of not having control of her work, work stress, or having experienced severe harassment. Younger women, those with the least work control, and those having been severely harassed had the greatest job dissatisfaction.

It is also apparent that job satisfaction is not solely an issue for U.S.-based physicians. Sibbald *et al.* have found in Great Britain that, for both male and female physicians, overall job satisfaction declined from 1987 to 1990, with a slight improvement from 1990 to 1998, although satisfaction in 1998 remained below that in 1987.[146] They note that, while there has been some improvement in job satisfaction from the low point in 1990-91, the "reported levels of stress in relation to many aspects of work have continued to increase."

Factors Contributing to Physician Dissatisfaction

Myriad factors have contributed to physician unhappiness or dissatisfaction. In the section of an NCQA report[96] called "Fulfillment," the Practicing Physicians Advisory Council identified a number of factors contributing to physician job dissatisfaction. At least half, if not more, of these reasons are directly or indirectly related to money, income, or time pressures (which relate to money).

■ Anger about decreasing reimbursement.

■ The press and recent reports on medical error rates.

■ The feeling of "being attacked."

■ The feeling that "everybody wants to tear the profession down."

■ Concerns that patients will leave their practice in January when the health plans switch.

■ Managed care "carving out your EKG or your x-ray or your lab."

■ "Working harder, seeing more patients, their billing is up 10 percent, but their income is flat.

■ No ability to negotiate with major payers.

■ Feeling angry and helpless; they have no clout and "they're being dictated to."

■ Being forced into large practices when they would prefer to stay in small, community-based practices.

What do we do about these things? In Chapter 3 we discussed how to enhance personal and professional credibility by acknowledging and being more transparent about the business aspects of medicine. In the long term, one thing *not* to focus on is efficiency. One focus might be to begin to connect to the value in the profession beyond money—the intrinsic motivation that led us into medicine to begin with. Finally, we can focus on personal leadership, becoming increasingly proactive, and looking for solutions to our problems "out of the box," because medicine is no longer "business as usual."

Decisions We Make: Understanding We Are Responsible

The medical profession seems to miss the fact that *we* have ended up "where we are" in part because of decisions we have made. Decisions we have made as individuals, and decisions we have made as a profession have put us where we are as a profession.

Covey has noted: "All organizations are perfectly aligned to the results they get."[3] If an organization is wildly successful, it is because the organization is aligned for wild success. If an organization is failing, it is because the organization is aligned for failure. Medicine is in its current state because it is aligned to obtain such results.

Earlier we talked about efficiency in medicine and how it is not the place to focus. How many times have you heard someone make the statement: "I am so busy I can't even take new patients" or "I wish I were not so busy." Why don't individuals in such a position choose to recruit another partner? Usually when I have asked such individuals this question, the response is something along the lines of "The practice wouldn't support another person." Hilfiker succinctly describes this thought process and what drives it (at least for many):

"In addition, the desire to maintain my financial position inhibited many of the changes that might have made my work more tolerable. One response to the intensity of medical practice, to the need to be constantly available, and to the demand to know more would have been to add more physicians or physician assistants to the practice.... With more physician time available for the same number of patients, I could have taken longer with my patients, dealt with their problems in a more leisurely fashion, looked up information, or consulted with my partners about problems I faced. Yet in our situation, extra help could not be hired without reducing our incomes.... Despite the enormous pressure each of us was feeling in our work, we never seriously considered that option."[147]

If one chooses not to hire more help in order to keep income at its current level, it is a conscious tradeoff. One will continue to feel the pressures described by Hilfiker. Alternatively, the physician could hire additional help and have more time. Two ironic things would probably occur with this latter choice: the physician would be happier and more satisfied, and the "new help" will almost invariably draw new patients into the practice, ultimately adding income over time.

Another choice is whether to schedule as many patients as possible to maintain or increase one's income, or to take one's time with each patient, attending to each patient's physical and emotional needs. As in some managed care environments, does one schedule a patient to be seen every 6 minutes, or does one schedule 15 or 20 minutes out of respect for individual and the individual's schedule? The choice will affect your satisfaction and your income, usually in opposite directions, and has a lot to do with "intrinsic" vs. "extrinsic" motivation. We must take personal responsibility for our choices. As Covey notes: "While we are free to choose our actions, we are not free to choose the consequences of those actions."[148] For most choices, we have a pretty good idea of what the consequence will be.

Practice is so unpleasant to a substantial portion of physicians that many work as hard as they possibly can—see as many patients as possible, maximize efficiency, etc.—to earn enough to retire or leave the profession as soon as possible. If those physicians hired more doctors, the evidence suggests they would feel less pressure and still earn a very reasonable income. The question becomes: "Would they still want to leave the profession early if their satisfaction and fulfillment were higher?"

An illustration of abdication of professional responsibility appeared recently in a monthly medical publication. The article's alleged focus was on how medicine has gotten away from a patient focus and how much patients crave the "laying on of the hands." "The business community and the country decided it simply did not want to pay for the increasing cost of health care. Thus, the Right joined with the Left to begin the systematic degradation of the medical profession."[149] According to the author, physicians, as a profession, had nothing to do with this. We are innocent bystanders.

The article then turns to how important it is to "identify best practices and to partner with business in an attempt to identify quality and base medical practices on our concept of that quality." The crux of the article—money—raises its head. "We must demonstrate that we will partner with them [business] in promoting best practices, and when we do not know what best practices are, conduct clinical trials and patient-oriented research in an effort to identify them. I am hopeful that business will join with us and even pay for such research if they correctly perceive that this may save them money in the long run."[149] In the interest of our patients, and in the name of "quality and best practices," shouldn't physicians pay for the research and development that is focused on improvements in the way we do our jobs?

The most disturbing part of the article follows: "…if we do this [i.e., define quality and best practices in conjunction with business], we can return to our historical role as advocates for the patient." This statement is disquieting for several reasons. I am unaware that physicians ever lost the role of "advocates for the patient." That is our primary job. Also, the author's implication is that "laying on of the hands" is something that requires us to study and understand "quality and best practices." Both of these things can be accomplished without any understanding of quality or best practices.

This article is a good example of the current paradigm in medicine; it highlights how we as individuals and a profession consistently fail to see the bigger picture, often not accepting responsibility for the consequences of the decisions we have made. We do not see the real problem: how we think and how we make decisions. For literally decades the profession has not well understood the ramifications of their decisions… how each decision has a consequence and how the decision-maker is responsible for the consequence. Recall the story of the Nalle Clinic's failure in Chapter 3; the disconnect between decisions (i.e., choices) made by the clinic's physicians and the subsequent consequences was a prime lesson learned by the organization. We must, as individuals and as professionals, broaden our thinking to clearly understand this relationship and assume full accountability.

An important step in changing our thinking is to focus on our personal leadership as it relates to the choices we make and the consequences that ensue.

Non-Monetary Value in Medicine

The danger of conceiving of personal relations in terms appropriate to marketplace exchanges is that it hastens the depersonalization of personal relations by fostering the intrusion of economic values into such relations.[150]

Intrinsic vs. Extrinsic Motivation

Non-monetary value is something or some activity from which one derives some form of gratification that is not based on the amount of money it either generates for the individual or requires the individual to pay. Hock writes a great deal about value and community: "One concept…I have puzzled over is an ancient, fundamental idea, the idea of community. The essence of community, its very heart and soul, is the non-monetary exchange of value; things we do and share because we care for others, and for the good of the place. Community is composed of that which we don't attempt to measure, for which we keep no record and ask no recompense. Most are things we cannot measure no matter how hard we try. Since they can't be measured, they can't be denominated in dollars, or barrels of oil, or bushels of corn—such things as respect, tolerance, love, trust, beauty—the supply of which is unbounded and unlimited. The non-monetary exchange of value does not arise solely from altruistic motives. It arises from deep, intuitive, often subconscious understanding that self-interest is inseparably connected with community interest; that the individual good is inseparable from the good of the whole; that in some way, often beyond our understanding, all things are, at one and the same time, independent, interdependent, and intradependent—that the singular "one" is simultaneously the plural 'one.'"[151]

Hock continues: "Community is not about profit. It is about benefit. We confuse them at our peril. When we attempt to monetize all value, we methodically disconnect people and destroy community.

"The nonmonetary exchange of value is the most effective, constructive system ever devised. Evolution and nature have been perfecting it for thousands of millennia. It requires no currency, contracts, government, laws, courts, police, economists, lawyers, accountants. It does not require anointed or certified experts at all. It requires only ordinary, caring people."[152]

We—medicine and society—have put virtually an infinite number of price tags on life and health. The health care consumer values health so highly that he or she will pay large portions of his or her income to maintain it. The question for me as a health care provider is: "Is this the way it should be?" Should everything I do—every bandage I change, every conversation I have with a patient, every waking moment I spend at work—be something that I *must* be paid for? Hilfiker has an entire chapter entitled "Money." The final paragraph of the chapter reads: "Like the medieval monastic practitioners, many (I think even most) of us physicians entered medicine with the desire to serve our patients, to be altruistic healers sacrificing ourselves for their good. Clearly, even the servant should be paid for working, so there is nothing contradictory between some remuneration and our calling. Yet as the profession has become wealthier and wealthier, a contradiction has arisen. As we physicians accumulate wealth, as we earn more than we really need, we become entrepreneurs and can no longer hang on to our perception of ourselves as servants. Yet we are not willing to let it go either, to embrace the Hippocratic ideal of self-interest. So money becomes for us the hub of a very serious contradiction. At some hardly conscious level, my income proved paradoxically to be little more than an additional drain on my energies."[153]

The concepts of "nonmonetary" and "monetary" lead to a discussion of "intrinsic" vs. "extrinsic" motivation as it relates to the practice of medicine. Let's define "intrinsic motivation" as pursuing an activity because one enjoys it or derives some level of personal gratification by doing it—enjoyment of work or an activity for its own sake. "Extrinsic motivation" is induced: "If you do this, you'll get that." The idea of extrinsic motivation is that, if a positive reward is given for a task, it will lead one to continue wanting to do the task, usually to keep getting the reward. It is a method of controlling behavior and is no different than the promise of punishment if one does not do something.[154] The promise of a reward could be reworded to, "If you *don't* do that, you *won't* get this," in essence a form of punishment.

Kohn spends a great deal of time systematically destroying the myth that awards (extrinsic motivation), whether financial in the sense of "pay-for-performance" or "gold stars" for the good behavior of children, fail at achieving their intended effect. The evidence overwhelmingly suggests that rewards fail miserably in efforts to induce lasting change. Kohn cites multiple studies that support this conclusion:

Undergraduate students who were asked to perform certain tasks without compensation performed the tasks significantly better than those who received compensation.

The performance of college students who were paid for turning out school newspaper headlines stopped improving, while those who were not paid continued to get better.

Fourth graders who were asked to perform a task they "liked" performed poorly at the same task when offered toys or candy as a reward for doing the task. [155]

Rewards—extrinsic motivations—significantly affect not only the *quantity* but also the *quality* of one's work. Intrinsic motivation, conversely, is a powerful predictor of work *quality* and *success*. Koestner has noted: "Intrinsically motivated people function in performance settings much the same way as those high in achievement motivation do: They pursue optimal challenges, display greater innovativeness, and tend to perform better under challenging conditions."[156]

Thus, extrinsic motivators are a poor substitute for genuine interest in what one is doing. But Kohn points out: "What is likely to be far more surprising and disturbing is the further point that rewards, like punishments, actually undermine the intrinsic motivation that promotes optimal performance."[158] Even when an individual enjoys a particular job and is intrinsically motivated, providing extrinsic rewards to that individual to do the work results in reduced motivation to do the work they were previously motivated to do, and a reduction in the quality of the results obtained. Kohn uses an "old joke" to illustrate this point: "It is the story of an elderly man who endured the insults of a crowd of 10-year-olds each day as they passed his house on their way home from school. One afternoon, after listening to another round of jeers about how stupid and ugly and bald he was, the man came up with a plan. He met the children on his lawn the following Monday and announced that anyone who came back the next day and yelled rude comments about him would receive a dollar. Amazed and excited, they showed up even earlier on Tuesday, hollering epithets for all they were worth. True to his word, the old man ambled out and paid everyone. 'Do the same tomorrow,' he told them, 'and you'll get 25 cents for your trouble.' The kids thought that was still pretty good and turned out again on Wednesday to taunt him.

At the first catcall, he walked over with a roll of quarters and again paid off his hecklers. 'From now on,' he announced, 'I can give you only a penny for doing this.' The kids looked at each other in disbelief. 'A penny?' they repeated scornfully. 'Forget it!' And they never came back again."[157]

The fact that the old man began to pay the children for something they had been doing voluntarily, "something they thought was fun," changed the manner in which they viewed the activity. Suddenly, they came to seem themselves as harassing him in order to get paid, not because they enjoyed the activity. The old man's goal, and in fact the result, was to sap the kid's intrinsic motivation.

This premise is directly relevant to medicine today. Almost everyone who goes into medicine is driven by some substantial degree of intrinsic motivation, whether it be scientific interest, interest in "doing good for humanity," or Hock's "community." In the process of accumulating an average of nearly $100,000 of educational debt,[25] observing the money that physicians "have" in the form of clothes, cars, houses, and other accoutrements of wealth, and listening to physicians complain about the discrepancy between what they get and what they deserve, our medical school graduates and residents have their intrinsic motivation sapped before they are out of training. They graduate with expectations of extrinsic rewards that can never be met. This loss of intrinsic motivation due to extrinsic rewards is the primary reason we have a profession stuffed with successful individuals who are not happy or fulfilled in what they do. Their intrinsic motivation gets "sapped" in the process of their becoming physicians.

Reflecting on my father's group, I don't believe they ever fought about money. In more than 35 years, they never had a malpractice suit filed against them. They never argued over or competed for patients. Yet their practice spanned the incredibly difficult periods of the introduction of Medicare, the fee-for-service era, the transition period into managed care, and the period when the average physician expected to be sued three or more times in his or her career. But one thing struck me more than any of these other impressive facts: it was apparent that they were all driven by the intrinsic motivation of their profession.

In a time when so many other physicians seemed to be solely motivated extrinsically, unknowingly sapping their intrinsic motivation, resulting in unhappiness, infighting, inter-group and intra-group rivalry, and rampant malpractice, why was this group different? In part, it is because these men were of the World War II generation. It was also in part because the meager means of the farming community they practiced in would not allow "extrinsic motivation" to develop, even if the physicians had wanted it. Of course, these physicians were not oblivious to the fact that they could double-to-quadruple their incomes by moving to one of the larger cities in the region. Basically, the financial "rewards" that were available to them would allow them to sustain the practice, send their children to school, and pay their mortgages, but the disposable income known by most physicians today was simply not available. Ironically, in this environment, intrinsic motivation simply occurred; it wasn't something they had to be vigilant to maintain.

I don't think these individuals would have been any other way, even if they had practiced in a large city. Their personal qualities and their intrinsic motivation were deeper than the harsh economic realities of the community. It also had to do with their personal leadership qualities, which allowed them to avoid falling into the trap of extrinsic motivation.

I don't mean to imply this group was without problems. I was blissfully unaware of the difficult times they had as a group and between each other on occasion, but I never heard them complain about "needing more money." When they spoke of "needing more money," it was because they were having trouble paying the electric bill, not because they wanted a Mercedes. Further, I don't mean to imply that there are no physicians practicing today who are not primarily intrinsically motivated.

I think nurses, as a profession, may have retained greater degrees of intrinsic motivation than physicians because of a similar mechanism related to compensation. It has often puzzled me how nurses continue to go to work each day and take good care of people who are often demanding and difficult, and show levels of compassion that some physicians can't even comprehend. My impression is that this is because they have been able to maintain their intrinsic motivation to a greater degree.

One plausible explanation is that they have a relatively fixed income. In general, a nurse can only make so much per 40-hour workweek. They have no incentives to see more patients or do more in less time (efficiency) in order to earn more money. Acting in this way holds no power over them because there is no financial incentive. The reward they gain is less tied to financial considerations than it is for physicians as a group. A study referred to in Chapter 2 demonstrated that nurses changed jobs mainly due to job-related stress, convenience, and work schedule.[47] While this study did cite "salary or benefits" as being a reason nurses left one job for another, the fact that, after one to two moves, the nurses became "more satisfied" implies that it is something about the culture that increases their satisfaction. Most nurses do not receive substantial increases in pay for lateral moves.

This discussion begs the question: "How do we return intrinsic motivation to medicine?" One possibility is to avoid destroying the intrinsic motivation of our medical students and residents. If I don't complain about the discrepancy between "what I make and what I should be making," it goes a long way to avoid instilling such thinking in a young physician.

Kohn has some suggestions on how to maintain the intrinsic motivation of individuals that have tremendous merit. "Here are the basic principles I would propose to those responsible for setting policy: Pay people generously and equitably. Do your best to make sure they don't feel exploited. Then do everything in your power to help them put money out of their minds. The problem with financial incentives is not that people are offered too much money; earning a hefty salary is not incompatible with doing good work. Rather, the problem is that money is made too salient. It is pushed into people's faces. Moreover, it is offered contingently—that is, according to the principle

"Do this and you'll get that." To end this practice is to take the first step—but only the first step—toward fixing what is wrong with organizations."[158]

He goes on to say "decouple the task from the compensation." Managed care and fee-for-service compensation systems are exactly counter to the concept of "uncoupling!"

Personal Leadership and Increasing Physician Gratification and Job Satisfaction

Part of my goal in attempting to emphasize the importance and benefits of personal leadership and interpersonal skills in medicine has to do with increasing the amount of intrinsic motivation, non-monetary gratification, and satisfaction physicians have with medicine. I have eluded to the concept that strong personal leadership can be helpful in avoiding the trappings of "extrinsic motivation." Success can be very empty without fulfillment. The profession needs to be reminded that there is value that is not monetary. One of those values is how it feels to connect with another human being, to help people.

The Linzer study,[144] in which 54 percent of family practice physicians felt they needed more time with patients, is indicative of the profession's desire to connect and reestablish the concept of non-monetary (intrinsic) value of their practices. Eliason *et al.* studied the personal values of primary care physicians and how they related to their satisfaction with their practices.[159] They defined personal values as "desirable goals varying in importance that serve as guiding principles in people's lives." They also wished to see how these values affected a physician's willingness to care for the underserved. They randomly surveyed a stratified sample of 1,224 practicing family physicians about their personal values, practice satisfaction, practice location and type, demographics, and other characteristics. They examined three separate groups based on the characteristics of *benevolence* (motivation to help those closest to you), *universalism* (motivation to enhance and protect the well-being of all people), and the *underserved* (defined as Medicare, Medicaid, and indigent populations). They found that family physicians as a group rated benevolence the highest and that the ratings of the benevolence value were positively correlated with practice satisfaction ($p = 0.002$). Those whose practices consisted of 40 percent or greater underserved rated tradition (motivation to maintain customs of traditional culture and religion) significantly higher than those not having an underserved population. Physicians whose practices were at least 30 percent indigent people rated universalism higher than those who did not have this percentage of indigent people.

Motivations such as benevolence and universalism are important, if not crucial, to physician job satisfaction. Second, none of these values is defined in monetary terms. These traits are a reflection of and markers for intrinsic motivation. Further, one can consciously develop and work on being more benevolent and universal by having a greater personal awareness.

There are other aspects of personal leadership that are worth mentioning. The impact of improving our personal leadership in relationships with our loved ones is one of them. The concept that "nothing is more important than our patients" is misguided. In the end, our families are the most important thing. With rare exception, no patient will attend to us at our deathbed. Being able to keep things in perspective is crucial, and good personal leadership skills help one do that. Knowing when to "say no" to yet another referral—even if it means you may be sacrificing future "business" with that referring physician—in order to keep a promise to your husband, wife, or kids requires personal leadership of the highest order. It requires understanding what your priorities are and that the "bill of goods" that physicians are sold in training is incorrect. If we can't take care of the emotional needs of our loved ones, how can we expect to be sensitive to the emotional needs of our patients?

Think of this concept—that physicians should take care of themselves and their families first—from the perspective of a patient. If you were a patient, whom would you rather have as your physician? A physician who has not focused on his or her own priorities and is upset because he or she have failed to meet a family obligation in order to see you? This is a situation that might result in a physician's hurrying, or even being careless, in order to "get this over with" and return to the family and salvage part of the day. Or would you rather have a physician who clearly understands his or her priorities and the importance of family and who, when pushed, will make decisions according to these priorities. This scenario is much more patient-focused than the first example, because the physician is "totally present." He or she is not distracted by the guilt of not being where he or she feels they should be. This does not mean we always get to do what we want, it merely means we must make choices daily that balance honoring those most important to us and our jobs. We should err on the side of our family, except in the most extreme circumstances. As one's relationships with those at home improve, the ability to be "totally present" with patients and staff will improve, as will job satisfaction.

My point in this chapter is this: As we begin to focus on intrinsic motivators in medicine—our personal values and motivations—those moments in which we "connect" with our staffs and patients as individuals will increase. As the number of times we connect increases, our gratification will increase, as will our job satisfaction. Those around us will have greater satisfaction too. This is what I mean by focusing on "non-monetary value." The beautiful thing is, it appears that our patients and employees want the same things we do. Focusing on personal leadership will help get us to where we all want to be.

Lost Leaders in Medical Organizations: A Case Study in Identifying "The Problem"

It has been contended that personal and organizational leadership is an important issue in health care and that it needs greater emphasis on the basis of experience and observations. We have pulled extensively from the literature to provide data supporting this position. Now it is time to start looking at data we have collected on current physician leadership and how it functions.

The Stated Problem

A large medical center (more than 600 beds, 800+ physicians, 4,400+ staff, and nearly 30,000 discharges annually) sought our help in streamlining patient care from admission to discharge. It was the hospital's observation that the discharge process was slow, resulting in a backup of patients in the admissions office. As a result, the admissions office had no beds for patients scheduled for admission, let alone emergency department admissions. It was suspected that problems in the system were most likely related to process.

We met with the chairs of the various medical departments as a group to take them through an exercise to help them better define the issues related to the problem. They were asked to write down everything they could think of that contributed to the problem of delayed patient discharge. In addition, they were asked to assign points to each issue they identified, with more points being assigned to issues they felt were more important to the issue at hand. After they had finished writing, the physicians grouped all identified issues under headings that captured each issue in a general category.

The next morning we met with nursing department heads, managers from the environmental services (housekeeping) group, and other nonphysician administrators from the hospital. We took them through the same process the physicians had completed, identifying and grouping issues into general categories. In each case, the issues were identified and categorized by them. They identified the problems and issues as they saw them in their current environment.

After the general categories were identified, two of the categories were randomly selected as a starting point by each group (in separate rooms), and two basic questions were asked of the participants:

1. Are these two categories related to each other in some way?

2. If yes, which category "drives" the other?

This process was repeated until all categories had been included in the model. This exercise allows participants to answer two major questions for the organization:

1. Where do they feel the "pain" of the problems? "Pain" is the manner in which a problem or issue is experienced by an individual, group, or organization. It is the visible manifestation of an identified problem.

2. What is the major "driver" of the current situation? A "driver" is defined as something—a person, a quality, a process, or a piece of technology—that is required to achieve a desired outcome.

Gaining Clarity:
Where Is the "Pain" and What "Drives" It?

The major categories related to this organization's stated question of "enhancing patient flow" turned out to be fairly similar for the physicians and the staff. The "pain" that the organization feels is determined by the number of points the participants assigned to each of the issues they identified during the process described above. The points are totaled under each major category and the categories are rank-ordered to determine which is most visible to the members of the organization. Visibility is essentially interpreted as the issues for which the greatest amount of "pain" is being felt.

The three categories with the greatest number of points, that is, those causing the greatest amount of "pain" per group, are listed below.

The Physicians' "Pain"

1. We must optimize the services intended to support and handle patient volume and intensity of care (25 percent of point total).

2. We must have a streamlined process for discharge (22 percent of point total).

3. We must be able to accurately and quickly track patient flow (12 percent of point total).

The Staff's "Pain"

1. We must identify and appropriately use critical personnel and required resources to support patient care from admission to discharge (21 percent of total points).

2. We must anticipate patient discharge (18 percent of total points).

3. We must have a single group empowered to determine appropriateness of admission based on predefined criteria and bed availability (15 percent of total points).

The entire list of categories is noted below by group. The number one item is the primary driver in the process, related to the question of "enhancing patient flow." The second item is the next most important driver, and so on.

Drivers within the System: Physician Data

1. Patients must be our number one concern.

2. We must have effective leadership that understands and is accountable for outcomes.

3. We must have a user-friendly plan for continuous improvement of health outcomes, satisfaction, and profit.

4. The processes to achieve our common goals must be agreed upon by the hospital and physicians.

5. We must align organizational incentives to be focused on health outcomes, satisfaction, and profit.

6. We must have accurate, easy-to-find tracking data of patient flow.

7. We must understand profit and cost efficiencies and be able to measure and respond to them.

8. We must have a faculty willing to lead the house staff both clinically and with regard to the change process.

9. We must optimize communication and collaboration throughout the system, including patients and their families.

10. We must optimize all patient services to handle the volume and intensity of required care

11. We must be able to anticipate discharge and carry it out efficiently.

Drivers within the system: Staff Data

1. We must make patient care our most important driver.

2. We must agree on defined business processes, and the physicians must agree to follow them.

3. We must have educational standards related to process for which we hold key stakeholders (MDs, RNs, etc.) accountable.

4. We must efficiently communicate and maximize trust among departments.

5. We must evaluate critical functional areas and resources needed to support total patient care as determined by the analysis.

6. We must have a single group empowered to determine appropriateness of admission based upon predefined criteria and bed availability.

7. We must anticipate hospital discharges.

8. We must identify and provide needed ancillary services around the clock.

The Results of Clarity:
Patient Focus and Leadership as Drivers

The similarity between the physician group and the staff group as it relates to both pain and drivers in the system is remarkable. It speaks to the common goal of high-quality patient care in this and probably most health care organizations.

Understanding and optimally utilizing resources to enhance patient flow from admission to discharge appears to be the "common pain" of both groups. The number one inducers of pain for both groups' center on understanding/optimizing patient support services and how to best deliver or utilize those services. Discharge is a major focus of each group. The focus on discharge is the visible manifestation of a problem that relates to the entire process of admission through discharge, because patients cannot be admitted without available beds. Admission and discharge exists in symbiosis in this setting, as all health care systems are an ecosystem where the whole is composed of multiple, distinct, but inseparable parts that don't function when isolated from the others. Finally, the physicians state, "We must have accurate, easy to find tracking data of patient flow," while the staff group says "We must have a single group empowered to determine appropriateness of admission based on predefined criteria and bed availability." This is essentially the same "pain" being stated in a different manner. A "single group" or center would be core to any method of "tracking data" on patient flow.

It is clear that the groups equally value the importance of patient care and recognize this as the most important driver and number one priority in their goal of high-quality health care delivery. It is also clear that each of the groups appreciates that leadership is the second most important driver.

The physicians have unequivocally stated, "We must have effective leadership," implying that effective leadership is either lacking or needs substantial enhancement. The fourth point of the physicians, "The processes by which to achieve common goals must be agreed upon by the hospital and physicians," is also a leadership issue, as such agreement requires effective negotiation and the seeking of "win-win" results. As we have seen, failure to seek win-win results is a common leadership misstep for physicians. Driver #8 of the physicians is, again, a direct acknowledgement that more effective leadership is needed, and Drive #9 speaks of optimizing communication and collaboration, again a leadership and interpersonal skills issue.

The staff also focuses on issues related to physician leadership. The second and third drivers of the staff group are both about leadership, with both implying greater integrity in their physician leaders is needed, especially related to following predefined and agreed-upon processes. The statement by the staff, "We must agree on defined business processes, and the physicians must agree to follow them," implies that physician integrity is not always apparent. "Actions don't match the words," or agreements about how business is to be conducted or how processes are to be followed are not honored. The third driver of the RN-Others group is: "We must have educational standards for which we hold key stakeholders (MDs, RNs, etc.) accountable." "Accountability" is a pure leadership issue. The staff's fourth driver is concerned with communication and trust, both core personal leadership issues

In summary, the major drivers of the current situation in this large medical center appear to be concerns for patient care and leadership. In fact, physician leadership will drive delivery of quality patient care. It can't be the other way around.

Conclusion:
The DEPO Principle^{SM}—Leadership is Always a "Driver"

The leadership in this large medical center was identified by those within this organization as the major driver of all other desired results in the system, after customer, or patient, focus. Naturally, patient focus is going to be the number one driver in all health care organizations if you ask physicians and staffs. Realistically, however, patient focus is not a driver as much as it is an intended result. But leadership is the driver that gets one to that end—The DEPO Principle^{SM}. Personal leadership allows a complete customer focus—complete meaning the patient *and* the staff—and allows individual physicians to obtain excellent results with their customers even if the organization doesn't commit to a personal leadership focus. In order for such a cultural change to occur and "stick," "on-the-ground" physician leaders must appreciate their vital role and buy into it. In the end, regardless of what "the organization wants," change will not occur without such "on-the-ground" buy in.

We have just learned (at least in this organization) that physicians and staff essentially feel the same pain and have the same goals. In the last chapter, we concluded that high-quality time and relationships were desired by both patients and physicians as a means of enhancing both patient and physician satisfaction. Physicians, staff, and patients all have the same needs and goals. Improving personal leadership will help the "on-the-ground" physician leaders in guiding all parties—patients, staff and themselves—to greater satisfaction.

Section Four
Action Planning for Personal and
Organizational Improvement

*The significant problems we face today cannot be solved at the
same level of thinking we were at when we created them.*
—Albert Einstein

CHAPTER 9 ⊂⊃⊂⊃⊂⊃⊂⊃⊂⊃

How Successful People Get Even Better
Part I: Seeing the Problem

We can't solve problems until we realize we have a problem of not seeing the real problem.[88]

Admitting There Is a Problem

We have seen that success is distinct from personal satisfaction, happiness, and fulfillment. One can be successful without having happy, satisfied employees or patients. And we all know that current success does not ensure future success. Success is also distinct from "optimal." Success does not imply that improvement is not possible, or in fact necessary.

If we have wealth, social status, education, and other outward signs of success as physicians, why do we see:

- 38 percent of physicians over the age of 50 years polled in one survey planning to leave medicine in the next three years?

- Of that same group of physicians over the age of 50, a remarkable 56 percent not encouraging their children to enter the profession of medicine?[160]

- The front page of the Oct. 20, 2000, *Philadelphia Enquirer* declaring, "Departures rattle Temple med school," detailing the fact that 49 senior staff members took an early buyout and 30 others were leaving the school voluntarily, "only accentuating widespread unhappiness with what is perceived as a high-handed management style"?

■ A study published in 1998 found that, of 16 forms of alternative health care therapies examined, 33.8 percent of individuals surveyed used at least one form of alternative therapy in 1990. By 1997, that number was 42.1 percent. Likewise, the probability of an individual's visiting an alternative health care provider in that same period increased from 36 to 46 percent.[161]

■ 48 percent of upper-income families and 37 percent of lower-income families change doctors because of dissatisfaction with some aspect of their care, including unwillingness of doctors to spend time talking with them, hostile feelings toward doctors, and unfavorable attitudes about doctors' personal qualities?[116]

Physicians are successful as a profession, but it appears that many of us are not happy. It appears that our ultimate customer—the patient—isn't too thrilled either. And the nonphysician employees who work in medicine aren't very satisfied with their occupations or work environments. If our patients aren't happy, our employees aren't happy, and we are successful but not happy, what needs to change? Personal leadership and interpersonal skills development would be of tremendous value in furthering the success of physicians and enhancing job satisfaction. We should strongly consider utilizing leadership training and try to improve our personal leadership and interpersonal skills.

Many physicians will say, "I am already successful, so why do I need personal leadership development?" Goldsmith has found that it is both easier and harder for successful people to change their behaviors.[162] It is easier for them to change because successful people are familiar with setting and achieving goals. If they choose to improve their personal leadership or interpersonal behaviors, they will. However, it is also harder for successful people to change, because they are, in fact, already successful. Goldsmith states that successful people are usually successful in spite of themselves and their behaviors. They are successful despite having behavioral shortcomings, such as arrogance, intolerance to even minor mistakes, closed-mindedness, etc. Further, he states, successful people are inherently fearful of change—if they change what they are doing, they fear they will no longer be successful.

A point-by-point illustration of this mode of thinking follows:

Point #1: Physicians are reasonably successful people.

Point #2: We tend to go about our daily activities, play our roles and behave in a certain manner.

Point #3: We often assume our behaviors have resulted in our success.

Point #4: This leads us to believe that we are successful because we behave the way we do, regardless of what that behavior is.

However, we can choose a different way to think about our behaviors and ourselves—one that allows us to form a reasonable set of expectations for personal development. Think about the above points in two, parallel ways.

1. I am successful *because* of doing many things very well…	2. I am also successful *in spite* of doing one or two things (or behaviors) that are not helping…
A (being honest)	**X** (being arrogant)
B (being punctual)	**Y** (being stubborn)
C (being intelligent)	**Z** (not listening)

Successful professionals need to acknowledge the things that we are doing well and that enhance our results and celebrate them. But we also need to be aware that there may be one or two behavioral issues that are not contributing to or enhancing our success—in fact, they are hurting how others perceive our effectiveness—and put an action plan in place to make some changes.

Resisting Change

We think too small. Like the frog at the bottom of the well. He thinks the sky is only as big as the top of the well. If he surfaced, he would have an entirely different view.— Mao Tse-Tung[163]

Quinn has observed that people often resist in a predictable sequence when confronted with new, potentially transformational ideas proposed by "change agents" (i.e., individuals). First, Quinn says, people will laugh at the new idea; however, when they see that the change agent isn't laughing, they subsequently move to the second defensive strategy of providing reasons why the idea won't work—rationalizations. The third and final step for those who wish to resist the change agent is to resort to "moral indignation," calling into question the individual's motives, morals, qualifications, ethics, or abilities in order to maintain the status quo or defend the current system.[15] These visceral responses are related to the current culture, which defines the environment in which the people being asked to change operate. The suggestion that the culture of a profession needs to be changed is extraordinarily threatening to individuals within that culture, because it redefines the expectations of people within the organization. People no longer know how to act, what their responsibilities are, and how to play by the rules.

Steinem has added a fourth step to the resistance to change equation. She noted that, after failure of all of the arguments against social movements that rely upon things such as God, religion, country, and "tradition," people who have resisted begin to congratulate you on "all you've done" and "your progress." She notes this is the last form of resistance: attempts at getting the change agent to think he or she has "reached the goal," when, in reality, social or cultural movements are a continuum of change or evolution.[164] The intent is to get the change agent to quit pushing suggested changes and to kill the agent's momentum by making him or her think the mission has been accomplished.

Kriegel and Brandt provide another view of how people act when confronted with change.[79] They refer to the skepticism of suggested change, especially change of deeply entrenched behaviors, as "firehosing." They state that "firehosing" of new ideas or suggested change is meant to dampen people's enthusiasm, "douse the sparks of creativity, and just plain put out the fire, killing excitement and motivation on the spot." They point out that "firehosing" is not legitimate dissent—that those with genuine differences of opinion attempt to extend the debate, not quash it. "Firehosing" is relevant not only to incremental change, but also to the transformational change to which Quinn refers.[15]

Kriegel and Brandt's list of common firehosing illustrates skepticism toward change:

■ **Yeah, but...** This is code for "I think the idea stinks." Anything that comes after the but is bull.

■ **The toos.** It's too hard, too complicated, too expensive, too quick, slow, showy, takes too long. Anytime you hear the word too it's too late.

■ **They'll never buy it.** Who's "they," and why presume how someone else will react?

■ **It's unrealistic.** Our favorite. Was Galileo unrealistic? Was Einstein? How about Alexander Graham Bell or Ted Turner? Realism is just a name for yesterday's thinking.

■ **It's just a fad.** Yes, and so were the compact car, the microwave oven, the fax machine. Today's fad is tomorrow's household word.

■ **It'll never work; it can't be done.** If these naysayers are so smart, how come they never come up with any ideas of their own?

■ **If it ain't broke, don't fix it.** If you wait until it's broke to fix it, you'll end up with nothing left to fix.

■ **Don't rock the boat.** Huge waves of change are already rocking the boat and will sink it if you're not prepared to change course.

■ **Don't stick your neck out.** An ostrich strategy that can't possibly work in a competitive environment. If you don't stick your neck out, you'll lose your head.

■ **It's not in the budget.** Of course not. This year's budget was made up last year when circumstances were different.

■ **Let's wait and see.** A delay tactic based on the hope that, down the road, the whole idea will be forgotten.

For the interventions that need to be instituted in medicine, there may be substantial resistance and many arguments from successful physicians and organizations as to "why we can't do it," or why it "isn't relevant." There will be resistance because what is being suggested is a social movement to change the personal leadership culture in medicine and enhance the intrinsic, non-monetary value (i.e, gratification) that physicians receive from their occupation. Basically, it is an attempt to get individuals who are successful to commit to becoming even better.

A point made by Quinn jumps to mind: "If one person can do this, it destroys the credibility of the universal argument, 'But you do not understand....'"[17] I know this can be done. Not only have I realized my own shortcomings related to personal leadership and interpersonal skills and committed to overcoming them, but I've also seen many others do it successfully.

Leadership and Self-Deception

Haw knew he had left a trail for Hem and that he could find his way, if he could just read The Handwriting on the Wall.[165]

The Arbinger Institute approaches resistance to change a bit differently, and it cannot be overemphasized how important these concepts are to the issue of leadership in medicine. It convincingly argues that many problems of personal and organizational leadership begin with self-deception. "Identify someone with a problem and you'll be identifying someone who resists the suggestion that he has a problem. That's self-deception—the inability to see that one has a problem. Of all the problems in organizations, it's the most common—and the most damaging."[88]

The Arbinger authors claim that our self-deception leads us to "be in the box," and "being in the box" results in us treating people as objects, things, or tools. Four points lead to our "being in the box."

1. An act contrary to what I feel I should do for another is called an act of "self-betrayal."

2. "When I betray myself, I begin to see the world in a way that justifies my self-betrayal.

3. When I see a self-justifying world, my view of reality becomes distorted.

4. So—when I betray myself, I enter the box.[88]

An example of Arbinger's four points relative to medicine is as follows: I walk into the exam room to see a patient who is scheduled for the standard 6-to-10 minute slot I have asked my scheduling assistant to keep for me. As the time approaches 10 minutes, I glance at my watch, because this patient is not even close to wrapping up the conversation. I know I should ignore the time and be completely present for my patient, attending to his needs and desire to be heard. But, in an act contrary to what I feel I should do for another, I stand-up to begin the process of shutting-down the conversation so I can exit the room and get on to the next patient. I have just self-betrayed myself. In order for me to suppress the negative feelings of my self-betraying act, I tell myself that I can't keep other people waiting just because of this one person and that I have a responsibility to them too. I ignore, suppress, or fail to see that it was my decision to schedule patients every 6 to 10 minutes, but I have successfully justified by self-betrayal on behalf of my other patients. Because I have vindicated myself with this act of self-betrayal and am able to justify my actions, my view of reality becomes distorted. The next time a similar situation occurs, it is easier from me to handle. I have just "entered the box."

I have arrived at the following conclusion: Very few physicians understand the importance of personal leadership and interpersonal skills and how it can affect our daily lives, our patients, and our staffs. Now is the time to embrace personal leadership and the cultural changes it will bring, allowing us to be happier, more satisfied, and fulfilled as physicians. In the process of getting there, we will find our employees and patients have willingly followed us—the "on-the-ground" leaders in medicine—to the same end.

CHAPTER 10

How Successful People Get Even Better
Part II: Feedback and Behavioral Coaching

The one quality that can be developed by studious reflection and practice is the leadership of men.—Dwight D. Eisenhower

"Seeing the Problem(s):"
Assessments and Behavioral Coaching to Improve Leadership Behavior and Skills in Medicine

If one is to get better at something, one must have a mechanism by which to receive feedback that identifies developmental needs. In Chapter 4, we expanded on the inability of physicians to accurately self-assess. We also learned of Kruger and Dunning's finding that individuals who are incompetent at a certain skill in a particular life "domain" can increase their self-assessment skills if they are helped to "recognize the limitations of their abilities."[110] What we are going to discuss now is how individuals raise their awareness and assess their current developmental needs related to personal leadership and interpersonal skills, as well as their strengths in each of these "domains." If a person's personal insight is increased by 10 percent, he or she will see the difference, particularly if the person is willing to see his or her blind spots—to recognize lack of strength in a particular area. Great opportunities for both individual and organizational growth exist in such exercises.

What can be done about personal leadership and interpersonal skills in medicine? As Eisenhower stated, leadership behaviors can be learned, and leadership strengths already present can be enhanced. There is one crucial element in instituting any change regarding leadership in medicine: one must admit as an individual (and perhaps medicine as a profession) that we can do much better than we currently are doing, even if we are successful. The key to change is being willing to open our minds and commit to change and address our developmental needs.

A Personal Commitment to Change

Becoming self-aware forces an individual to make a choice. One can choose or choose not to address the issue one is now aware of. Choosing to ignore an issue is a choice to do nothing about the situation.

Successful behavioral change requires an individual to be prepared to change, which implies that the individual sees areas for needed improvement. James Prochaska at the University of Rhode Island has studied behavioral change in more than 30,000 people and found that there are four stages or levels of readiness to accept behavioral change[166]:

1. **Oblivious:** Basically, these people are not ready for change because they deny the need to change in the first place. They actively resist attempts to help them.

2. **Contemplation:** People at this stage appreciate a need to change and begin to contemplate how to initiate the change. While being open to discussing the needed change, they may not be willing to wholeheartedly pursue improvement. "Ambivalence is rampant; some wait for a 'magic moment' of readiness, while others leap into action prematurely, but meet failure because they are half-hearted." People in this stage can also remain in the cycle of deciding to take action "next month." Prochaska relates that it is not unusual for people "to spend years telling themselves that someday they are going to change."[167]

3. **Preparation:** People in this stage begin to formulate a plan to improve—and to develop a solution. Not only do they perceive and understand the problem, they also see ways to solve it and "palpably anticipate doing so." People occasionally enter this stage because of some dramatic precipitating event, such as a disaster on the job or a crisis in their personal lives. Their awareness has been raised, and they prepare for action.

4. **Action:** At this stage, visible change becomes a focus, as individuals embrace the plan and enact the steps required for change. This stage forms the basis for long-standing visible change.

While leadership requires technical and managerial competence, most physicians don't seem to have problems with these things. The room for improving their leadership competence is in addressing behavioral issues through recognition of their developmental needs and feedback concerning their behavior.

Feedback is not criticism or judgment. In general, successful people love getting feedback in the form of suggestions and ideas. Successful people hate to be judged.

Physicians have perhaps the most vehement, gut-wrenching response to judgment (real or perceived) of any occupational group. We can thank our educational system for this response. Ironically, we are taught to question everything, but we hate to be questioned. The reason we hate to be questioned is because it can sound as if or imply that we are being judged.

Also, in the clinical environment, questioning by peers or staff can often appear to be referring to patient care or practices, and no physician ever makes patient care decisions lightly. As patients go, so go our egos. Think of morbidity and mortality (M&M) conferences or morning reports. We often witness someone attempting to defend a patient care decision that was less than optimal for a patient when they should have simply said, "I made a mistake."

Focused feedback offered as a suggestion, even outside a formal behavioral modification setting, is experienced very differently from statements that are overt judgments or judgments disguised as questions. Let's use the setting of an M&M conference as an illustration. Suppose a procedure in which a complication occurred is being presented by Dr. Smith, and, in the procedure, he did not move the duodenum out of the way, as would have been a standard part of this procedure. Suppose someone makes the following statement: "Dr. Smith, not moving the duodenum was really unwise." That is a judgment of Dr. Smith's actions disguised as a "benign" statement. It would immediately put Dr. Smith on the defensive—even if the statement is made in a benevolent tone, as if to "educate" Dr. Smith.

Compare the dynamics of that statement to the following: "Dr. Smith, do you think in the future you would consider moving the duodenum before attempting that procedure?" While this statement focuses on the same issue—i.e., the complication—the interpersonal dynamic and the way in which Dr. Smith perceives the statement are very different. Instead of putting Dr. Smith on the defensive, the statement leaves an opening for discussion—breathing room—and may actually allow Dr. Smith to say, "Yes I would consider it—in fact I should have done it in this case, and it was a mistake."

There is never a reason to be demeaning, condescending or aggressive in a professional or a personal situation. If that is a physician's pattern, there may be (probably are) destructive inter- or intra-group political rivalries in the medical environment leading to "win-lose" one-ups-manship behavior, or the physician is exhibiting one of the missteps and would benefit from coaching.

How the Process of 360-Degree Assessment and Behavioral Coaching Works

How does one go about changing the current leadership environment in medicine? We can attack in any direction and at all levels. But even one physician at a time will ultimately get us to where we need to be.

Perhaps the best place to start any change effort is with a baseline assessment of where one's strengths and developmental needs lie, as seen from the perspective of our followers. A multi-source assessment process, often referred to as "360-degree feedback," is a concept foreign to most physicians, but one that is frequently used in business to help people develop their personal leadership and interpersonal skills. The process uses a questionnaire to provide feedback to an individual about his or her work-related behavior (not technical performance). This feedback comes from coworkers, such as supervisors, subordinates, peers, team members and other individuals who work with the individual being assessed. The 360-degree multi-source assessment process provides the "wake up call" needed for the individual to raise awareness and get serious about undertaking a personal leadership development effort. It is difficult to remain in denial that "we are the problem" when we see, in black and white, how our colleagues and peers view us as leaders relative to our own perceptions about our abilities. It is a humbling albeit rewarding experience, and it is an essential first step to personal growth and change.

While both experience and formal training are important sources of learning, formal training, such as a 360-degree multi-rater feedback program with follow-up behavioral coaching, has been shown to increase productivity in the area covered by the training by 30 percent in the first year.[12] This effect is illustrated in figure 10-1, below.

The Woods Development Institute has developed a 360-degree feedback process specifically for physicians called the LeadeRx[SM] Personal Development Program, which is designed to raise awareness about how The Seven Common Leadership Missteps[SM]

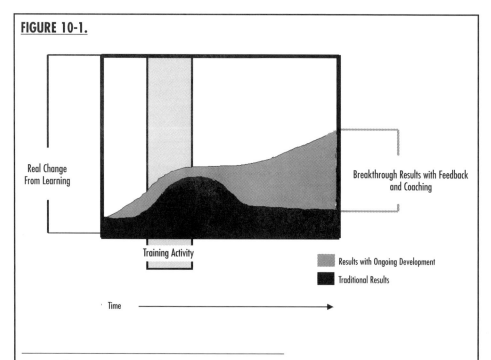

FIGURE 10-1.

Real Change From Learning

Breakthrough Results with Feedback and Coaching

Training Activity

Results with Ongoing Development

Traditional Results

Time

Continued improvement in performance is seen with behavioral coaching (i.e., follow-up and accountability). Without such follow-up, the performance level is just slightly higher than before the training.

work in a physician's life and to help physicians make and sustain positive change. Physicians receive feedback on critical aspects of leadership from various constituencies, such as physician administrators, hospital-based nurses and other health care personnel, their office staffs, residents or medical students, and their physician partners, even physicians from outside their group. The only feedback that is not confidential is from the individual's supervisor. All other feedback is anonymous and is provided to the participant as aggregate scores from each rating group (e.g., peers, nurses, support staff). Respondents must be assured that no retaliation will occur in order to obtain honest, frank feedback. This can be a problem in politically charged situations and in training programs, where residents and medical students may be reluctant to respond honestly.

This feedback process is coupled with a one-on-one debriefing session, in which interpretation of the report is discussed with the physician being rated. A personal "coach" assigned to each physician participant goes over the results in private with the physician. The physician participant identifies one to three behaviors in the feedback report related to his or her personal leadership behaviors to work on over the ensuing 12 months. These behaviors can be tied to strengths for the physician to leverage, or to critical deficiencies and developmental needs that have the greatest likelihood of having an impact on the physician's overall leadership ability. An action plan is created that is a roadmap for the physician to make change. Ongoing feedback helps maintain the changes.

Perceptions of those around you, even if wrong in your eyes, are still their perceptions—and they must be addressed. It is crucial to provide assistance to the physician in interpretation of the report, because receiving feedback may be difficult and most people have a difficult time maintaining the proper perspective without coaching. Further, behavioral change is most likely to be sustained in an environment in which training and coaching are available. Research shows that holding people accountable for change is effective.[168] This is accomplished through action planning and by re-surveying the original raters of the physician as to improvements in behaviors targeted for change.

This process will only result in changing the behaviors of individuals who are interested in changing. The LeadeRx℠ Personal Development Program—or any 360-degree assessment tool—will clearly identify strengths and developmental needs if the raters of the individual answer honestly. However, change will occur only if the individual being assessed chooses to embrace the feedback and commits to change. Second, the instrument should not be used as a performance appraisal system; it is designed to assist individuals in understanding their current personal leadership traits and in identifying behaviors they can leverage or improve.

Individuals who take these assessments, commit to change, and engage in periodic, ongoing follow-up with their colleagues on the issues or behaviors they are working to develop will be perceived as improving as leaders by the vast majority of those with whom they work (figure 10-2, page 132).[169]

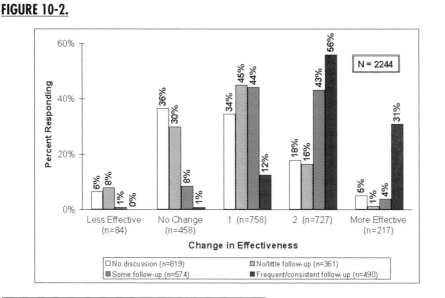

FIGURE 10-2.

Frequent, consistent follow-up with constituents by individuals completing a 360-degree assessment process has consistently been shown to result in the perception of enhanced leadership effectiveness by 99 percent of those observing the person. Follow-up is simply the act of the person receiving feedback taking a few minutes to reiterate what he or she learned and is doing about it and soliciting additional ideas for improvement from those who initially rated him or her.

These results are reproducible. Keilty, Goldsmith, & Company (KGC) has found the same results. In KGC's results with 8,208 direct reports responding about their managers' perceived leadership effectiveness and development, relative to managers' follow-up with them, there is a definite correlation between the dedication of individuals in responding to and following -up with their raters and behavior improvement (table 10-1, page 133).[170]

University- and/or training program-based physicians—even the chairs of departments—are no different in this regard from other physicians. Fritts writes, "The attitude a chair should try to cultivate may charitably be called self-delusion or, uncharitably, arrogance. When a chair sits home and reflects on the way his or her job is going, the chair should be able to say he or she is doing the job about as well as most people could. Here, chairs must use common sense and compare themselves to contemporaries in similar jobs."[171]

Sitting at home and reflecting is not the same, nor is it as valuable, as getting honest, frank feedback from peers, office staff, residents, and medical students. A major fear is that university-based physicians will not get accurate, honest feedback from staff, residents, and students because of fear of retaliation by those they are rating, even when those being rated are genuine in their commitment to improve. Chairs and

TABLE 10-1.

Degree of "Response and Follow-up" "My manager did..." (% of Direct Reports' Responses)	% of Managers achieving +1 or greater improvement in Leadership Effectiveness
...not respond and did no follow-up (19%)	48%
...did respond and did no follow-up (6%)	45%
...did respond and did a little follow-up (17%)	66%
...did respond and did some follow-up (30%)	89% (7% + 3 points)
...did respond and did frequent follow-up (17%)	95% (21% + 3 points)
...did respond and did consistent (periodic) follow-up (11%)	95% (55% + 3 points)

If an individual responds to feedback and requests even some additional feedback concerning his or her performance from employees (e.g., direct reports in industry or office staff of a physician), there is a 90 percent chance of the individual's being perceived as more effective as a leader. Leaders who do not engage in the follow-up process show only slightly more than random improvement.

attendings being evaluated are responsible for making sure that subordinates know there will be no retaliation for their candid feedback, otherwise the results will be predictable—inflated ratings.

It is always dangerous to compare yourself to others for several reasons. One reason is that we will always find those who are worse at some things and better at some things than we are.

This smacks of "The Physician Hierarchy" and "The Chairman's Syndrome" that make up 2 of the original 20 missteps in physician leadership and that are partially responsible for the Seven Common Leadership Missteps℠ of Physicians.

Finally, the point in personal leadership development isn't to "be better than someone else" or to even "compare ourselves to others." The point is to improve yourself, as an individual, simply because you want to and it is the right thing to do.

Most things printed about "leadership in medicine" are 20 years behind leadership thought in other professions. To ultimately address the problem of leadership in medicine, we must push leadership development down into the medical education system. There are signs that this might be happening, but there is a long way to go and much more is needed.

The Potential Drawbacks of 360-Degree Assessment

When people are part of the evaluation of another individual, there is potential for abuse. This type of evaluation can be used as a weapon in office or departmental political wars or, worse, as a mechanism to falsely praise or lift up friends.

In the nonmedical business world, it can be difficult for executives to get candid feedback for a variety of reasons, not the least of which is related to the power they wield.[13] This can foster a sense that one has no areas of personal leadership to improve.

These executives become somewhat insulated from reality because subordinates fear offending them. This is particularly relevant for physicians, because essentially all physicians are "executives" of their business.

This is of special concern in university programs in which medical students and residents participate in the review of staff physicians. Because of the "Captive audience phenomenon" we discussed in the Seven Common Leadership Missteps℠ chapter, where medical students and residents have few if any options outside of their current training program, they may perceive significant motivation (i.e., self-preservation) to be less than truthful in giving feedback concerning the behaviors of attending staff.

Another potential concern is whether medical students and residents will be able to accurately judge leadership and developmental needs of physicians in the system in which they are training. They are being steeped in the same culture that has resulted in many of the personal leadership deficiencies that are the basis of this book. Do they have the perspective to remain objective enough to give accurate feedback?

The university system and its trainees are not the only group with this problem, however. Office staff members who might perceive themselves to have few employment options outside of their current jobs may have the same reluctance to be forthright with their comments concerning a physician's personal leadership behaviors.

Most of these concerns can be minimized by getting evaluations from multiple sources of which several may be less likely to be intimidated by the individual being evaluated. This should be easier in medicine than in nonmedical businesses, because it is uncommon to have a single physician wielding an inordinate amount of power in any single setting.

Return on Investment: What Do We Get for This Money?

What's my return on investment on e-commerce? Are you crazy? This is Columbus in the New World. What was his ROI?—Andrew Grove, Intel Chairman

Unquestionably, some are wondering why they should spend hard-earned money on personal leadership development for physicians. But leadership training in medicine is about like Andrew Grove's take on the value of e-commerce; it's a new world.

Showing a return on investment (ROI) is essential, and a return can be shown for a personal leadership development program. One thing is certain: employers increasingly consider leadership development a sound, holistic approach—and a strategic advantage—to dealing with growing demands for profits, increasing competition, a shrinking labor pool, and accountability.[30]

Surprisingly, an increasing focus on ROI as it relates to development programs and personal coaching has uncovered some astonishing findings. Patton notes: "ROIs that continue to astonish even the most results-oriented employer and prove, hands down, the worth of executive coaching—picking the tool that will give your employer the most accurate assessment of the effectiveness of this training depends largely on the characteristics and needs of your company."[30]

ROI for a personal development program with coaching can vary dramatically—from 150 to 1,000 percent. Usually, the higher the ROI, the more likely that the company has previously neglected personal development training. It is not uncommon, however, to see numbers in the 200-400 percent range. In fact, some organizations now expect such ROIs for their development programs. Boyd Owens of Invensys Energy Metering has been measuring ROI for executive training since 1997. His organization has seen an average ROI of 150-200 percent. The ROI for the company's training program targeted at hourly workers has seen an ROI of 400 percent.

While there are no data on ROI for physicians in such a development program, there are data from health care systems. Robertson noted one such system. He recalls a large employer in health care being "stunned" by the rate of return for a personal leadership program that incorporated coaching. By working with the top 200 individuals in this health care organization, the company saved between $30 and 60 million dollars.[30] Robertson feels that most organizations are "missing the point" when it comes to personal leadership development. Such programs provide an "undeniable competitive advantage," he says. The TRIZ Principle tells us that these same sort of advantages will occur in other industries where personal leadership development is applied.

Lishansky points out that an analysis of ROI needs to be done in view of the team's performance and not just of the individuals being coached.[30] Evaluating a single person may not be sufficient. For physicians, this may be partially true; increased personal effectiveness for a physician developed through personal leadership training and coaching may directly affect the bottom line through enhanced patient and employee retention and reduced malpractice liability. On an organizational level at which many, if not all, physicians are involved in such a program, the benefits and ROI should be magnified.

Measuring ROI can be done in many ways, both tangibly and intangibly (table 10-2, page 136). It is clear that, however it is done, it must be consistent throughout the organization and must be an on-going process. Two different types of tracking should be put into place: one to track the individual's behavior (in this case, the physician) and two, a program to measure the impact the physician's training has on the staff and the organization's performance. The first type of tracking can be done with a mini-survey follow-up process, as we have described. The second can be accomplished in the manner outlined in table 10-2.

Finally, in order to maintain a high level of functioning, as well as to continue to reap the benefits of personal development and coaching programs, one needs to appreciate the need for on-going coaching and "refresher" courses. Robertson notes: "I measure the lifetime-quality benefit of the coaching...since all of these good lessons or thinking skills in many ways will fade. The effect of coaching will not go on forever.[30] This is the reason for on-going, maintenance programs in personal development, including coaching.

TABLE 10-2.	Tangible and intangible measures of ROI for personal development and coaching programs for executives.

Tangible Measures of ROI

Steps*

1. Calculate all direct costs associated with the training program.

2. Calculate lost productivity while trainees are in the program.

3. Calculate the total cost of the program.

4. Estimate expected hourly, weekly, or monthly benefits per trainee.

5. Estimate the actual quality benefit from the training.

6. Using a standard discount rate formula, estimate the time length of the training's effect.

7. Calculate the profit per employee.

8. Calculate benefits of the total training program

9. Calculate return on investment.

Intangible Measures of ROI

When measuring ROI for coaching, Remember…†

1. Measure any result that is meaningful.

2. Recognize that not everything you measure will be objective (e.g., customer or employee satisfaction). [This is especially critical for health care and physicians.]

3. Clearly define the most important results an executive (or physician) can influence or achieve.

4. Align your plans and outcomes for coaching with an executive's existing development plan.

Key ROI Measurements

1. Increase in profits, sales, and gross margin.

2. Decrease in expenses.

3. Improvement in productivity, such as dollars generated per employee.

4. Increase in customer (patient) and employee satisfaction.

5. Increase in employee retention.

6. Improvement in communication effectiveness.

7. Increase in leadership effectiveness.

8. Improvement in teamwork at all levels.

9. Improvement in processes such as product introduction cycle time or financial reporting; In medical environments, things such as decreased patient waiting times.

---

*Source: Gordon, E., "Skill Wars." In Patton, C., "Rating the Returns." *HR Executive* 15(5):40-3, April 2001.

†Adapted from Steve Lishansky, president, Success Dynamics and the Executive Coaching Institute, Concord, Mass. In Patton, C., "Rating the Returns." *HR Executive* 15(5):40-3, April 2001.

Gaining Self-Perspective: The LeadeRx^{SM} 360-Degree Inventory for Physicians

Still the question recurs "can we do better?" The dogmas of the quiet past are inadequate to the stormy present. The occasion is piled high with difficulty, and we must rise with the occasion. As our case is new, so we must think anew, and act anew.—Abraham Lincoln[172]

LeadeRx^{SM} Personal Development Program

The LeadeRx^{SM} Personal Development Program was developed to specifically assess the personal leadership skills of physicians regardless of setting. Part of the LeadeRx^{SM} program is the LeadeRx^{SM} Inventory, a 360-degree multi-rater feedback tool. The LeadeRx^{SM} Inventory is broken-down into seven sections, aligned with the Seven Common Leadership Missteps^{SM} of Physicians, as follows:

1. Seek Win-Win Solutions

2. Demonstrate Respect

3. Demonstrate Personal Leadership

4. Practice Flexibility

5. Be a Team Player

6. Develop Others

7. Be Open

The LeadeRx℠ Inventory is designed to help the physician overcome difficulties in appreciating or recognizing developmental needs in the domains of personal leadership and interpersonal skills. It gives physicians greater insight into the competencies needed to effectively lead the practice or organization, thus enabling them to more effectively self-monitor their own effectiveness within these areas. This insight facilitates the development of strategies to enhance their competence in these domains. The physician begins to appreciate the value and importance of seeking regular performance feedback concerning personal leadership and interpersonal skills.

The LeadeRx℠ development process begins with an introductory training seminar that takes the physician through The Seven Common Leadership Missteps℠, the economic aspects of The LECO and DEPO Principle℠—how leadership translates into value—and why enhanced personal leadership can dramatically affect their practices and their lives. The LeadeRx℠ Inventory is introduced to the participant in this session, and a demonstration is provided on how to fill-out the survey and recruit raters.

After completing the LeadeRx℠ Inventory, and 4 – 6 weeks after the initial seminar, participants attend a debriefing session at which they are taught how to interpret their results, how to keep the results in perspective, and how to develop an action plan focused on leveraging their strengths and improving in areas of developmental need. They then receive their report of the results and participate in their first face-to-face coaching session.*

Performance of the LeadeRx℠ Inventory: Samples from Practice

Let's examine an aggregate report and some specific findings concerning the behaviors of a small group of physicians using the LeadeRx℠ Inventory.

The American College of Physician Executives (ACPE) provided the Woods Development Institute with the names of 200 physician members with email addresses, generated randomly from its membership database. An unsolicited email inviting participation in a physician leadership research project was sent to each of these 200 individuals and included a detailed description of the LeadeRx℠ Inventory and the 360-degree process. Of these 200, 47 initially agreed to participate. On the date the study was closed, 8 individuals had completed the LeadeRx℠ Inventory. The data from this group are the basis for the following discussion.

Obviously, we are examining a very small sample. This was anticipated. However, the purpose of this effort was not to generate a sample size large enough to obtain any statistically significant results, but rather too:

■ Document that the instrument can highlight strengths and developmental needs of individuals, based on others' perceptions.

---

*Both the introductory seminar and the debriefing seminar are available as e-learning modules.

■ Demonstrate that individuals rating the physicians would give honest, open feedback.

■ Demonstrate that the instrument would be able to illustrate differences in perspective between rater groups from different functional areas in health care

The aggregate results highlight areas of strength and developmental needs of the aggregate group of physicians. Additionally, individuals rating the physicians appeared to give honest feedback, as manifested by the broad range of responses noted on multiple questions within the data set. The assessments did not routinely "cluster" at any one point in a discernable fashion, nor did the raters tend to collectively "crucify" or, alternatively "deify" the physicians. It is also clear that different rater groups clearly have different perspectives on these physicians, as one would expect, based on their very different job functions in the health care system and on how they interact with these physicians.

It should also be noted that, while only 8 physicians participated, 72 raters participated with these physicians, providing a very respectable average of 9 raters per physician. Additionally, the raters were from diverse groups, including the physician's partners, administrators, office staff, nurses/PAs, and chief medical officers/department heads. This provides additional confidence in the combined dataset.

Finally, the physicians who participated in this project are a highly selected, biased sample of physicians who all had specific interests in leadership, either stated overtly, or implied tacitly by their participation in the project. The only incentive provided for physicians to participate was their being offered copies of this book. The participation of these 8 individuals implies a certain degree of commitment to the concepts promoted in this book and a substantial degree of intrinsic motivation. It is likely results obtained with the more "general, unselected physician population" will appear much different from those of this group.

General Observations from the LeadeRx℠ Inventory

In reviewing this information, attempts have been made to avoid making specific, sweeping conclusions unless the data unequivocally allow such a conclusion to be made with some reasonable degree of certainty from experience or the literature. Instead, the focus is on general trends noted in the aggregate data, as well as the data broken-down into the seven major sections of the LeadeRx℠ Inventory.

The largest rater group was partners (18) followed by administrators and chief medical officers/department heads (16), nurses/PAs (11), office staff (10), and students (1). Individuals who tend to have the greatest contact with physicians on a daily basis (office staff and Nurses/PA's) generated scores that were consistently lower than those provided by physicians or by other groups rating them. The office staff scores were lower than the physicians' self-rating on 42 percent of the items, and the scores from nurses/PA's were lower than the physicians' rating 33 percent of the time. The partners and administrators' scores were also lower than the physicians' self-ratings on 29 percent of the items.

Conversely, the chief medical officers/department heads consistently (93 percent of the time) scored the rated physicians higher than the physicians rated themselves. Their ratings were higher than the scores provided by any other group rating the physicians. Possible reasons for what appears to be a consistent, perhaps inflated scoring pattern on the part of the chief medical officers/department heads are:

- The chief medical officers/department heads may not have sufficient, routine contact for as accurate a view of the rated physician's personal leadership and interpersonal skills as those working more closely with the physician, e.g., office staff and nurses/Pas.

- There may be a tendency toward inflated ratings by the chief medical officers/department heads because they are aware the rated MD would see "the bosses' response" in the survey report and do not want to offend the rated physician (Misstep #6).

- The chief medical officers/department heads might have an inaccurate sense of their own effectiveness as leaders. The ability of the chief medical officers/department heads to assess their own effectiveness may be impaired (Missteps #3 and 7).

- The chief medical officers/department heads may have difficulty in seeing the "developmental needs" of their staffs because of a pervasive belief within hierarchical medical systems that all physicians are competent and that the chief medical officers/department heads have only "good people" on their staffs. (Missteps #6 and 7)

- The chief medical officers/department heads could simply view their scoring of the rated physician as being "supportive" of their staff (which is, of course, critically important for a leader), as opposed to seeing the inventory as a tool to assist their staffs in development of personal leadership and interpersonal skills. (Misstep #6)

Logically, each of these possible reasons may be at work, and probably no single answer will ultimately explain the ratings provided by this group.

Some surprising "Hidden Strengths" were identified in the aggregate group. Partners, administrators, nurses/PAs, and chief medical officers/department heads all consistently scored the rated physicians at least 20 percent higher than the rated physicians scored themselves concerning:

- Avoiding defensiveness

- Avoiding political and self-serving behavior

- Avoiding making destructive comments about others or the practice

Physicians acknowledge that they may be engaged in political or self-serving behavior and that they may not always avoid defensiveness or making destructive comments about their practices. Their raters are not as critical of them as they are of themselves—although these areas did emerge among the lowest rated items from most rater groups. This suggests that these physicians are generally insightful about their shortcomings and recognize that they can, at times, react in a defensive way.

For this group of physicians, there were no blind spots—i.e., items for which they rated themselves 20 percent higher than their raters rated them. This further supports the notion that, as a group, these physicians are fairly insightful.

This group of physicians was rated very highly by all rating groups on demonstrating an interest in continuous learning. Given that this small pilot sample consisted only of physicians who volunteered for this assessment process, this is not surprising. Members of the group are most appropriately characterized as "early adopters" and as people who embrace change and innovation. Their profile in general is likely to be quite different from those of groups for which this process is bought and "sold" to the staff from within an organization. This group of physicians also seems to be respectful, open, flexible, honest, and team players who make people feel like winners.

While this group is effective in many domains, there are areas that appear to be developmental opportunities:

■ Avoiding bureaucracy

■ Better management of conflict

■ Seeking win-win solutions

■ Being a little more patient

■ Being more willing to admit mistakes

■ Establishing clear performance expectations of their staffs

■ Avoiding making destructive comments

A Word about "Outliers"

Ultimately, looking at one isolated rater group, one section, or even mean scores cannot give physician participants all of the information they need to optimally utilize feedback from the LeadeRx℠ Inventory. During feedback and coaching, participants are encouraged to look at the spread of the scores across all rater groups. It is important to note and attempt to explain overall trends. It is also crucial to understand the perspective of raters who have given exceedingly low or high scores. If 9 raters scored a physician as a "role model" and 1 person scored the physician as "needs significant improvement," the physician should not simply ignore this one, perhaps, very unhappy person with whom they work. After all, the physician thought highly enough of this individual to ask him or her to provide feedback. Often there is a reason behind the outlier's score, and the additional feedback the physician solicits may allow the physician to understand a different perspective, resulting in a very powerful learning experience for the physician. A saying in the pharmaceutical industry is relevant to the topic of "outliers" or "extremes:" "In questions of efficacy (whether a drug does what it is supposed to do in the majority of people—the 'good things'), it is a question of means (or averages). In questions of safety (the side-effects or "bad things" that drugs can do to even one person), it is a question of looking at extremes (the unusual cases, or outliers).

Relative to interpreting the data from a 360-degree inventory, such as the LeadeRx℠ Inventory, both strengths and development needs are clearly identified by mean data and "clustering" of perceptions from the raters. However, the outliers highlight a clearly different perspective and should be explored in greater depth, as they may be pointing out important developmental needs.

Results by Domain

Let's now look at some of the results found by category (mirroring the Seven Common Leadership Missteps℠ of Physicians) in the LeadeRx℠ Inventory. The possible responses to each question include:

■ Significant Improvement Needed

■ Slight Improvement Needed

■ Skilled/Competent

■ Particularly Talented

■ Outstanding: A Role Model

Seek Win-Win

Many of the lowest rated items from all rating groups were from the category of "seek win-win solutions." This means that of all the items in the survey that received ratings, these issues were on or near the bottom from the perspective of all who work with the physicians being rated. Recognizing and avoiding destructive win/lose situations was among the lowest rated items from all four rating groups. Administrators and partners gave less favorable ratings than on other items on the physician's ability to effectively work through conflicts. Reacting well to situations with conflicting demands is another area where partners' ratings' were less favorable, as were the ratings from nurses/PAs/nurse clinicians. A telling finding is that "making people feel like winners" was among the lowest rated items from office staff. Table 11-1, page 143, depicts the ratings of this category and drives home the unfavorable ratings in this domain.

Demonstrate Respect

Office staff members gave physicians particularly high marks for treating others the way he or she would like to be treated, being polite and courteous, and demonstrating appropriate humility. Nurses responded very favorably regarding the extent to which physicians involved them in decisions that affect their work. Note, however, that the lowest rated item for physicians on the inventory from office staff was "willing to admit mistakes," which received an average rating below the "competent" level and is clearly an area of developmental need. One-third of the raters in this category rated their physicians as "needing improvement."

TABLE 11-1.

Seek Win-Win Solutions	Partners	Administrators	Nurses/PAs	Office Staff
Strives for win-win relationships.		L		
Recognizes and avoids destructive "win/lose" situations.	L	L	L	L
Effectively works through conflicts.	L	L		
Reacts well to situations with conflicting demands.	L		L	
Rewards others for taking informed initiative.				
Makes people feel like winners.			H	L
Gives people the information they need to be effective.				
Recognizes and avoids destructive "win/lose" situations.	L	L	L	L

Of the seven domains, seeking win-win solutions received the lowest overall rating across all groups of raters. Only the nurses/PAs gave a "high" rating on a single item in this group. H = High score, L = Low score.

Demonstrate Personal Leadership

For three of the four rating groups, avoiding making destructive comments about others or the practice was one of the lowest rated items. Partners also gave lower ratings to items relating to avoiding political or self-serving behavior and avoiding bureaucracy and striving for brevity, simplicity, and clarity. On the other hand, possessing and sharing functional/technical knowledge and expertise was highly rated by both partners and nurses/PAs/ nurse clinicians. Office staff also rated their physicians highly on "creating a positive work environment."

Practice Flexibility

For three of the four rating groups, demonstrating awareness of the role of a leader was seen as a strength of the physicians. Office staff also credited their physicians for embracing processes that require an investment of time in order to see the benefits. This strength is, in fact, manifested by this group's being willing to participate in this exercise. Partners gave the physicians they were rating high marks for promoting shared ownership for the group/clinic/university, although they rated over-reliance on administrative skills less favorably than other areas (as did office staff). In a very vivid illustration of how different groups perceive an individual, it was discovered that willingness to adjust style/methods to achieve long-term results and listening and demonstrating understanding of needs and views were among the lowest rated items from nurses/PAs/nurse clinicians. Several of the lowest rated items in the survey from administrators and nurses/PAs/nurse clinicians were related to flexibility: willingness to adjust style to achieve long-term results; demonstrating patience and understanding; and listening/demonstrating an understanding of others' views.

Be a Team Player

Items relating to teamwork generally received high marks from all rating groups. Partners, administrators, and nurses/PAs/nurse clinicians responded particularly favorably regarding the informal working relationship physicians had established with their staffs. Nurses/PAs/ nurse clinicians also gave physicians high marks for demonstrating a willingness to cooperate and work as team players.

Develop Others

Establishing clear performance expectations was one of the lowest rated items from office staff. Nurses/PAs/nurse clinicians and office staff rated the physicians very high on giving positive recognition for a job well done and on possessing and sharing functional/technical knowledge. Expertise was highly rated by both partners and nurses/PAs/nurse clinicians.

Be Open

Results of this survey suggest that being open and interested in personal development are strong suits of the participating physicians. Demonstrating an interest in continuous learning; being open to discussing issues, alternative treatments, and ideas; welcoming directness, openness, and honesty; and promoting open and free exchanges of ideas were among the highest rated items from several of the rater groups. Administrators also rated the physicians highly on asking for feedback. On the other hand, avoiding defensiveness was among the lowest rated items for all four rating groups. Administrators and office staff also rated physicians less favorably on demonstrating an awareness of their own strengths and shortcomings. Note also that recognizing the value of different opinions was among the lowest rated items from nurses/PAs/nurse clinicians, whereas partners were more critical of physicians' ability to respond positively to changes and ambiguity.

Verbatim Comments from the LeadeRx^SM Inventory

At the completion of the "fixed response" questions on the LeadeRx^SM Inventory, each rater is given the opportunity to provide additional verbatim feedback to the physician in a text-entry box. The raters are aware that this feedback will be given, in a blinded fashion, to the physician. Some of the most beneficial and powerful feedback on the inventory emanates from the verbatim comments. The rater is asked to complete three different text-entry boxes, each having a different focus. Each text-entry box is preceded by a partial sentence that the rater is asked to complete:

■ This individual is especially effective in (please provide 2-3 specific examples)…

■ This individual could be more effective if (please provide 2-3 specific examples)…

■ Other comments…

Each of the three sections of text-entry boxes will have the verbatim comments broken-out by rater group (i.e., partners, administrators, etc.). Each bullet represents a verbatim response from a single rater.

"This individual is especially effective in..."
Partners

■ …taking multiple viewpoints and considering all sides.

■ …developing others. The Administrative Colloquium is an excellent example of his dedication to the growth of others, both personally and professionally, with the ultimate goal of strengthening the organization.

Administrators

■ …looking at ways to improve herself.

■ …development of the team approach to problem solving.

■ …including people in the decision-making process. Excellent at recognizing staff contributions.

■ …exciting the staff in moving with the vision (i.e., walking the talk with integrity by even facilitating the course, walking throughout the clinic and interacting with staff and patients).

Office Staff

■ …growing the common goals of the team. She has coordinated off-site meetings and involved her previously formed contacts to assist in developing and presenting the group's plan, thereby providing the building blocks to grow the team goals. The individual is effective in ability to start from grass roots of an idea and then form a working committee.

■ …in leading people with differing goals toward identifying similar goals and implementing a program to serve all interests. An example is his initiative in establishing an ad hoc committee to study the needs of advanced leadership training for physicians, other professionals, and paraprofessionals and presenting a proposal to meet the training needs to upper management.

Nurses/PAs

■ …working with other physicians to understand the quality processes we work with. Getting them to make decisions. Getting all to come to consensus in win-win situations.

■ …providing positive feedback to others readily on a one-to-one basis. She is very enthusiastic in her feedback. She takes the time to learn about staff on a personal level. She treats staff with respect and seeks out their opinions. She listens to others. She does not gossip, nor does she promote it.

Chief Medical Officers/Department Heads

■ …staying committed to ideas she believes are important. She has a very strong belief in improving patient care and doing what it takes to make sure physicians do that. She has invested, for the 8 years I have worked with her, significant time to this effort through her commitment to quality improvement, outcomes assessment, and performance measurement. Specific examples include her decision to get a master's degree in management and to take a course to seek additional skills development.

■ …building consensus and creating harmony from staff dissonance. During board meetings, he leads well and can allow others to lead. He doesn't dominate, but neither does he shirk. He is optimistic and helps staff morale by letting others know when they've performed a particular task well.

Discussion

In these verbatim responses, we can see these physicians successfully avoid the missteps and serve as role models for others. The verbatim remarks of nurses/PAs noted the ability of one of the physicians to address Misstep #1 by "seeking win-win solutions." One administrator commented that the rated physician clearly understood the importance of interpersonal relationships (Misstep #2), as they "include people in the decision-making process." Misstep #2 is dodged by one of the physicians, as noted by the nurses/PAs, who find, "She treats staff with respect and seeks out their opinions." An administrator acknowledges that the rated physician "walks the talk with integrity." This avoids Misstep #3. One of the partners describes how the physician being rated takes "multiple viewpoints" and considers "all sides" when making a decision, a behavior that promotes avoiding Misstep #4. The office staff and administrators note avoidance of Misstep #5 by several of the physicians who are focused on a team approach to problem solving and gaining consensus. Developing others is a strength of at least one physician who successfully side-steps Misstep #6, as noted by the nurses/PAs. Even Misstep #7, lack of openness is addressed, as one administrator notes that the physician being rated is always looking to improve.

"This individual could be more effective if..."

Partners

■ …he wasn't self-serving.

■ …he was not perceived as being argumentative and confrontational by some co-workers.

■ …he listened more closely to what people are trying to say before he starts trying to explain the "state of the nation."

■ …he was more tolerant of opposing views. When someone introduces an opposing viewpoint, he tends to become defensive and to begin almost to argue rather than to calmly discuss the issues. He is passionate about some views and comes across as inflexible or insensitive to another's views, occasionally.

- …he were a bit less righteous—i.e., he unintentionally leads with his answer, at times, which is the right answer but is conveyed in a tone that can be perceived as judging others' solutions as not worthy.

Administrators

- …she would practice what she preaches, i.e., take the time to elicit subordinates' ownership of the process. She knows that step is critical, but in her impatience she often dictates the solution instead.

- …she would learn to listen and understand others before insisting on being heard. She often interrupts staff, before hearing what they are trying to say. The implicit message is "what you say isn't important, I'm the Medical Director, listen to me."

- …she was less judgmental/self-righteous in dealing with others with opinions contrary to her own.

- …he did not humiliate people—even if they ask for it. Sometimes the ears should be larger and the mouth smaller.

Office Staff

- …he said, "I don't know," if he doesn't know the answer, rather than winging it.

- …she provided more feedback on my performance.

Nurses/PAs

- …he didn't sometimes make others feel they have nothing to contribute or that decisions are being made for them.

- …she didn't use the defensive attitude she sometimes displays if her ideas are not used and then criticizes the outcome. She will tend to say that if you did it my way, it would be right. Verbalizes lack of inclusion in some processes, but does not recognize that her personal time commitments to other projects inhibits co-workers from getting her opinion at each step of the project.

- …he built alliances and tried to mend more fences when faced with conflict.

Chief Medical Officers/Department Heads

- …she didn't have such a forceful demeanor that can be confused for rudeness. Her sometimes gruff style can keep her from being recognized as the outstanding leader and professional she is. She could benefit from learning to listen a bit better and understanding the frame of reference of those she hopes to influence in positive ways.

- …he learned to delegate authority and avoid micro-managing. Although he chairs many committees, one often gets the sense that committee members play a very small role in various decisions that are made. He listens well, but it is clear that he makes most decisions and leaves very little up to the various chairs and leaders in the group.

Discussion

While this group of physicians is clearly effective, it is clear from the verbatim remarks that they have room for improvement in a number of areas. This finding demonstrates that even those who have good personal leadership and interpersonal skills have substantial opportunity to get better.

Let's examine the verbatim material in terms of each of the missteps:

Misstep #1: Failure to Seek Win-Win Solutions

One of the partners notes that one of the physicians would be more effective if he was "more tolerant of opposing views." He goes on to state the physician can become defensive, as opposed to more calmly discussing the issue. Another partner observes the tendency of the physician to be "righteous," often giving people the answer he wants to hear, "judging others' solutions as not worthy." These are both Misstep #1 and are reminiscent of Shell and Klasko's research on the difficulty of getting physicians to look for win-win solutions.[72]

Misstep #2: Failure to Consistently Demonstrate Respect for the Individual

An administrator suggests the rated physician would be more effective if "she would learn to listen and understand others before insisting on being heard." A rater in the nurse/PA group found the rated physician made "others feel they have nothing to contribute or that decisions are being made for them." In a perfect example of "Chairman's Syndrome," one administrator remarks about a physician who "interrupts staff, before hearing what they are trying to say." The implicit message is, "What you say isn't important, I'm the Medical Director, listen to me." These are all examples of not demonstrating respect for the individual, illustrating how Misstep #2 can creep into our daily activities.

Misstep #3: Lack of Personal Leadership

A partner notes that the rated physician would be more effective if he were not self-serving, while an administrator describes a classic example of lack of integrity by finding a physician who should "practice what she preaches." Integrity—doing what we say we will do—is critical to personal success. When violated in public, others clearly notice.

Misstep #4: Lack of Flexibility

A partner describes the rated physician as being passionate about his views. Unfortunately, it "comes across as inflexible to other views." A rater in the nurse/PA group illustrates an example of lack of flexibility shown by a physician who becomes defensive when her ideas are not used. A rater in the chief medical officer/department head group comments about a physician who could benefit "from listening a bit better and understanding the frame of reference" of other people. Demonstrating flexibility would enable these individuals to open themselves up to new possibilities and points of reference.

Misstep #5: Inability to Be a Team Player

A perceptive nurses/PAs rater comments that one of the physicians would be more effective if he were able to build an alliance and tried to "mend more fences." Another rater writes that the rated physician complains about not being included in some of the processes, yet her availability severely limits the other team members. Sometimes, being part of a team means empowering your fellow team members to make decisions when you aren't available.

Misstep #6: Failure to Develop Others

In developing others, sometimes we have to let go of some of our own responsibilities—and delegate effectively. A rater in the chief medical officer/department head group comments that the rated physician needs to learn to delegate authority and quit micro-managing. He goes on to note: "He listens well, but it is clear that he makes most decisions and leaves very little up to the various chairs and leaders in the group." Clearly, a developmental opportunity for this physician is to help others develop by empowering them to make decisions. Another example of this misstep is given to us by a rater in the office staff group, who observes that a physician would be more effective if "she provided more feedback on my performance."

Misstep #7: Lack of Openness

This misstep is, in many ways, very difficult for a person at work to assess. Part of this misstep is the inability to accurately self-assess, and we do see a mention of this in the verbatim. A rater in the office staff group notes that the rated physician would be more effective if he said "I don't know" when he didn't know the answer, rather than "winging it." This is related to self-assessment, as well as to growing as a person—being comfortable with not knowing everything and being able to admit it. Helping the physicians to understand that "not knowing all the answers" is not a sin would be useful.

"Other Comments..."

Partners

- ◼ ...he needs to be in a position and organization that values and better uses his many talents.

Administrators

- ◼ ...one of, if not the most, dynamic physician leaders I have worked with in my 30 years of health care. My current employment is based on a desire to work with this physician leader.

- ◼ ...her defensiveness and lack of demonstrated courtesy severely limit her effectiveness with professional staff. While she intellectually accepts constructive criticism, her emotional reaction is to become defensive and to point to errors the other party committed that "forced" her to act.

Office Staff

- ...he is a wonderful person who cares about his patients and staff.

Nurses/PAs

- ...a rebel before her time. A trail blazer with an unpopular message that needed to be shared.

Chief Medical Officers/Department Heads

- ...she stands out as one of those rare physicians who is approachable, honest, smart, and willing to tackle a number of "sacred cow" issues in the physician communities. I am impressed at her level of insight about the culture of medicine and her commitment to trying to improve a system in which physicians typically are blame-oriented.

- ...overall, he has provided very good leadership to the Clinic, and job satisfaction and financial performance seems to have benefited from his leadership. I think that he still has a tendency to exclude physicians from the ultimate decision-making process. Hopefully, this will improve with time.

Discussion

The general comment section provides additional insight into both strengths and developmental needs, and is a fascinating amalgamation of responses. An administrator acknowledges he is working with one of the most effective physician leaders he has encountered "in my 30 years of health care." He literally is motivated to continue working by this person. We see the humanness of the physician group in these comments, where one physician is described as "a wonderful person who cares about his patients and staff." We see innovativeness and cutting-edge thinking in a "rebel before her time." A rater in the chief medical officer/department head group describes a woman who is "willing to tackle a number of "sacred cow" issues in the physician communities" and is "committed to trying to improve a system in which physicians typically are blame oriented." There is also commentary, however, on developmental needs. An administrator observes that the rated physician becomes so defensive that it severely limits her effectiveness with other staff.

Concluding Remarks

It is clear that the physicians who participated in this exercise are a highly biased sample of individuals. Clearly, they are interested in good personal leadership skills and represent an above-average segment of the physician population. Some are board members with experience in leading teams, facilitating relationships, and building coalitions. One individual has helped implement and foster cross-departmental teamwork to achieve better patient care. One of the individuals who participated has established an ad hoc committee to study "the needs of advanced leadership training for physicians." One of the individuals is a Lieutenant Colonel in the Army Reserves, who has had tremendous leadership experience. One of the individuals went back to school to get a master's degree in management—often associated with leadership training—and has continually sought "additional skills development" opportunities. Each of these eight individuals clearly understands the crucial importance of effective personal leadership and interpersonal skills.

Despite these accomplishments and clear personal success, each of them saw an opportunity in this exercise to learn more about themselves, and to potentially utilize the information and insights gained to achieve even greater personal and professional success—to achieve positive, measurable, and sustainable changes in their personal leadership and interpersonal skills. Regardless of how good we think we are as an individual, there is always room for improvement, as long as we are open to asking for, receiving, and acting upon feedback from the diverse and unique set of people surrounding us.

While this is an above-average group, the LeadeRx℠ 360-degree Inventory still clearly identified areas in which each of the physicians could improve. The most obvious area of development need for the group in aggregate, based on the fixed-response questions, is seeking win-win solutions. Every group of raters had the perception that these physicians were less skilled at seeking win-win than the physicians thought they were, based on their self-scores. Many of the individual ratings of this group of physicians were in the "needs improvement" category.

Any area in which a physician feels he or she needs either slight or significant improvement represents an opportunity for personal development. This occurred 46 times in the physician group. At least two of the physician participants felt they needed slight or significant improvement (the lowest end of the rating scale) in the following areas:

■ Not being arrogant (3 physicians).

■ Not making destructive comments about others (4 physicians).

■ Not having such a "quick-fix" focus in order to achieve long-term results (3 physicians).

■ Being more patient when others speak (2 physicians).

■ Realizing that there is more to leadership than technical skills (2 physicians).

■ Avoiding political and self-serving behavior (3 physicians).

■ Not being defensive (4 physicians).

Did we accomplish what we intended at the outset of this project? The goals were to:

■ Document that the instrument can highlight strengths and developmental needs of individuals, based on differences in perception between the raters and the individual being rated.

■ Demonstrate that individuals rating the physicians would give honest, open feedback, as manifested by a broad range of responses.

■ Demonstrate the instrument would be able to illustrate differences in perspective between rater groups from different functional areas within health care.

Unequivocally, the instrument demonstrated the ability to detect the strengths and developmental needs of physicians, based on the perceptions of those with whom they work most closely. A broad range of responses by all rater groups on the inventory—including both extremes of the scale—indicates that no rater group felt "intimidated" into falsely "raising-up" or "trashing" the physician. The one exception to this, as mentioned earlier, may be the chief medical officer/departmental head group, but it is doubtful that "intimidation" played a role in this phenomenon. If there was any residual doubt concerning whether this goal was achieved, and about the possibility of inhibited responses on the part of the rater groups, it should have evaporated upon reviewing the verbatim responses. It is clear "the gloves came off" and the raters were brutally honest. Finally, the third goal was also clearly achieved. There can be no doubt that the LeadeRx℠ Inventory can delineate commonly held views and views that vary on the basis of the perspective of the rating group. In this sample, the office staff and nurses/PAs—those who perhaps work most closely with the physicians—held perspectives different from those of the administrators, whose perspectives were different from those of the partners. For example, all rater groups viewed the physician they rated as being open and respectful. On the other hand, the perspective of these physicians and the chief medical officers/department heads were generally more favorable than the perspective of the office staff. The chief medical officer/department heads were different from all other groups as well.

This chapter should give great comfort to physicians and medical organizations that are committed to assisting their physicians to understand their personal leadership strengths and see their developmental needs. A 360-degree inventory such as LeadeRx℠ is the first step to establishing a program to help physicians enhance their personal leadership and interpersonal skills and to institute positive, measurable, and sustainable change in the leadership culture of medicine.

Section Five

Thoughts and Observations from the Edge

CHAPTER 12 ⊂∞∞∞∞⊃

The Kinder, Gentler Sex:
Women's Advantage in Medical Leadership

Strength based in force is a strength people fear. Strength based in love is a strength people crave.—Nerburg[173]

Gender Differences and Personal Leadership Skills

In a survey of 9,250 physicians who had been insured for malpractice for at least two years, male physicians were three times as likely to be in a high-claims group as were their female physician counterparts, even after adjusting for years at risk and other demographic variables. The authors conclude: "We suspect that the most likely explanation for this finding is that women interact more effectively with patients." [174]

In a separate study of 667 graduates of Jefferson Medical College between 1982 and 1986, it was found that "women, in general, valued psychosocial aspects of medical care higher than did men." In this same study, paradoxically, men considered "interpersonal interactions" as being the least problematic to them.[175] Recalling the work by Argyris presented earlier relative to the way "we think we are" and the "way people really see us,"[63] it isn't that men don't see the problem; they apparently are convinced they don't have any problem related to interpersonal interactions. This is also the issue that Kruger and Dunning speak of concerning "incompetence" within certain "domains" of our lives and the inability to recognize that "incompetence."[110]

What accounts for such differences between men and women? And what relevance does it have to leadership in medicine? Miller writes: "It is fair to say that in our history, those people who have concentrated on finding ways to foster the growth of other people have been women. Women have long practice in the complex, emotionally and cognitively integrated activity of helping other people to develop."[176]

This is apparently true for how female physicians treat their patients, not just their family and friends. In a large national survey of physicians (n = 2,326), women physicians in ambulatory settings felt greater time pressure related to their jobs and, on average, felt they needed 15 percent more time than their male counterparts to provide what they considered high-quality care.[177] This indicates a greater need—and skill—of women in fostering the doctor-patient relationship compared to men. Further, female physicians are more likely to report satisfaction with their specialty and with patient and colleague relationships compared to their male counterparts. Women seem to gain more satisfaction in the nonmonetary aspects of their jobs and to maintain a greater degree of intrinsic motivation than do their male colleagues. Women do, however, have less satisfaction with their autonomy, relationships with community, income, and resources compared to male physicians.

Some male physicians may think, "So what? I'm technically competent, and that's more important. Besides, look how successful I am!" While technical competence is certainly important, consider what an impact this "typically female" approach would have if applied to teaching roles in residency programs, roles currently predominantly held by men. There is probably no better place to begin to "foster the growth of people" and to assist our medical students and young physicians to develop greater understanding of interpersonal relationships and personal leadership through "complex, emotionally and cognitively integrated activity." Perhaps more women in teaching positions would result in our students' communicating more effectively and maintaining greater degrees of intrinsic motivation.

While some male physicians may scoff at these "softer qualities," there is no question that such qualities are important in the doctor-patient relationship. Miller points out: "Women have provided growth-fostering relationships for many people—children, husbands, and other women and men in their home and in the workplace. Equally important, women have carried out this kind of activity within an "institutional" context.... Despite obstacles and difficulties, women have tried to learn how other people feel and what their needs are. Struggling to understand these many varied feelings, they have often mediated skillfully among family members."[176]

It is such traits that allow women to have a unique approach upon entering medicine. Women have a "realistic history of practice" that brings needed values into medicine and that brings to leadership positions approaches that are "softer" and that medicine lacks and needs most at this time. Many of the interpersonal skills that women manifest are either tied to or directly reflective of personal leadership skills.

Why are women physicians better able to relate to patients? Miller states: "Most women want the kinds of connections with others that allow them to hear and understand the perceptions and desires of others, and in which the other person is able to hear their perceptions and desires. Emerging out of the psychological experience, most women feel a greater sense of well-being, self-worth and effectiveness if they feel their actions arise from a context of relationship and, in turn, lead on to a greater sense of connection with others, as opposed to a sense of distance or so-called "independence." This is to say that women feel better and more worthwhile if we feel that our activities have come out of the interchange and workings of a relationship."[176]

Basically, female physicians seem to have a greater tendency to genuinely attempt to "connect" with their patients than do men. Again, the value of such connection is non-monetary and retention of greater degrees of intrinsic motivation.

So, do male physicians not have these abilities? Do male physicians simply not need such relationship connections? Do male physicians simply not have the emotional capabilities to maximize emotional characteristics such as empathy? Men can develop—and in fact already have—such characteristics, but males have a tendency to suppress such characteristics for a variety of reasons. "Men need these kinds of relationships, too, but at this point in history most men have been led to feel that each is more worthy and effective, if he believes that he, personally, is a strong, highly developed individual, that he 'is his own man.' Men have not been raised to feel that it is their primary responsibility to foster the growth of others; and their own development has not focused on preparing them for building relationships which benefit others as well as themselves. Instead, men have been encouraged to concentrate on developing and advancing themselves."[176]

Miller says that men are socialized in a manner contrary to many of the traits physicians should have to develop effective interpersonal relationships—this includes the ability to be team players, to collaborate, to negotiate, and to deal with patients. How many of The Seven Common Leadership Missteps[SM] are due, at least in part, to the issue of socialization either as a male in growing up or in medical training, largely controlled by male physicians?

Goleman's work in emotional intelligence is relevant to these issues. Goleman points out that "emotional intelligence" does not mean merely "being nice" or "giving free rein to feelings—'letting it all hang out.'"[14] Rather, he states, it is the careful and appropriate management of feeling, expressed effectively, that allows people to work together. While Goleman goes on to point out that women are not "smarter" than men related to emotional intelligence, he does acknowledge that women are, on average, "more aware of their emotions, show more empathy, and are more adept interpersonally." Women are also better at detecting another person's feelings than are their male counterparts. On average, women perform 80 percent better than men at the task of guessing what emotion an individual is experiencing at any one time.

It appears that men are able to be empathetic to the same degree as women, but are less motivated to be empathetic in any given situation compared to their female counterparts. Men may view the showing of empathy as weakness. "If men appear at times to be socially insensitive, it may have more to do with the image they wish to convey than with the empathic ability they possess."[14]

Often, physicians, especially males, say they need to "remain objective" or to avoid becoming "to close" to the patient or family in order to make the best medical decision, to avoid "transference." There appears to be an underlying belief that if one shows some feeling or personal involvement, one cannot make decisions as well as if one does not show feeling or personal involvement. In other words, demonstrating feelings may result in indecisiveness.

Miller describes a situation in which the hospital emergency department staff was not able to find a physician to see a patient after calling the on-call physician and the next three backup physicians.[176] Obviously, this upset the staff. When the administrator of the emergency department was apprised of the situation, she held a number of debriefing and exploratory meetings, all very time-consuming. All parties were encouraged to share their feelings about the situation, prior to working out a solution. Ultimately the problem was solved, with no recurrence of the problem. Miller observes: "Here, too, all of the meetings and expressions of emotions could have been seen as manifestations of indecisiveness by the leadership, of encouraging people to be emotional, and especially as inefficient. Instead, I'm certain that if measurements had been made they would have shown a decrease in actual time and money costs. Most important, the new programs benefited the people served."

The characterization of indecisiveness is inaccurate. Decisions were made. They were made by a different process. The common image of decisiveness need not be the only or the best guide to decision making. As mentioned above, the characterization of anything or anyone as 'too emotional' is also incorrect. It is more accurate to say that the existence of emotions was recognized and an attempt was made to provide pathways to deal with them in a productive fashion.[176]

We might refer to the typical quick, decisive, decision-making process as "testosterone-driven decision making," and there are clear examples in business of this mindset that are directly transferable to the medical profession. Clancy and Krieg describe at length the concept of "testosterone decision making." "We know from our experience and observation that testosterone-driven decision making tends to be what guys do. Testosterone-driven decision makers are the guys who assemble complex toys on Christmas Eve without reading the directions, cook without a recipe, make business decisions without research. This is the stuff of popular culture worldwide. It is the subject of Professor Deborah Tannen's books. Her bestseller *They Just Don't Understand* is a must read for all managers. There are T-shirts that say "Real Men Don't Use Road Maps." Women talk about the problem, and comics joke about it: 'Why does it take a million sperm to fertilize a single egg? Because they won't ask directions.'"[178] Testosterone-driven decision-makers feel that stopping to ask for directions—asking for help—is "tantamount to admitting weakness, and what real man admits weakness?"

Clancy and Krieg studied 293 senior marketing managers, equally divided among males and females and representing a cross section of the Fortune 1000 companies.

TABLE 12-1. Decision-making patterns among marketing executives.*

	% Males	**% Females**
Tends to make decision quickly	**82**	**48**
Tends to be a courageous risktaker	**81**	**53**
More focused on short-term rather than long-term results	**67**	**46**
Pays too much attention to what competitors are doing	**56**	**43**

*Adapted from K Clancy, K., and Krieg, P. Counter-Intuitive Marketing. New York, N.Y.: The Free Press, 2000, p. 33.

The study examined the perceptions of male versus female chief marketing officers (CMO) by the marketing managers who reported to them. They examined 34 different aspects of decision making and management styles of these CMOs as seen by their subordinates. Their findings supported their hypothesis: "most marketing decisions are rushed, rely on little research, and focus on short-term results." They also found that this decision-making pattern was more characteristic of senior male executives than of female executives. The actual numbers do not reflect subtle differences, as seen in table 12-1, above.[179]

On the flip side, female senior marketing executives were more effective in building consensus (84 percent versus 60 percent for men) and more thoughtful in their decision-making processes (90 percent versus 71 percent for men), being more careful about examining many options before acting. The authors summarize the attributes of testosterone-drive decision makers as:

- Make decisions quickly.

- Rely on intuition.

- Are uncomfortable with ambiguity.

- Tend to force their views on their subordinates.[179]

The authors go on to explain that these decision-making traits are not as successful as more considered approaches. They refer to companies and individuals who use such approaches as practicing "Death-Wish Marketing" because of the high failure rate of such decision-making approaches.

Why is marketing being discussed here—a topic many would consider almost antithetical to medicine? One reason is the TRIZ Principles—that is, problems or issues encountered in one industry or science are found in or repeated in other industries or sciences. These findings apply to medicine too. Males (especially) in medicine often follow the "testosterone-drive decision-making" pattern described above. It isn't simply that they make decisions quickly, rely on intuition, are uncomfortable with ambiguity, and tend to force their views on others that is the most bothersome, nor is it the point. As suggested in this chapter, males value such qualities of decision making despite the evidence that they are less effective than softer, more considered approaches. Further such decision making and "quick-fix" approaches can result in difficulties in other parts of our lives, e.g., relationship building, taking time to demonstrate compassion or concern, malpractice liability, etc.

Emotions, if they play a role in decision making, do not derail the decision-making process. They result in a different way of thinking about and solving any one problem and may actually result in better outcomes. This "new way of thinking" may or may not lead to the same answer. While the answer may not be the one you would have chosen, it does not mean it is wrong. It also may be better. Miller states: "These examples suggest one feature which is relevant for all institutions: no one knows the right way to do things. Further, because institutions are composed of people, they are alive and therefore always in motion, in a state of change."[176]

Hock has an exercise that drives home the point about institutions as "living organisms," that is, being made up of people.[18] He asks questions such as "What does your institution look like? Taste like? Smell like? Sound like? Feel like?" Obviously, one can't taste the Mayo Clinic. One can't hear Massachusetts General. Because physicians are so data driven, requiring "proof of existence," does the fact we cannot taste or smell or feel our organizations mean that these organizations do not exist? Of course they exist—in our minds. Because they exist in our minds, we can change them any time we want, depending on needs and external forces. Just as we can change our behaviors any time we want.

Organizations are made of, and are about, people. We don't deal with "the hospital." We deal with the people running the hospital. We don't deal with "the clinic." We deal with the people running the clinic. As has been laid out in this chapter, women appear to be either better equipped or more willing to deal with people on an interpersonal level. Therefore, women may actually have more inherent qualities relevant to being effective leaders than men do, on both the interpersonal and the institutional level. Males need to learn from them.

A Word About Power

It's worthy to note that leadership, by definition, omits the use of coercive power. When a leader begins to coerce his followers, he's essentially abandoning leadership and embracing dictatorship.[180]

Power is not what leadership is about, but often that is what one thinks of when discussing leaders. While leaders do have power, it is derived from the individuals who choose to follow them. It is not something to be "wielded" by the leader, like a sword. Miller says, "Closely related to the question of hierarchies is another overriding and unsolved topic: power—both the drive by those in power to keep things the way they are and simultaneously to seek greater power. This drive is clearly not the same as seeking the good functioning of the institution and the development of everyone in it."[176]

Men are more likely than women to seek power simply for the sake of power. During the socialization of men, they are taught to "concentrate on developing and advancing themselves." Miller points out that men are encouraged to seek their own advancement, status, and power, "usually including power over others."[176]

Women generally are not motivated to engage in such power-grabs. Women's emphasis on relationships makes such motivations less likely, as most women do not feel their "deepest pleasure in 'winning out' over others. Indeed, most women feel pain if their own enhancement results in another person's pain."[181]

Individuals who are power-hungry but "leadership-weak" don't fool very many people; they do, however, alienate a great number of individuals. Maxwell's "Law #5" states that it is apparent to everyone who the true leader is, regardless of their position within the organization. If the "chairman" is leading a meeting, but everyone listens more intently to another individual in the room—male or female—it is because the power—usually determined by stronger interpersonal skills and personal leadership—resides with that individual, not with the chairman. "The real leader holds the power, not just the position," Maxwell says. "If you see a disparity between who's leading the meeting and who's leading the people, then the person running the meeting is not the real leader."[8]

Even though women may not seek out power, their personal leadership skills and their ability to relate to individuals on an interpersonal level give them a great deal of power without their even trying to be powerful. I remember a female attending surgeon in my training program who was often viewed as being "weak and soft" (by male surgeons) because of her manner in the hospital and in conferences. Residents viewed her as being "indecisive." But I never knew anyone who did not have the utmost respect for her. The reason she was respected was because of all the things mentioned above, manifested by her ability to connect with patients and those with whom she worked.

Some male physicians may be puzzled by this line of thought and will wrack their brains trying to think of a female physician with power. This is very much a male perspective. Many of us may not have the degree of competence in this "domain" of our lives required to appreciate the importance and power of such individuals. My impression is that many female physicians are not concerned with demonstrating power with physician colleagues—male or female—even when in the position to do so. They are concerned about effectively interacting with and developing staffs, residents, students, and patients—the people they serve. If the female physician is in a "defined leadership position," she is concerned about her constituents or colleagues. It is those individuals who view her as powerful, not in the sense of "controlling power" but in the sense of earned respect, admiration, and trust—the same things that result in the success of "non-positional leaders" that Maxwell describes in The Law of E.F. Hutton.[8]

Imminent Impact II: Driving Personal Leadership Throughout Health Care

In the end, there is no set of rules or regulations so rigorous, no organizational hierarchy so great, and no individual so powerful to prevent us from behaving this way, providing you properly lead yourself.[18]

Instituting Leadership Training in Medical Curricula

There is virtually no medical organization, no hospital or practice, and no individual physician that couldn't benefit from at least some of the information in this book and from personal leadership development for the "on-the-ground" physician. It isn't hard to know where to institute a leadership development program in medicine, as it is a bit like the Battle of the Bulge in World War II, when General Creighton William Abrams made the observation: "For the first time in the history of this campaign we are surrounded on the East, West, North and South. We can now attack the enemy in all directions."

This is the attitude that we must take to personal leadership development in medicine—attacking it at all levels of the profession, in all directions, from the medical student to the resident to the attending, university chair, and physician administrator. We need leadership development everywhere in medicine.

We need to change the definition of what it means to be successful in medicine, starting, as Hock notes, with leading ourselves as individuals first and foremost.[18]

Solving the disconnect between what motivates physicians and what physicians' claim is their primary focus will be another key—admitting that we are in medicine and that medicine is a business, albeit one where we take care of people, is necessary. The final step will be to fully reconnect with our intrinsic motivations, which will only be possible after enhancing our personal leadership skills.

Schwartz outlines his vision for leadership in medicine with a surgery example. He summarizes very nicely what is needed in medical education: "...a cadre of surgical educators must be trained in such strategies so that we can model leadership roles while incorporating these principles into both undergraduate and graduate medical curricula. Heretofore the initial and subsequent development of physician leadership has occurred at random; in the future it must become an organized, conscious effort on the part of surgical educators in order that physicians may again lead the American health care system.

"Just as the surgical community embraces broad-based training for general surgeons in all core competencies, we must include basic leadership, organizational, and quality management skills in the undergraduate and graduate medical education curricula of the 21st Century.... Just as the surgical community demands systematic, intense fellowship training for the development of competent surgical specialists, we must encourage and support a similar leadership training period for interested surgeons that encompasses germane executive and financial skills. Without the development of such expertise, the direction and development of departments of surgery may be usurped by nonphysicians with managerial and financial skills."[22]

Schwartz is on the right track, but he stops short of where we need to be. He promotes these concepts for a single specialty—surgery—with no mention of the rest of medicine. Improving the personal leadership of surgeons is not sufficient for success in medicine. Internists are not what medicine is about. Or pediatricians or gastroenterologists or family practice doctors. The impact of managed care and other forms of organized medicine didn't affect just one special group—it hit all of us. We sink or swim together.

Schwartz also notes that such training should be focused only on "interested surgeons," not on "all surgeons," or as the Woods Development Institute proposes, all physicians. Physicians have perceived a lack of control over many aspects of their profession for years, yet relatively few have taken on leadership training or learned management skills. Medical schools need to be teaching personal leadership skills, as well as the business management piece of medicine to all medical students, while practicing physicians are catching up through external CME courses and 360-degree feedback and behavioral coaching.

My final point on Dr. Schwartz' comments concerns his worry that the profession may become "usurped by nonphysicians." This has already happened, whether physicians want to believe it or not. It already is reality.

Still, Dr. Schwartz and the University of Kentucky seem to be "ahead of the curve" compared to many other training programs. They have instituted a medical management course, focused on providing physicians with some of the skills required to be a physician in today's business climate. Their program focuses on five objectives:

1. Acquiring fundamental business and management skills for application in an integrated health care delivery environment.

2. Understanding current financial and market forces in the health care environment.

3. Developing ability to apply quality improvement concepts to health care.

4. Understanding the current health care environment, including organizations, trends, and legal and ethical issues.

5. Training effective team leaders/change managers, with knowledge of organizational behavior, effective communication, and negotiation and conflict resolution skills.

Missing from this training program is personal leadership development, which should form the foundation for each of these five very worthy objectives. Dr. Schwartz seems to understand the need for such training, but his omission may represent the tacit belief by physicians that their personal leadership skills are inherent with the job.

The Physician Executive and Physicians as "Followers"

There has been a huge focus on the training of physician executives in the past 5-10 years, with the education focusing on all of the things just mentioned in the Kentucky program: fundamental business and management skills, understanding finance and marketing, quality improvement, and legal and ethical issues. Some programs offer some training in personal leadership.

McCall has noted that the failure of physician executives almost always boils down to interpersonal skills—people management "does them in."[90] There is a bigger problem for physician executives in leadership roles: finding physicians who will willingly follow them. A physician executive friend, who is in the upper management of a large managed care system says that physicians have trouble selecting leaders because they are so unwilling to be led. Physicians are lousy team players largely because they are so unwilling to follow.

It is great to have physician executives, individuals who will learn all of the skills that the MBA programs and other training initiatives have to offer, but they need followers to accomplish their goals and to assist the organization in achieving its vision. Even the best vision is just blue sky unless "on-the-ground" constituents are willing to enable the mission—to accomplish the vision—to get behind the leader willingly. Too often, this is not the case. LeTourneau and Curry have noted: "Many physician executives are concerned that, if they do not maintain some semblance of a clinical practice, they will no longer be accepted by other physicians as a physician. This brings us to the second aspect of the dilemma. Physicians are notorious for demanding that one of them be involved in decision making; when a physician leaves practice to do just that, however, other physicians may reject that physician as a 'turncoat.'"[182]

The unwillingness to follow relates directly back to the Seven Common Leadership Missteps[SM] of Physicians. There are multiple issues at play here: failure to consistently respect the individual, lack of personal leadership, inability to be a team player, and certainly a basic lack of trust.

Personal leadership training of "on-the-ground" physicians should assist the physician executive in achieving "followership." Physician executives need good leadership and interpersonal skills themselves, but enhancing the ability of all physicians within the organization should assist in developing trusting relationships, focus physicians on their own areas of needed development, and help them to understand they don't "know all of the answers." Ultimately such an approach should enhance the likelihood that the constituency will empower physician executives to make decisions for the group. Simply getting physicians to understand the essence of "win-win" and trust would be a major step in enhancing their willingness to follow.

A Suggested Plan

Traditionally, academic medical centers have…spent an inordinate amount of time, money, and effort in faculty (leadership) recruitment as opposed to faculty development; however, lessons from private industry have clearly demonstrated this practice to be a mistake.[22]

Kohn has described the format for what is being recommended: "When something is wrong with the present system, you move on two tracks at once. You do what you can within the confines of the current structure, trying to minimize its harm. You also work with others to try to change that structure, conscious that nothing dramatic may happen for a very long time."[183]

The plan being suggested to incorporate personal leadership development into medicine has two tiers. First, we need to rapidly implement personal leadership training for physicians in practice and for residents in the second year of training and higher. This would be done through a feedback program, beginning with an organizational employee survey, followed by a 360-degree feedback program and leadership coaching of the individual physician. Follow-up is critical to assess improvement and enhance the likelihood of sustained benefits related to leadership behaviors. Once physicians begin to see the benefits, maintenance of a focus on personal leadership will be auto-catalytic for the individual and the profession. Such programs assist physicians to develop greater competency in self-assessment related to their personal leadership and interpersonal skills.

This first step can be accomplished through a variety of approaches, from a single individual who wants help, through an entire organization. On-site programs, in which trainers come to the organization for a one-day educational seminar concerning leadership skills, the Seven Common Leadership Missteps[SM], and interpretation of the 360-degree feedback program, followed by a debriefing period and one-on-one behavioral coaching, is a very effective method, having been used successfully and reproducibly in the nonmedical business world. Follow-up is usually through personal, face-to-face coaching, although other methods can be used, such as the telephone or internet-based video.

A second method for accomplishing this first step is through seminars and continuing medical education courses. Over a one- or two-day period, personal leadership training, much like the on-site courses, could be presented, including one-on-one coaching sessions. Follow-up behavioral coaching could be face-to-face, by videoconference, or by telephone. One attractive inducement to enhance the likelihood of physicians' adopting personal leadership development is offering CME, through accreditation of the training programs. This approach offers two benefits for the same dollar spent; leadership training and CME credit, which is required by most states for physicians to maintain their licenses.

Part of this initial wave of leadership training would be initiating the 360-degree program including behavioral coaching and close follow-up for a minimum of one year for all residents at the second-year level and above. After the first year of this program, all incoming second year residents would participate (as everyone from the previous class and upward would have received training the prior year). The rationale for not instituting this in the first year of residency is that residents would not have had any exposure to the workplace, including contact with peers, hospital or office staff, or attendings. Because of this, no one would be able to rate them on a 360-degree assessment.

The second step, ideally taken simultaneously with the first, is to institute personal leadership training in medical school. Leadership should be taught in the first year of medical school, with a refresher in the fourth year prior to graduation, and should be mandatory. It could consist of reading material, lectures by credible school faculty and outside leaders—both medical and nonmedical—as well as examinations. Mandatory one-on-one coaching sessions, which could be based on a "student 360-degree" evaluation, would be a part of this program. This could, in fact, be done annually, with a coach assigned (probably a faculty member akin to an advisor, who has undergone such training and understands personal leadership) to work with each student throughout his or her four years. Alternatively, student "mentors" from the classes ahead could be utilized effectively. Students should be coached to maintain their intrinsic motivations and shown how to uncouple "rewards" from their job.

Part of the difficulty with these recommendations is the fact that many medical students, like practicing physicians, seem to view these sorts of exercises as "fluffy" and without value to their impending profession. It is, unfortunately, far more important than the students could possibly know or than the faculty is currently able to see. What we are talking about here is greater emphasis on the more human elements of the profession, maintaining intrinsic motivation and respect for the individual.

The Long View

Success, like happiness, cannot be pursued. It must ensue. And it only does so as the unintended side effect of one's personal dedication to a cause greater than oneself.[20]

If the two-tiered program just described were implemented, what impact would the training have on the profession? We are basically talking about the potential to overhaul the profession. An "occupational rehabilitation." We could restore personal leadership and interpersonal skills to the position of importance they should have in the most people-focused profession there is, with an intense focus on respect for the individual, whether fellow physician, nurse, housekeeper, or patient.

Health care will continue to evolve, and it will require increasing levels of cooperation, collaboration, and teamwork, even among competing groups of physicians. In such a rapidly changing environment, personal leadership will be crucial. Hock has said: "The past is ever less predictive, the future is ever less predictable, and the present barely exists at all."[19] With such uncertainty in our world and in medicine, the only way for us to deal with change as individuals, groups, and a profession is to develop a strong core of personal leadership—"unconditional confidence."

Some of you may be thinking, "All those 'fluffy' concepts are great, but why should I pay good money to do this?" The answer is simple; the return on investment is substantial. The DEPO Principle[SM] tells us that these skills will enhance the bottom line. Ulrich says that research supports the contention that employee attitude is the lead indicator of customer (patient) and organizational attitude and results, and those seem to be lead indicators of profitability.[27] He also points out that improving the attitude and opinions about the business of each of these segments—employee, customer and organization, and investors—are, in themselves, results. Employee and customer satisfaction translates into dollars.

Ulrich's data shows that, if one enhances one's personal leadership, the people around the person are affected positively. People like their jobs and enjoy work more. Because this tends to result in more satisfied employees, and satisfied employees result in satisfied patients or customers, one would fully expect to see greater retention of patients and lower organizational staff turnover.

Leadership as Infrastructure

Developing personal leadership in medicine is an investment in the "infrastructure" of medicine that will allow long-term success and growth of our personal business and the profession. The investment in personal leadership development is "capital improvement" and has long-term benefits.

Physicians and their organizations spend thousands of dollars per individual annually on continuing medical education (CME) credits required to maintain their licenses and/or certification. For the most part, however, CME courses do not affect the manner in which physicians deliver care or how they practice. A study that examined this issue for a 10-year period following the introduction of mandatory CME for physicians found: "The paucity of change in CME habits and behaviors ten years after mandatory participation became law indicates no major changes in education resulting from the regulations. Moreover, there have been no demonstrable improvements in patient care, in frequency of malpractice suits, or in reduced health care costs."[184] Others have come to the same conclusion: "There is no evidence that current approaches to CME, mandatory or voluntary, produce sustainable changes in physician practices or application of current knowledge."[185]

In light of the ability to effectively and measurably improve behavior of an individual using feedback coaching, money spent on personal leadership and interpersonal skills development has greater potential for value-added results compared to the standard CME course. In the end, perhaps the question will be: "Can individual physicians and medical organizations afford not to initiate personal leadership training?"

Physician Executives: The Catalyst to Transmit Personal Leadership Throughout Organizations

Increasingly, physicians who are interested in regaining some control—and some understanding of business principles—are going back to school to get their Master's in Business Administration (MBA). Such education assists in the understanding of subjects such as finance, personnel, practice and organizational management, strategic thinking and other business-related topics not part of the typical medical education. However, while these skills are important, the vast majority of physician executives who fail do so because of personal leadership or interpersonal issues—not because of their technical management-related skills. Therefore, a significant emphasis should be placed on personal leadership development early in physician executive MBA programs.

Many physician MBA programs talk about the importance of "leadership" and may even have courses with the word leadership in the title. Upon closer review of the topics taught in those courses, one usually finds topics on everything but personal leadership. Mostly, these programs speak to management, organizational structure, human resource issues, innovation, and other "technical management skills." Rarely is more than a one-hour session devoted to personal leadership, despite data suggesting effectiveness seems to follow such personal leadership development.

My recommendations for physician MBA programs are similar to the recommendations made for physicians in practice. In essence, physician executives training in MBA programs should undergo the same personal leadership development training already described, with a few differences.

The Final Analysis

In the final analysis, there will always be reasons not to commit to enhancing personal leadership and interpersonal skills, and individuals and organizations that do not appreciate the value of such programs will always find those reasons. There are five points (realities), however, that individuals and organizations should keep in mind when pondering whether they will survive the changes occurring in health care today and whether to look into development programs for their "on-the-ground" physician leaders:

1. The first point is that regardless of how effective an individual thinks they are, everyone can improve their personal leadership and interpersonal skills and will obtain benefit from a personal development program. Everyone.

2. The second point is, attracting and retaining good non-physician employees will be a critical strategic focus in health care for the next two decades, and effective physician personal leadership and interpersonal skills will ensure the likelihood of an organization to effectively compete for the shrinking pool of

such individuals. Individuals and organizations that put physician personal leadership programs into place will gain a competitive advantage over individuals and organizations that don't have such programs. With time, patients and skilled employees will flock to the former. And be assured that health care insurers will either willingly have those physicians and organizations in their plans or patients will force insurers to include them.

3. The individual and organization that understand the relevance of the "flattened hierarchy" and the narrowing gap between patient and physician knowledge, resulting from freely available information, and is adaptable and can quickly adopt new technologies will have a competitive advantage over those who fail to understand and embrace technology.

4. Physicians who are capable of appreciating the fact that they are just part of the interdependent reality of health care and society and are clear about their critical but partial role will have competitive advantages related to efficiencies and effective relationships that will sustain them long after those who have failed to appreciate this have retired or left the profession.

5. Finally, and most important, physicians who are able to maintain or regain their sense of intrinsic motivation and forget about external motivations (money, prestige, power, etc.), will have a sense of professional gratification and personal peace as a result of more effective relationships with family, staff, and patients, and will survive *regardless* of their ability to live within the other four realities.

The individuals who are capable of living all five of these realities will be the most successful physicians in health care for the next two decades.

The only question remaining is: "Will physicians and health care organizations leverage these realities, or will the realities leverage them?"

CHAPTER 14 ⊂○○○○○⊃

Blue Sky:
A Social Movement Toward Better Medicine

Truth, virtue, honor, the dignity of human nature…are the touchstones by which the conduct of nations as well as individuals is to be tested.—John Quincy Adams

We can't just do a superficial "facelift" of medicine—a "remodeling effort" to change the outward appearance and ignore changing the core of the profession. What I am suggesting is *not* incremental change— it isn't a remodeling—it is a transformational shift in the current leadership culture of medicine. I view this as the beginning of a second Renaissance in medicine—a major step in the evolution of the profession—by starting with occupational rehabilitation through personal leadership development. We are, in many ways, tearing down the current "structure" of beliefs about what it means to be an effective individual and personal leader in medicine. Competence is no longer enough, and developmental needs related to behavior and personal leadership can no longer be ignored.

Enhancing personal leadership will lead health care to and through a dramatic evolutionary progression to a higher level. It will result in a unique rejuvenation and renewal of sustained professional credibility, accountability, and success. It will steal the malpractice attorney's most powerful weapon against doctors: their behavior and the ability to tap into patient's emotions related to those behaviors.

Many of the negative issues raised in this book emanate from the post-World War II generation of physicians—the baby boomers. Some of what we deal with, such as hierarchical medical education and the "Chairman's syndrome, are holdovers from a generation or more before that." But others are more recent. It makes me ponder the way my father's generation (World War II era) was raised, what they stood for, and how they conducted their lives. As Brokaw has suggested, perhaps they are "The Greatest Generation."[186] Humility was not a foreign concept to them, as it seems to be today.

Perhaps we need to understand some of the differences between then and now, and ask ourselves: "What should I (or we) be doing differently?" "What else should we do?" "What else can we do?"

Perhaps we should re-institute the concept of a "liberal arts education" in which there are requirements in pre-med education outside of the hard sciences, including personal leadership courses. This will require a different mindset for pre-med students. Perhaps we should teach ethics—not just medical ethics, but social ethics.

I would love to see mandatory public service included in the pre-med or medical curricula. It could be accomplished in an array of ways: working for a soup kitchen for a summer, volunteering at a VA hospital, assisting in the teaching of summer school in an area serving the disadvantaged, or being a hospice volunteer. This would help keep people going into medicine focused on people and relationships. This would have clearly remind them of their purpose and assist in maintaining intrinsic motivation.

What if we could develop an aptitude test for pre-med students that measures personal leadership qualities and the likelihood of an individual's maintaining intrinsic motivation and a humanistic approach in a medical career? Tying such a test to first- and fourth-year medical student personal leadership programs may help the profession immensely.

What I have proposed is a development program for individuals going into medicine that focuses on components of being a person and of personally leading oneself— almost a "rebirth of the individual" during the process of becoming a physician, leading to occupational rehabilitation of medicine and maintenance of intrinsic motivation.

Some people will argue that the educational process of a physician is already too long. It may be too long, but is it wise to produce physicians who are not as effective with people as they should or could be? This interpersonal ineffectiveness or, perhaps more accurately, suboptimal effectiveness, is expensive and cost-inefficient. What would it mean in economic terms to produce physicians with better personal leadership and interpersonal skills, in sheer dollars of reduced liability? Reduced organizational turnover? Reduced patient waiting time and its effect on society's productivity as a whole?

Physician's Incomes

It is hard to discuss how to make medicine better and how to enhance access to affordable care for all without addressing the topic of the physician's income. It has already been mentioned that physicians make huge margins on every dollar they take in, especially compared to other workers in this world. What is a fair and reasonable income for a physician? How should physicians be compensated? How do we avoid killing intrinsic motivation?

Perhaps we should eliminate all fee-for-service and managed care plans that provide incentives for any behaviors related to patient volume or treatment. Perhaps there should be an annual salary with increases tied to the annual rate of inflation. Perhaps this salary should be the same for every physician, regardless of specialty, adjusted only for regional cost-of-living differences. Incomes would be "transportable." If a physician leaves a practice in the Midwest for a practice in the Southeast, he or she would receive the same income, with the new regional cost-of-living adjustment. This strategy would ensure that, for instance, if a medical student decides to apply to a surgery residency program, he or she is doing so out of interest (i.e., intrinsic motivation), not because surgeons can earn twice what a family practice doctor can.

If such a scheme is not acceptable, perhaps there should be a tax on a physician's income, based on a sliding scale and increasing with increasing income. The revenue from the tax would be put back into health care for the uninsured, to compensate residents, and to pay for medical research.

This taxing approach is not unheard of. Over-the-road truckers pay a higher tax on their vehicles than the rest of us because of the wear-and-tear their trucks inflict on the roadways. Physicians are at least partially responsible for the high and increasing costs of health care. If their incomes are to be maintained at some cost to consumers and society, should they not give something back? Obviously the answer to this question is elusive, but it is something that needs to be explored. Physicians can't ask everyone else to sacrifice and not willingly put something meaningful on the auction table themselves. For too long, we have been the last in the value chain to feel pain and make sacrifices.

Medical Education Costs

The debt one incurs in the process of becoming a physician is obscene. The average premedical student has $17,155 and the average medical student has $89,127 in educational debt upon graduation, for an average total educational debt of $94,901—before earning a single dollar with their medical degrees.[25] This is equivalent to a home mortgage, only the pay-off period is often a mere 5 to 10 years. To pay off this amount of debt over 10 years, assuming an 8 percent rate of interest, results in a monthly payment of more than $1,100.

There is pressure on the new physician to repay this debt as quickly as possible. This results, understandably, in a financial focus for those coming out of training. If we could make medical education more affordable, the perceived need for and expectation of a 6-figure income might decrease.

Another, and perhaps more powerful and pragmatic, reason to decrease tuition costs and control earning expectations of graduating physicians is the fact that reimbursement for medical services continues to decline. The cost of education continues to rise, while reimbursement to working physicians continues to decline. This is an unsustainable economic model. If we don't change it, economic realities eventually will. If we don't, only the independently wealthy will be able to go into medicine.

The salaries of residents should be increased, perhaps allowing them to begin paying off the educational debts while still in residency. These two steps would take some of the debt pressure off graduates. Besides, for what they do, the abuse they endure, and the hours they work, they are grossly underpaid.

Medical Malpractice Costs

Physicians pay $20,000 to $80,000 per year or more in medical malpractice insurance premiums. If an individual is to have an after-tax income of a modest (for physicians) $50,000 and pays $80,000 in malpractice insurance premiums, as many surgical specialties do, it would require earning $215,000 annually. That assumes they do not have to pay any office staff or other overhead, which of course they do. If malpractice costs were less, in this simple model, physicians would have to earn less to take home the same number of real dollars. This could be savings passed on to the patient (or "health care consumer") or invested back into the medical business infrastructure.

Prescription Drug Costs

Prescription drug costs must be better controlled, either by a conscious effort on the part of the pharmaceutical industry or by federal regulation. There are ways to do this, but they would require cooperation between the industry and the government. For example, part of the reason new drug prices are often so high is so the pharmaceutical company can recoup its development expenses as quickly as possible and begin to make a profit on the new drug. Part of this urgency is driven by the limited patent life of the drug, pushing the company to recoup costs and generate profit within a specific time. Some of the profits go to other drug development programs within the company, but the industry has seen profit growth of 15-25 percent in the past 1-2 decades.

What if the government extended patent life of any newly approved compound by 5 years in return for a reasonably negotiated, consumer-friendly price on the drug? It could eliminate the need of the company to recoup all its investment in the first several years, yet result in the same absolute dollar profit for the pharmaceutical companies across time.

For the Health Care Consumer (Formerly Known as Patients)

None of what has been written here is meant to demean or degrade the relationship between the patient and the physician, and none is meant to minimize the reverence most physicians hold for patients. Most physicians began their training with every intent of upholding the idealism of the profession—intrinsic motivation. It just tends to get "trained out" of them. More often than not, they allow it to happen, usually without overt complicity.

Everything I have proposed concerning personal leadership development in medicine should translate into greater satisfaction and better care for patients. These things could clearly enhance the ability of patients to interact on a more personal and authentic level with their physicians, because the physicians would be better able to relate to patients. The physician who is personally led well will have a staff that is much happier and more in-tune to patient needs, wants, and concerns. This will result in more satisfaction on patients' parts, a sense of partnering with providers in their care, and ultimately will make them less susceptible to malpractice considerations. Many malpractice cases emanate out of expectations of perfection by patients, combined with the sub-optimal personal leadership and interpersonal skills of physicians. This expectation has been created in part by physicians, in part by the legal profession, and in part by the media, and patients have bought into this concept with lustful support of sometimes less-than-scrupulous attorneys.

Where Can We Go?

Successful people can improve, if they are willing to see what they need to work on and are willing to commit to change. If you don't think you have a problem, you probably have a problem, because there are always developmental needs and room for improvement in our personal leadership skills. Physicians tend to over-rate their personal leadership and interpersonal abilities compared to the perceptions of those around them.

If enough individuals believe there is value in this material, perhaps we will start to see a change. If enough medical organizations adopt personal leadership development, the change could be sweeping. And if universities and medical schools understand this, the change would transform health care delivery and patient satisfaction in this country.

I can see physicians running hospitals and large health care organizations better and more effectively than they have been run in the past 20 years. I can see physicians becoming less worried about their incomes and more concerned with their effectiveness as it relates to patients, their families, and their communities. I can see physicians donating their time for the betterment of their communities. I can see universities developing physicians who are as compassionate to their fellow residents and medical students as they are to their patients. I can see the systematic deconstruction of "win-lose" educational systems and department chairs who ask residents to call them by their first names, and see them first as individuals, second as friends and resources, and third as residents. I can see physicians carrying these traits home.

I can see physician office employees being happy about coming to work, because they see the big picture and how they "fit" into the organization. They receive positive feedback and guidance and are internally motivated. They call the physicians they work by their first names and feel they are part of a team, not just lining-up patients, filing the charts, and billing patients. I see office staffs working in the same office for 20 years instead of 20 weeks.

I see hospital-based staff members being happier and more satisfied because they are being treated as individuals on the team and not as "instruments of patient care." I see solutions to problems being solved because of physicians' increased ability to genuinely listen and seek feedback from their staffs. I see lower organizational and institutional turnover.

I can see patients being happier with modern medicine because their doctors are, for the first time, listening to understand and not simply to respond. I see fewer patients "doctor-shopping." I see patients understanding more about physicians and appreciating physicians' efforts to improve themselves and the profession. I see malpractice suits becoming rare because more effective interaction between health care providers and patients has closed the gap between health and care"

There is essentially nothing about medicine that would not be improved and no individual who would remain untouched by enhancing personal leadership effectiveness of physicians, the "on-the-ground" leaders in health care.

If we commit to improving personal leadership and interpersonal skills of those in practice and teaching hospitals and instituting leadership training in medical school, all of the problems facing us in medicine will not evaporate. But we will be much more prepared to accept, address, and ultimately solve the problems we do encounter, from reimbursement, to malpractice, to ensuring high-quality care and respect for all people. The personal leadership quality of proactivity is the key and first step to all other aspects of personal leadership and will ultimately lead individuals to begin to find solutions to other problems without waiting for management or the university or the clinic or the government to do it.

Epilogue

Many in medicine may either not care about this work and my concerns, or may not understand what I have attempted to do and say. Some will say I'm not living in reality, or I am on the "lunatic fringe." I have no illusions that this material or these concepts will be adopted lock, stock and barrel.

On the other hand, I have a classic physician tendency: impatience. I want this to happen yesterday because I see such a huge need. But I realize that this material will require some thought by most, and people will ultimately make their own decision as to whether I am on the right track. If I am able to convince one person or one organization, the effort will have been worth it. One person or organization will ultimately affect thousands of others—physicians, staffs, and patients.

Writing this book has energized me. Sooner or later, others will begin to understand my concerns. Until then, I hope this makes sense, serves you well, and stimulates you and your organization to take that first step.

The Hippocratic Oath

I swear by Apollo the physician, and Aesculapius, and health, and all-heal, and all the gods and goddesses that, according to my ability and judgment I will keep this oath and this stipulation. To reckon him who taught me this art equally dear to me as my parents; to share my substance with him, and relieve his necessities if required. To look upon his offspring in the same footing as my own brothers, and to teach them this art, if they shall wish to learn it, without fee or stipulation, and that by precept, lecture and every other mode of instruction, I will impart a knowledge of the art to my own sons, and those of my teachers, and to disciples bound by a stipulation and oath according to the law of medicine, but to none others. I will follow that system of regimen which, according to my ability and judgment, I consider for the benefit of my patients, and abstain from whatever is deleterious and mischievous. I will give no deadly medicine to anyone if asked, nor suggest any such counsel, and in like manner I will not give to a woman a pessary to produce abortion. With purity and holiness I will pass my life and practice my art. I will not cut persons laboring under the stone, but will leave this to be done by men who are practitioners of this work for the benefit of the sick, and will abstain from every voluntary act of mischief and corruption. And further, from the seduction of females or males, of freemen and slaves, whatever, in connection with it. I see or hear, in the life of men, which ought not to be spoken of abroad, I will not divulge, as reckoning that all such should be kept secret. While I continue to keep this oath unviolated, may it be granted to me to enjoy life and the practice of the art, respected by all men, in all times. But should I trespass and violate this oath, may the reverse be my lot.

The 20 Original "Missteps" in Personal Leadership

1. "Win-lose" paradigm

2. "Win-lose" Education—competition

3. "Perfectionist" Mentality—setting unrealistic expectations

4. The Media—"Best Doctors List" (rating of doctors and hospitals)

5. Inability to Negotiate

6. "Challenge" Syndrome

7. The Physician Hierarchy—the "frozen bureaucracy"

8. "Chairman's Syndrome"—positional "leadership"

9. "Captive Audience Phenomenon"—the abuse of residents, medical students, and staff

10. "Quick-fix Attitude"—the acute care paradigm

11. "Quick-fix attitude"—time

12. Physician Self-Deception—"I have the Most Important Job in the World Syndrome," and the failure to understand interdependence in the larger world

13. "Physicians Are Autonomous"—a persistent fallacy

14. Inability to Self-Assess

15. Difficulty in Providing Behavioral Feedback to Other Physicians

16. Over-Focus on Technical or Intellectual Ability as a Proxy for Leadership

17. Information Overload

18. Reluctance to Trust—resulting in self-protecting, self-serving behavior

19. Failure to Appreciate the Importance of Interpersonal Relationships

20. Skepticism of "Softer Sciences" that Have Contributed to Current Leadership Concepts—e.g., sociology, management science, organizational analysis, etc.

References

1. Philips, D. *Lincoln on Leadership.* New York, N.Y.: Warner Books, 1992.

2. Gill, S. "Managing the Transition from Clinician to Manager and Leader." In LeTourneau, B., and Curry, W. *In Search of Physician Leadership.* Chicago, Ill.: Health Administration Press, 1998. p. 84.

3. Covey, S. *The 7 Habits of Highly Effective People.* New York, N.Y.: Simon & Schuster, Inc. 1989, p. 51.

4. Berger, W. "Physician Leadership in the New Millennium." *Annals of Allergy, Asthma, and Immunology* 82(6): 507-10, June 1999.

5. Souba, W. "Academic Surgery@Leadership.You." *Journal of Surgical Research* 90(1):5-9, May 1, 2000.

6. Souba, W. "Taking a New Job—The Leadership Transition." *Journal of Surgical Research* 92(2):143-9, Aug. 2000.

7. Souba, W. "Editorial: The Core of Leadership." *Journal of Thoracic and Cardiovascular Surgery* 119(3):414-9, March 2000.

8. Maxwell, J. *The 21 Irrefutable Laws of Leadership.* Nashville, Tenn.: Thomas Nelson Publishers, 1998.

9. Federman, I. "A Personal View of Leadership," presentation to the Executive Seminar in Corporate Excellence, Santa Clara (Calif.) University, Oct. 16, 1983.

10. Cashman, K. *Leadership from the Inside Out*. Provo, Utah: Executive Excellence Publishing, 2000, p. 20.

11. Lynch, R. "How to Foster Champions." In Hesselbein, F., and others, *Leading Beyond the Walls*. San Francsico, Calif.: Jossey-Bass, 1999.

12. Kouzes, J., and Posner, B. *The Leadership Challenge*. San Francisco, Calif.: Jossey-Bass Inc., 1995.

13. Goleman, D. *Working with Emotional Intelligence*. New York, N.Y.: Bantam Books, 1998.

14. *Ibid.*, p. 318.

15. Interview with Robert E. Quinn by www.ededge.com on his book "Change the World."

16. Torbert, W. *Managing the Corporate Dream: Restructuring for Long-Term Success*. Homewood, Ill.: Dow Jones-Irwin, 1987.

17. Quinn, R. *Change the World*. San Francisco, Calif.: Jossey-Bass, 2000.

18. Hock, D. Leadership Development Conference, "Birth of the Chaordic Age: New Leadership Concepts to Manage Institutional Change," Washington, D.C., June 12, 2000.

19. Hock, D. *Birth of the Chaordic Age*. San Francisco, Callif.: Berrett-Koehler Publishers, 1999.

20. Frankl, V. *Man's Search for Meaning, An Introduction to Logotherapy*. New York, N.Y.: Washington Square Press, 1963.

21. Palmer, P. "The Courage to Teach: Exploring the Inner Landscape of a Teachers Life." In Quinn, R., *Change the World*. San Francisco, Calif.: Jossey-Bass, 2000.

22. Schwartz, R. "Physician Leadership: A New Imperative for Surgical Educators." *American Journal of Surgery* 176(1):38-40, July 1998.

23. "Practical Innovation: Applying the Concepts of TRIZ to Accelerated Innovation," presentation by Ellen Domb, Ph.D., to the Keilty, Goldsmith Network, Rancho Sante Fe, Calif., Jan. 8, 2001.

24. Ulrich, D., and others. *Results-Based Leadership*. Boston, Mass.: Harvard Business School Press, 1999.

25. Division of Medical Education, Association of American Medical Colleges. *Medical School Graduation Questionnaire, All Schools Report 2000*. Washington, D.C.: Association of American Medical Colleges, 2000.

26. *Random House College Dictionary, Revised Edition, 1975.* New York, N.Y.: Random House, 1975.

27. Interview with David Ulrich, Jack Zenger, and Norm Smallwood by www.ededge.com on their book *Results-Based Leadership.*

28. Kathryn Jashinski, ASK Marketing, Personal Communication, March 15, 2001.

29. LeBoeuf, M. *How to Win Customers and Keep Them for Life.* New York, N.Y.: Berkley Publishing Group, 2000.

30. Patton, C. "Rating the Returns." HR Executive 15(5):40-3, April 2001.

31. Gaddy, R., and Bechtel, G. "Nonlicensed Employee Turnover in a Long-Term Care Facility." *Health Care Supervisor* 13(4):54-60, June 1995.

32. Bureau of National Affairs' *Bulletin to Management,* Dec. 6, 1999,

33. Zesiger, S., and others. "Fortune Writers on Speed." *Fortune* 142(4):48-54, Aug. 14, 2000.

34. "Our People, Our Assets." *Chief Executive* 1999, p. 5.

35. Kaye, B., and Jordan-Evans, S. "Retention Tag, You're It!" *Training & Development* 54(4):29, April 29, 2000.

36. "How Much Does Turnover Really Cost." *HRFocus* 77(5):9, May 2000.

37. Kiel, J. "Using Data to Reduce Employee Turnover." *Health Care Supervisor* 16(4):12-9, June 1998.

38. Fisher, C. "New Paradigms." *Leader to Leader,* Summer 2000.

39. Johnson, C. "The Skills of Interpersonal Relationships." Presentation at the 86th Annual American College of Surgeons, Postgraduate Course, Oct. 24, 2000, Chicago, Ill.

40. Dean, B., and Krenzelok, E. "The Cost of Employee Turnover to a Regional Poison Information Center." *Veterinarian and Human Toxicology* 36(1):60-1, Feb. 1994.

41. Pascale, R., and others. *Surfing the Edge of Chaos.* New York, N.Y.: Crown Publishing, 2000.

42. Niedz, B. "Correlates of Hospitalized Patients' Perceptions of Service Quality." *Research Nursing and Health* 21(4):339-49, Aug. 1998.

43. Stewart M, Brown JB, Boon H, Galajda J, Meredith L, Sangster M. Evidence on patient-doctor communcation. Cancer Prev Control 1999; 3:25-30.

44. Leiter, M., and others. "The Correspondence of Patient Satisfaction and Nurse Burnout." *Social Science and Medicine* 47(10):1611-7, Nov. 1998.

45. Jones, J., and others. "Stress and Medical Malpractice: Organizational Risk Assessment and Intervention." *Journal of Applied Psychology* 73(4):727-35, Nov. 1988.

46. Bratt, M., and others. "Influence of Stress and Nursing Leadership on Job Satisfaction of Pediatric Intensive Care Unit Nurses." *American Journal of Critical Care* 9(5):307-17, Sept. 2000.

47. Baggs, J., and others. "Nurse-Physician Collaboration and Satisfaction with the Decision-Making Process in Three Critical Care Units." *American Journal of Critical Care* 6(5):393-9, Sept. 1997.

48. Cangelosi, J., and others. "Factors Related to Nurse Retention and Turnover: An Updated Study." *Health Marketing Quarterly* 15(3):25-43, 1998.

49. Peltier, J., and others. "Using Relationship Marketing to Develop and Sustain Nurse Loyalty. A Case of a Rural Health Care Institution." *Journal of Health and Human Services Administration* 22(1):83-104, Summer 1999.

50. Buerhaus, P., and others. "Why Are Shortages of Hospital RNs Concentrated in Specialty Care Units?" *Nursing Economics* 18(3):111-6, May-June 2000.

51. Buchbinder, S., and others. "Estimates of Costs of Primary Care Physician Turnover." *American Journal of Managed Care* 5(11):1431-8, Nov. 1999.

52. Hunter, J., and others. "Individual Differences in Output Variability as a Function of Job Complexity." *Journal of Applied Psychology* 75(1):28-42, Feb. 1990.

53. Levinson, W., and others. "Physician-Patient Communication. The Relationship with Malpractice Claims among Primary Care Physicians and Surgeons." *JAMA* 277(7):553-9, Feb. 19, 1997.

54. Beckman, H., and others. "The Doctor-Patient Relationship and Malpractice. Lessons from Plaintiff Depositions." *Archives of Internal Medicine* 154(12):1365-670, June 27, 1994.

55. Hamel, G. *Leading the Revolution.* Boston, Mass.: Harvard Business Press, 2000, p. 85.

56. Huycke, L., and Huycke, M. "Characteristics of Potential Plaintiffs in Malpractice Litigation." Annals of Internal Medicine 120(9):792-8, May 1, 1994.

57. Witman, A., and others. "How Do Patients Want Physicians to Handle Mistakes? A Survey of Internal Medicine Patients in an Academic Setting." Archives of Internal Medicine 156(22):2565-9, Dec. 9-23, 1996.

58. Robin, M., and others. "Truth-Telling, Apology, and Medical Mistakes." Medical Journal of Allina 7(3):1-6, Summer 1998.

59. Krupat, E., and others. "The Practice Orientation of Physicians and Patients: The Effect of Doctor-Patient Congruence on Satisfaction." Patient Education and Counseling 39(1):49-59, Jan. 2000.

References

ᘌ◯◯◯◯◯ᘍ

60. Hilfiker, D. *Healing the Wounds*. New York, N.Y.: Pantheon Books, 1985, 137-8.

61. Berwick, D. In Crounse, B., "Intellectual Capital," Health Forum, San Diego, Claif., July 31, 2001.

62. Holleman, J. "The Demise of the Nalle Clinic." *Physician Executive* 27(1):26-31, Jan.-Feb. 2001.

63. Argyris, C. "Crafting a Theory of Practice: The Case of Organizational Paradoxes." In Quinn, R., and Camerson, K., Editors. *Paradox and Transformation*. Cambridge, Mass.: Ballinger, 1988.

64. Arygyris, C. "Teaching Smart People How to Learn." *Harvard Business Review* 69(3):99-109, May-June, 1991.

65. Leitch, K., and Walker, P. "Surgeon Compensation and Motivation." Archives of Surgery 135(6):708-12, June 2000.

66. Kerr, S. "On the Folly of Rewarding A, While Hoping for B." *Academy of Management Executive,* 9(1):7-14, Jan. 1995.

67. Schenke, R., and others. "A New Philosophy of Management: Leading Beyond the Bottom Line." *ACPE News* 3(5):7-8, Sept.-Oct. 2000.

68. Pascale, R., and others, *op. cit.,* p. 5

69. *Ibid.,* p. 6.

70. *Ibid.,* p. 22.

71. Hilfiker, D., *op. cit.,* p. 169.

72. Kohn, A. P*unished by Rewards*. New York, N.Y.: Houghton Mifflin Co., 1993, p. 260.

73. Shell, G., and Klasko, S. "Negotiating. Biases Physicians Bring to the Table." Physician Executive 22(?):4-7, ? 1996.

74. "America's Best Hospitals." *US News,* July 17, 2000. http://www.usnews.com/usnews/nycu/health/hosptl/tophosp.htm.

75. Hilfiker, D., *op. cit.,* p. 154.

76. *Ibid.,* p. 153.

77. Pascale, R., and others, *op. cit.,* p. 32.

78. Brookhiser, R. *Founding Father. Rediscovering George Washington.* New York, N.Y.: Free Press, 1996.

79. Kriegel, R., and Brandt, D. *Sacred Cows Make the Best Burgers.* New York, N.Y.: Warner Books, 1996.

80. Waldrop, M. *Complexity. The Emerging Science at the Edge of Order and Chaos.* New York, N.Y.: Touchstone, 1992, p. 151.

81. *Ibid.,* p. 167.

82. Hilfiker, D., *op. cit.,* p. 157-8.

83. *Ibid.,* p. 144-5.

84. *Ibid.,* p. 127.

85. Fritts, H. *On Leading a Clinical Department.* Baltimore, Md.: Johns Hopkins University Press, 1997.

86. Collins, J. "And the Walls Came Tumbling Down." In Hesselbein, F., and others, *Leading Beyond the Walls.* San Francisco, Calif.: Jossey-Bass, 1999.

87. Kohn, A., *op. cit.,* p. 193.

88. Arbinger Institute. *Leadership and Self-Deception. Getting out of the Box.* San Francisco, Calif.: Berrett-Koehler Publishers, Inc., 2000.

89. Cohn, L. "Becoming a Surgical Leader." *Journal of Thoracic and Cardiovascular Surgery* 119(4Pt2):S42-44, April 2000.

90. McCall, M. "Why Physician Managers Fail—Part I." Physician Executive 16(3): 8-11, May-June 1990.

91. Hock, D. *The Chaordic Organization.* San Francisco, Calif.: Berrett-Koehler Communications, Inc., 1999.

92. Hawken, P. *Growing a Business.* Wichita, Kan.: Fireside Press, 1988.

93. Gill, S., *op. cit,* p. 91.

94. Anderson, P. In Waldrop, M., *Complexity. The Emerging Science at the Edge of Order and Chaos.* New York, N.Y.: Touchstone, 1992, p. 81.

95. Armstrong, K. *Buddha.* New York, N.Y.: Penguin Life Press, 2001, p. 5.

96. NCQA 1999 Annual Report, "Reflections on the Past, A Vision for the Future. A Decade of Quality Work. Washington, D.C.: National Committee for Quality Assurance, 1999.

97. Waldhausen, J. "Leadership in Medicine." *Bulletin of the American College of Surgeons* 86(3):13-9, March 2001.

98. Kohn, A., *op. cit.,* p. 55.

99. *Ibid.,* p. 137.

100. *Ibid.,* p. 110.

101. "Coordination of Care: Creating a 'System' That Works for Patients." *New Visions for Health Care* (The Picker Institute), Number 8, Aug. 1999.

102. Young, G., and others. "Best Practices for Managing Surgical Services: The Role of Coordinator." *Health Care Management Review* 22(4):72-81, Fall 1997.

References

103. Hilfiker, D., *op. cit.,* p. 162.

104. Cummings, K. "Building Trust in Contentious Times." In LeTourneau, B., and Curry, W., *In Search of Physician Leadership.* Chicago, Ill.: Health Administration Press, 1998. p. 115.

105. Hilfiker, D., *op. cit.,* p. 161.

106. Drucker, P. "Managing Knowledge Means Managing Others." *Leader to Leader* Spring 2000.

107. Kohn, A., *op. cit.,* p. 158.

108. Cashman, K., *op. cit.,* p. 80.

109. Personal communication, Marshall Goldsmith, Founder, Keilty, Goldsmith, and Company, 2000.

110. Kruger, J., and Dunning, D. "Unskilled and Unaware of It: How Difficulties in Recognizing One's Own Incompetence Lead to Inflated Self-Assessments." Journal of Personality and Social Psychology 77(6):1121-34, Dec. 1999.

111. Hilfiker, D., *op. cit.,* p. 119.

112. See any issue of "New Visions for Health Care." At www.picker.org.

113. "Eye on Patients: A Report by the Picker Institute for the American Hospital Association."

114. American Hospital Association. "Reality Check II: More Public Perceptions of Health Care, Change, and Hospitals." *New Visions for Health Care* (Picker Institute), Number 8, Aug. 1999.

115. Lawrence, D. "Improving Patient Safety: Building Teams, Trust, and Technology." *New Visions for Health Care* (Picker Institute), Number 20, Aug. 2000.

116. Kasteler, J., and others. "Issues Underlying Prevalence of "Doctor-Shopping" Behavior." *Journal of Health and Social Behavior* 17(4):329-39, Dec. 1976.

117. Carlson, M., and others. "Socioeconomic Status and Dissatisfaction among HMO Enrollees." *Medical Care* 38(5):508-16, May 2000.

118. Hulka, B., and others. "Correlates of Satisfaction and Dissatisfaction with Medical Care: A Community Perspective." *Medical Care* 13(8):648-58, Aug. 1975.

119. "Access: Reducing Patient Waiting Time." *New Visions for Health Care* (Picker Institute), Number 15, March 2000.

120. "Improving Patients' Access to Health Care Providers." *New Visions for Health Care* (Picker Institute), Number 3, March 1999.

121. Herzlinger, R. *Market Driven Health Care.* Reading, Mass.: Addison-Wesley Publishing Co., 1997, p. 16.

122. *Ibid.*, pp. 17-8.

123. *Ibid.*, p. 25.

124. Waitzkin, H. "Doctor-Patient Communication. Clinical Implications of Social Scientific Research." *JAMA* 252(17): 2441-6, Nov. 2, 1984.

125. Hamel, G., *op. cit.*, p. 138-9.

126. "Continuity and Transition: Preparing for Discharge." *New Visions for Health Care* (Picker Institute), Number 6, June 1999.

127. Reiley, P., and others. "Learning from Patients: A Discharge Planning Improvement Project." *Joint Commission Journal of Quality Improvement* 22(5):311-22, May 1996.

128. Hickey, M., and others. "Payer-Hospital Collaboration to Improve Patient Satisfaction with Hospital Discharge." *Joint Commission Journal of Quality Improvement.* 22(5):336-44, May 1996.

129. Birenbaum, A. *Managed Care: Made in America.* Westport, Conn.: Praeger Publishers, 1997, p. 116.

130. Tucker, J. "The Influence of Patient Sociodemographic Characteristics on Patient Satisfaction." *Military Medicine* 165(1):72-6, Jan. 2000.

131. "Physician/Patient Rapport Concerns Administrators." *ED Management* 12(6):68-70, June 2000.

132. Crounse, B., "Being the Most Wired," Health Forum, San Diego, Calif., July 31, 2001.

133. James, J., Leadership Skills for a New Age," Health Forum, San Diego, Calif., July 31, 2001.

134. Kathryn Jackson, Assessment Plus, Inc. Data on file and personal communication.

135. "Valuing Employees to Improve Performance Quality." *New Visions for Health Care* (Picker Institute), Number 24, Dec. 2000.

136. Ulrich, D., and others, *op. cit.*, p. 55.

137. *Ibid.*, p. 53–4.

138. *The Seven Habits of Highly Effective People Year 2000 Daily Calendar,* Aug. 10, 2000.

139. Maxwell, J., *op. cit.*, p. 99.

140. Ulrich, D., *op. cit.*, p. 57.

141. Larson, E., and others. "Hospitalk: An Exploratory Study to Assess What Is Said and What Is Heard Between Physicians and Nurses." *Clinical Performance and Quality Health Care* 6(4):183-9, Oct.-Dec. 1998.

142. Haas, J., and others. "Is the Professional Satisfaction of General Internists Associated with Patient Satisfaction?" *Journal of General Internal Medicine* 15(2):122-8, Feb. 2000.

143. Mirvis, D., and others. "Burnout among Leaders of Department of Veteran Affairs Medical Centers: Contributing Factors as Determined by a Longitudinal Study." *Journal of Health and Human Services Administration* 21(3):390-412, Winter 1999.

144. Linzer, M., and others. "Managed Care, Time Pressure, and Physician Job Satisfaction: Results from the Physician Worklife Study." *Journal of General Internal Medicine* 15(7):441-50, July 2000.

145. Frank, E., and others. "Career Satisfaction of U.S. Women Physicians: Results of the Women Physicians' Health Study. Society of General Internal Medicine Career Satisfaction Study Group." *Archives of Internal Medicine* 159(13):1417-26, July 12, 1999.

146. Sibbald, B., and others. "GP Job Satisfaction in 1987, 1990, and 1998: Lessons for the Future?" *Family Practice* 17(5):364-71, Oct. 2000.

147. Hilfiker, D., *op. cit.,* p. 180-1.

148. *Quotes and Quips.* Provo, Utah: Covey Leadership Center, Inc., 1993, p. 12.

149. Fischer, J. "Laying on of the Hands. *Bulletin of the American College of Surgeons* 86(1):24-8, Jan. 2001.

150. Kohn, A., *op. cit.,* p. 22.

151. Hock, D. *Birth of the Chaordic Age, op. cit.,* p. 42.

152. *Ibid.,* p. 43.

153. Hilfiker, D., *op. cit.,* p. 183.

154. Kohn, A., *op. cit.,* p. 5.

155. *Ibid.,* p. 37.

156. *Ibid.,* p. 69.

157. *Ibid.,* p 71-72.

158. *Ibid.,* p. 182.

159. Eliason, B., and others. "Personal Values of Family Physicians, Practice Satisfaction, and Service to the Underserved." *Archives of Family Medicine* 9(3):228-32, March 2000.

160. James Davis of Development Dimensions International. "Necessary Competencies for Physicians in Health Care Organizations," presented at the 86th Annual American College of Surgeons, Postgraduate Course, Oct. 24, 2000, Chicago, Ill.

161. "Alternative Medicine." *JAMA* 280(18):1569-75, Nov. 11, 1998.

162. Personal communication, Marshall Goldsmith, Founder, Keilty, Goldsmith, and Company Jan. 7, 2001.

163. *Quotes and Quips, op. cit.,* p. 30.

164. Steinem, G., "The Millennial Revolution," presentation at the Women in Leadership Summit, San Francisco, Calilf., 2000.

165. Johnson, S. *Who Moved My Cheese.* New York, N.Y.: Penguin Putnam Inc., 1998, p. 73.

166. Goleman, D., *op. cit.,* pp. 326-8.

167. Prochaska, J. In Goleman, D., *Working with Emotional Intelligence.* New York, N.Y.: Bantam Books, 1998, pp. 327-8.

168. Data on file, Assessment Plus, Inc. "Guidelines for Developing a Multi-Source Assessment Process by Welyne M. Thomas, PhD.

169. *Ibid.*

170. "The Impact of Direct Report Feedback and Follow-up on Leadership Effectiveness. A Study Involving over 8,000 Respondents in One of the 100 Largest Corporations in the United States" by Keilty, Goldsmith & Company.

171. Fritts, H., *op. cit.,* p. 78.

172. Phillips, D., *op. cit.,* p. 137.

173. O'Neill, H. Much Obliged." *Men's Health,* July-Aug. 1996.

174. Taragin, M., and others. "Physician Demographics and the Risk of Medical Malpractice." *American Journal of Medicine* 93(5):537-42, Nov. 1992.

175. Hojat, M., and others. "Gender Comparisons of Young Physicians' Perceptions of Their Medical Education, Professional Life, and Practice: A Follow-Up Study of Jefferson Medical College Graduates." Academic Medicine 70(4):305-12, April 1995.

176. Miller, J. "Women Administrators: New Hope and New Dilemmas." In *Women Physicians in Leadership Roles,* Dickstein, L., and Nadelson, C., Editors. Washington, D.C.: American Psychiatric Press, Inc., 1986.

177. McMurray, J., and others. "The Work Lives of Women Physicians. Results from the Physician Work Life Study. The SGIM Career Satisfaction Study Group." *Journal of General Internal Medicine* 15(6):372-380, June 2000.

178. Clancy, K., and Krieg, P. *Counter-Intuitive Marketing.* New York, N.Y.: Free Press, 2000, p. 30-6.

179. *Ibid.,* p. 33.

180. Philips, D., *op. cit.*, p.38.

181. 176. Gilligan, C. *In a Different Voice*. Cambridge, Mass.: Harvard University Press, 1982.

182. LeTourneau, B., and Curry, W. *In Search of Physician Leadership*. Chicago, Ill.: Health Administration Press, 1998, p 10.

183. Kohn, A., *op. cit.*, p. 206.

184. Stross, J., and Harlan, W. "Mandatory Continuing Medical Education Revisited." *Mobius* 7(1):22-7, Jan. 1987.

185. Donen, N. "No to Mandatory Continuing Medical Education, Yes to Mandatory Practice Auditing and Professional Educational Development." *Canadian Medical Association Journal* 158(8):1044-6, April 21, 1998.

186. Brokaw, T. *The Greatest Generation*. New York, N.Y.: Random House, 1998.

Index

A Successful Management Career Is No Accident

It takes careful attention to development of basic management skills in the beginning, and then ongoing learning as your career progresses. Success has to be built step by step. ACPE offers an array of books, its own and the best from other publishers, that cover the context and the content of successful career building. No matter where you are in your management career, we have information that can help you analyze and hone your management skills. Check them out.

MD/MBA: Physicians on the New Frontier of Medical Management
$35/members, $45/nonmembers

In Search of Physician Leaders
$45/members, $50/nonmembers

Get the Job You Want and the Money You're Worth—Second Edition
$20/members, $25/nonmembers

Hope for the Future: A Career Development Guide for Physician Executives
(book and audiotape)
$40/members, $48/nonmembers

Women in Medicine and Management: A Mentoring Guide
$30/members, $38/nonmembers

Physician Executives: What, Why, How
$18/members, $28/nonmembers

Physicians in Managed Care: A Career Guide
$20/members, $25/nonmembers

The Physician Leader's Guide, Second Edition
$85/members, $99/nonmembers

For more information, or to order books,
Call **800/562-8088**
Visa, Mastercard, and Discover accepted.

THE WORLD OF MEDICAL MANAGEMENT OPENS AT WWW.ACPE.ORG

If you're already in medical management or are in the process of pursuing a medical management career, information on the tools for success are at
www/acpe/org

The ACPE Publications Catalog.

Peruse descriptions of the many medical management offerings of the College and order copies on line.

Line-Up of Educational Offerings.

Complete descriptions and advanced schedules for the College's nationally recognized medical management curriculum are provided. Also described are College-sponsored advanced degree programs.

Myriad Ways to Manage and Advance Your Career.

Up-to-the-minute position postings, services for resume construc-tion, and other career services are designed to promote medical management and help physicians move into management positions.

This is a jam-packed Web site.
See for yourself.

www.acpe.org